Travels
Sor

Discovering the
Amalfi Coast and Capri

David M. Addison

Other Books by
David M. Addison

A Meander in Menorca
Misadventures in Tuscany
Bananas About La Palma
An Innocent Abroad
Confessions of a Banffshire Loon
The Cuban Missus Crisis
Still Innocent Abroad
Exploring the NC500
Travels Through Time in Italy

TRAVELS AROUND SORRENTO

Discovering the Amalfi Coast and Capri

David M. Addison

Travels Around Sorrento: Discovering the Amalfi Coast and Capri by David M. Addison.

First edition published in Great Britain in 2018 by Extremis Publishing Ltd., Suite 218, Castle House, 1 Baker Street, Stirling, FK8 1AL, United Kingdom. *www.extremispublishing.com*

Extremis Publishing is a Private Limited Company registered in Scotland (SC509983) whose Registered Office is Suite 218, Castle House, 1 Baker Street, Stirling, FK8 1AL, United Kingdom.

A CIP catalogue record for this book is available from the British Library.

ISBN: 978-0-9955897-3-5

Typeset in Goudy Bookletter 1911, designed by The League of Moveable Type. Printed and bound in Great Britain by IngramSpark, Chapter House, Pitfield, Kiln Farm, Milton Keynes, MK11 3LW, United Kingdom.

Front cover artwork is by Greg Montani at Pixabay.
Incidental stock images sourced from Pixabay.
Cover design and book design is Copyright © Thomas A. Christie.
Author images are Copyright © Fiona Addison.
The copyrights of third parties are reserved. All third party imagery is used under the provision of Fair Use for the purposes of commentary and criticism.
Internal photographic illustrations are Copyright © David M. Addison and Fiona Addison, unless otherwise indicated.

Contents

Map of Italy
Showing Campania Region
and the Province of Napoli

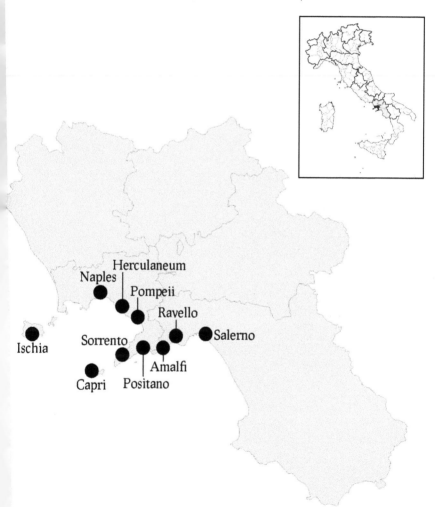

For Fiona

TRAVELS AROUND SORRENTO

Discovering the Amalfi Coast and Capri

David M. Addison

1

Scarily to Sorrento

WHENEVER you are in Naples or its vicinity, you can't ignore the omnipresent bulk of Vesuvius. At the moment it is on our left-hand side as we speed down the A3 towards Sorrento in our minibus, just centimetres from the car in front. A swish Mercedes, this; not one of those Italian Uglymobiles we had had as a taxi in Rome, but the passengers are the same. I, in the death seat beside the driver, am an alert co-pilot – the driver's extra eyes, and both feet braced ready to brake. In the back, Bill and Pat – whom we'd met on our tour of Italy the previous week[1] – and my wife, Iona (aka *La Belle Dame Sans Merci*), chat unconcernedly about pleasures past and those still to come this week. Hopefully. If we don't crash into the back of this thing in front.

I risk a glimpse of Vesuvius' towering cone illuminated by the slanting rays of the setting sun as it prepares to go to a watery bed in the Bay of Naples to our right. Just as it's hard to take one's eyes off the volcano, it's impossible not to be

---

[1] See *Travels Through Time in Italy: Eight Cities Past and Present* by David M. Addison (2017).

reminded of other things, more sombre things – the havoc, death and destruction which it wreaked in '79 – and also to reflect that it's the main reason we came on this holiday. If not for Pompeii, if not for Herculaneum, would we be here now? Probably not. Ironic to think their destruction is the cause of our pleasurable excursion.

One of the things we're intending to do this week is go to the top of this, Nature's weapon of mass destruction, and peer into the crater. Hopefully we will not spark off another eruption. In October, we had been up Etna – which erupted a couple of days later. It's not nearly as energetic or as daunting as it sounds – climbing Vesuvius I mean, not creating an eruption. You can get a bus pretty much to the top, or so I've read.

Now we are passing Ercolano – there's the sign to the *Scavi*. We'll certainly be going there. In fact, in some ways I am looking forward to Herculaneum more than I was to Pompeii. I'd seen it on television recently. It looks more compact, more intimate, gives me the feeling I can get a complete picture of it, unlike Pompeii which is so sprawling that our half-day there was sufficient to see only a fraction of it. Hopefully, we'll be able to combine Herculaneum with our ascent of Vesuvius on the same day and – at some stage – return to Pompeii also.

The fate of the residents of Herculaneum, because it was so near to Vesuvius, was different and – in my view – worse than those of Pompeii. They were buried in mud, not ash like the victims of Pompeii, and – according to the television programme I saw – the heat was so intense that the victims' brains evaporated. Too horrible to imagine, but I think I'd prefer that instantaneous option to the slower death by

Vesuvius (Image Credit: Pixabay)

drowning in that boiling mud. Besides, being of little brain (according to Iona) it might not have hurt too much.

After the Pompeii turn-off, we take the SS145 to Sorrento. The motorway driving was relaxing compared to this. As we weave along the road which clings to the cliff, I hang on to my seat for grim life. Naples to Sorrento via Alton Towers. The passengers in the rear have fallen strangely silent. Painted on the road is a continuous double white line with occasional signs saying to permit overtaking when, instead of blind bends, you can see the road snaking ahead for a few yards. But, as we had discovered on our first day, in Naples these road markings are not for demarcation but for decoration – yet another example of the Italian disregard for rules which had intrigued me last week.

Even where they do not permit it, drivers overtake. Whilst I hold my breath and press frequently on my imaginary brake pedal, our driver seems not in the least fazed by

3

the oncoming motorbikes and scooters he encounters on our side of the road as he rounds yet another bend. He seems to regard them as perfectly normal road-traffic users with every right to be there.

It is practically a three-lane road, the middle lane too narrow for cars, but wide enough for two-wheeled vehicles. It's almost as if those white lines down the middle are their designated lane, as it seems to be more or less permanently occupied by them as they streak past us with a deafening roar or come hurtling towards us, which is just as terrifying.

Not to be left out, on one short stretch, our driver makes a daring overtaking manoeuvre himself, squeezing back to our side of the road just in time. Incredible that there are no accidents! Why do I say that? I bet there are: I have already seen so many near misses that, statistically speaking, it must happen – and happen often. But perhaps the laws of probability do not apply in Italy. Why should they? After all, as I had been told last week, none of the EU laws which are devised in Germany, ignored by France, and obediently observed by the British, have yet to be heard of in Italy.

We had thought in this, the second week of our Italian holiday, we might possibly hire a car and drive down the Amalfi coast, to which purpose I have brought my driving licence. For the record, I have driven without incident all over the European continent – not to mention four crossings of Canada and the United States, New Zealand top to toe, and Italy to boot – and I've never had an accident in thousands upon thousands of miles. It follows therefore, according to the laws of probability, that my luck is bound to change sooner rather than later. And if it that is the case, this looks the very place where it will run out.

Here and now, I resolve to resign from my use as driver on this holiday. And if that also renders me useless on this trip, it scarcely matters as our guide last week said that Karen, who would be our rep this week, would be able to organise a minibus for us.

"Us", apart from Iona and me, and Bill and Pat, also includes Tom and Harriet and their son, Dick, with, in addition, Donald and Helen, a young Scottish couple, all of whom had been on the tour with us last week. At a banquet in the sumptuous surroundings of the Palazzo Borghese in Florence, Napoleon's nymphomaniac little sister's little place, we had agreed this would be the most effective (and cheapest) way of sightseeing the following week since we were all going to be staying at the four-star Monte Somma, apart from Bill and Pat who would be slumming it in a three-star in Sorrento itself. Even now, the others are speeding their way in a matching minibus to Sorrento – or should be, barring accidents.

At last we arrive safely in Sorrento. Our driver pulls into a narrow lane by the side of the Hotel Isabella, thereby blocking it off completely. From outward appearances, I'm not impressed by the hotel. It may be central, but it doesn't look particularly inviting. I am glad we've forked out extra to stay out of town, up in the lush green hillside. In any case, there is a complimentary bus service down to town, so we've nothing to lose, apart from the extravagant extra euros we forked out for the posher hotel.

At this moment I am looking forward to the gin which I had bought in Rome (I deserve it after this harrowing drive), followed by a swim in the pool, then maybe another couple of *apéritifs*, if I am lucky – if I can sneak them past *La Belle Dame Sans Merci*, before we go down to have what I hope is going to be a delicious Italian meal.

I'm really looking forward to this week. It's going to be so much more relaxing. No more getting up at what is, for me, the crack of dawn (usually about 8 am, but sometimes even earlier), to sit in a bus for hours upon hours as we travelled from one city to another like the Grand Tourists of yester-year.

"The pool probably closes at 6 o'clock," warns Bill when I tell him of my intentions. Except I miss out the gin parts, so I don't shock him by reminding him of the time I had bought two bottles, while all he had bought was a bottle of iced tea. He's not teetotal, just totally addicted to tea like a lot of the English nation. I thank God I was born a Scot and my national drink isn't tea. Having said that, whisky only tends to be my winter, autumn and spring drink. I reserve gin for the summer and for drinking outside, when the sun is shining. That means due to the vagaries of the Scottish climate, whisky is what I usually drink in the summer too – unless I am abroad.

"Hmm! Well, see you tomorrow!" I say in farewell as he and Pat are decanted with their luggage onto the pavement. It's the one organised thing for the week – we have a tour of Sorrento thrown in as part of the package. It's at 9 o'clock, which isn't too bad. After that, we can have some long lies. Sounds like heaven to me.

Our driver reverses fearlessly into the oncoming traffic and, resuming our journey, we climb steadily out of Sorrento. On our right is the harbour, but at last we leave the bay behind and head up the mountain by a succession of hairpin bends. It does seem to be some distance out of the town – and steep. Perhaps it was a mistake to have picked the Monte Somma. I notice, in the passing, there is no pavement – so if we were to attempt the walk, we'd have to have our wits

6

about us, trusting to luck that the motorists, on these tight bends, would miss us. This road is clearly not made for pedestrians, except for those with a death wish.

At last we pull up in front of our hotel. Tall white flagpoles are sprouting from a rose bed set in the midst of an immaculately manicured lawn, from the top of which a selection of national flags fluttering gaily and colourfully in the breeze. *Welcome! Welcome! Wherever you are from, we are delighted to see you,* so they are saying. To our right, cascades of blue geraniums are tumbling over a wall. A gap in it leads to a pergola dripping with wisteria and, beyond, a meandering path can be seen threading its way through emerald-green lawns bordered by exotic vegetation. This knocks the plain, even austere, Hotel Isabella into a cocked hat.

Yes, this looks my sort of place. For once, it looks like I might have made the right decision. *I think I am going to like it here,* I say to myself, as if – in a lifetime of disappointments – I'd never ever heard of tempting fate before.

Or counting chickens, for that matter.

A Matter of Reflection

TO enter that foyer, with its vast expanse of marble, fleetingly gives me the feeling of what it must have been like to enter a Roman villa. In front of us is reception, the burnished wood of the desk gleaming richly. To our right are broad marble steps leading down to the dining room. To our left, over another seemingly endless floor of polished marble, is a bar with comfortable-looking sofas and chairs, while – away in the distance – I can just make out a fireplace with a brass hood set in the middle of the floor which they must light in the winter. How cosy and how opulent!

And from a door to the left of the bar, you can take your drinks outside and sit on the terrace and enjoy a view of the bay. Here in the foyer, guests can relax and see the gardens through the floor-to-ceiling plate-glass windows. The entire place conveys an atmosphere of light, spaciousness and luxury. It is, you might say, satisfactory.

I approach the reception desk, the wheels of my luggage rumbling on the smooth, polished marble. This is always a nervous moment for me. I am accustomed to things going awry whenever I approach officialdom. On our outward journey, when I rang the airport to check if our flight was departing on schedule, I was told we were not affected by the BA strike – only when we got there, it was to be confronted by a queue of disrupted travellers snaking its way through the terminal lounge. And yes, our flight had been cancelled too. We only managed to get to Heathrow, where we were to catch our onward flight to Naples, by switching airlines at an exorbitant cost. Whether the insurance will cough up or not remains to be seen. So, as I approach the desk, I half expect there to be a problem with our booking. And not to disappoint me, the gods have ensured there is.

"Have you a reservation for Addison, please?"

"Adamson... let me see."

"No, not Adamson. Addison."

"Ah, Anderson..."

"No, not Anderson; Add-i-son." I enunciate each syllable as if I were talking to someone hard of hearing, which clearly I am.

"Adderson... Nothing in that name either, sir..."

Good grief! "A-D-D-I-S-O-N," I spell out, trying not to show my exasperation and trying to keep my temper under control.

"Oh, ADDISON...!" (Why didn't you say so before, you mumbling idiot?) "Yes, we have a reservation in that name, sir."

Phew! At last! It's not his fault really; just the gods having a joke, teasing me, winding me up. The relief is so great I don't mind this momentary hiccup, now that our booking is confirmed, the panic over. What would we have done if he had said he'd no reservation in that name? Too horrible to contemplate. Plainly it's an unusual name for him. Quite possibly I am the first Addison ever to check into the Hotel Monte Somma, at least in his tenure. Imagine that!

I can imagine my illustrious namesake, the famous essayist, Joseph, and one of the pioneers of the Grand Tour, experiencing the same confusion over his name as me on my latter-day Grand Tour. Strange to relate, the Grand Tour did not end in Rome, as you might expect, but in Naples – and here I am, three-hundred years later, down the road a bit, as you might say, in both senses of the expression, but experiencing the same sort of difficulties as he might have had on his tour.

The receptionist busies himself behind the desk and produces our key. It's one of those credit card types. My mind, irrationally striking off at a tangent, recalls Bob Newhart's sketch of Walter Raleigh coming back from the New World and trying to explain the uses of tobacco, that new and exotic plant. I can imagine poor Joseph having some difficulty in recognising this slim rectangle as a key: *What? So, I swipe (?) this through the door handle and the door unlocks... Ha! Ha! Ha!... (You're kidding me!) And then I put it in a slot (?)... behind the door and then... no, no, don't tell me... and then all the candles in the room light up at the same time, is that right? Ha! Ha! Ha!*

"Room 374, sir. Have you your passports?"

Eh? I snap out of my reverie. Well, yes I do, somewhere. Somewhere in the depths of one of the suitcases, but I haven't a clue where, nor in which one. We haven't needed them for a week.

"It's all right, sir," replies the impeccably-dressed receptionist suavely. "If you would just like to bring them down when you are ready. Just leave your cases, sir," he adds hurriedly as I make to grab hold of the nearest, "I'll see they are taken up to your room."

Damn! I'm perfectly capable of carrying my own cases to my room, especially since they have little wheels and there is a lift to take me up to the third floor. Now I'll have to pay a tip and hang about waiting for them to arrive. Not that I have any plans for going anywhere – except to the pool, and the sooner the better.

The lift is roomy, as big as the third bedroom in some modern houses: you could get at least a couple of cots in here if you were unlucky enough to get twins from the single sexual experience. Unfortunately, it has a mirror in it. I hate that. I hate having to look at myself more than necessary. Can't understand why people have mirror wardrobes in their bedrooms, but then, not everyone looks like me, I reflect, as I catch sight of myself again in the mirror. I don't want to, but it's difficult not to.

Maybe La Belle Dame Sans Merci *has a point about my sartorial propriety after all*, I continue to reflect as we are borne upwards. I am some sight. I don't think the Panama hat really goes with the swimming trunks I am wearing as shorts, even although the light-green pilot shirt compliments the dark-green perfectly. My shoes, once light blue, now covered in a rich patina of dust, I have to admit, go with neither. My Panama, once sparkling white, now has a grimy brim, like the rim round a dirty bath.

What's a person like me doing in a place like this? I don't remotely look like a patron of such a swanky establishment, more like a tramp who has wandered in off the street – apart from the Panama, which, I hope, gives me a certain cachet and with a bit of luck and a bit of myopia on the part of the observer, might make me look more like a dissipated *roué* than a down-and-out.

It's a relief to get out of the lift and put that vision from hell behind me. We turn to the right along the thickly-carpeted corridor. The numbers of the rooms are written, not on the door, but on the floor. How bizarre! Maybe it's to help the drunks crawling their way back after their corporate entertainment. I'm sure a posh place such as this must host lots of conferences. We are in the low teens at the moment (apart from our ages), and a curve in the corridor ahead means we must be round the bend somewhere. Some say I am there already – and not just my wife.

Ah, here we are at last. 374. I unlock the door with the credit card, put it in the slot to the right of the door, and a thousand candlepower's worth of lights flicker on automatically. Hey, this is all right! The room is spacious, with a king-size bed and another one – a single – against the wall to the right. Much more luxurious than our little love nest at home! Who knows what heights of passion these walls may witness! Only there's an antidote – a mirror facing the king-size.

"Wow! Separate beds! Yours is a bit smaller than mine though," I remark to Iona, who chooses to treat the joke with silence – or perhaps she's merely struck dumb with the sumptuousness of it all.

To the right of the double bed are sliding doors, clearly leading to the balcony, but at the moment barricaded by metal shutters. I press a switch in the wall and, with a protesting clank, the shutters are drawn slowly upwards like a portcullis, permitting light to flood into the room. Well, this should certainly exclude pests, like insects and burglars.

The view from the balcony is disappointing. We are at the back of the hotel, looking onto a cliff only a matter of a few feet away, apparently gouged out of the hillside to make way for the new hotel. There is some vegetation, including palm trees, to lend a bit of an exotic atmosphere, and a few flowers to add a bit of colour. A sea view came as extra, and we thought the cost was not justifiable: most of the time we would spend in the room, we'd be asleep – or at least trying to be.

As balconies go, it's not one of the best, and there is not much chance of me getting a tan on it – the sun is unlikely to penetrate the trees during the day, though there is a possibility that in the evening it might just strike it, which would be nice for the downing of the G&Ts before we go down to dinner. It doesn't really matter, though. I am not likely to be here during the day – and any time I do spend at the hotel, I'm more likely to be at the pool than on the balcony.

I am anxious to be off, to see the pool and to explore; but, of course, I can't – not until the luggage comes up, because Iona says it's the man's job to give the tip. Oh, is it? I never knew that before. What's the price likely to be? A euro a case, I suppose. I make sure I have a couple of them in one of the pockets of my swimming trunks, and a couple more, in the other pocket, just in case the porter gives me a drop-dead-you-mean-bastard sort of look.

As it happens, I am christening the facilities when there is a tap at the door. It's our cases already! A euro a case seems to be about right as the man goes away without looking at me.

Or perhaps he couldn't bear to.

3

A Cry in the Night

MAY as well unpack. Ah, the luxury not to be living out of a suitcase, as we have been doing for the past week – where a two-night stay had been our maximum! But the main priority is to get the gin and tonic chilled. There is an ice compartment in the baby fridge, but no ice, so I fill the tray with water from the bought bottle. No flies on me: no bugs for us from ice made from tap water. I had learned that dire lesson at the appropriately-named Cataract Hotel in Aswan.

I slip out of my dusty blue shoes which had cost me 50p out of Lidl's – and by the state of them, I would not put any money on them not making the return journey to Scotland – and slip into my *pantoufles*, a present from Iona. No, not the island, but the dearly-beloved trouble and strife. They are burgundy in colour and have pictures of wine bottles on them with labels saying Burgundy and Bordeaux and Chardonnay and Chablis, to preserve political correctness in terms of colour. I may have drunk enough wine in my time to float a battleship, but this is proof I don't let it go to my head.

It was an inspired present. She knows me so well, my lovely wife. She knows what I like. I am very attached to them. Wheresoever I go, they go also, as my feet are in them.

But forget the present; right now I am off to see what the pool is like and to see if there is any possibility of a swim before dinner. I may as well take the passports to reception at the same time.

The semi-hard-of-hearing man (or slow-on-the-uptake man) at reception is amazed I have brought them so quickly, and thanks me graciously for my promptness. What a nice man! I think I am going to like this hotel.

But where is the pool? I head off to my right, down the flight of steps that leads to the dining room. May as well check that out, see what is on the menu tonight; sample the ambience, stimulate the saliva glands.

Acres of marble surround me as I slide my *pantoufles* over the shiny surface. It's so friction-free I can't resist sliding them over it in the manner of an ice-skater. Far ahead of me I can see what I presume is the pool and, in the intermediate distance, what appears to be an ice floe harbouring a waddle of penguins.

The reality turns out to be a bit more prosaic. It's a table with crisp white napery on which reposes the salad bar. The penguins turn out to be merely waiters – unsurprisingly enough. I stop skating, because the temperature seems to have dropped so many degrees I fear I may fall through the marble. There is something about the way the penguins are looking at me which gives me an uneasy feeling, just like the one you get when you walk into a car showroom through salesman-infested waters.

"Yes, can I help you?"

The oldest, a small man with thinning hair swept back from his forehead and with a bit of a paunch and an overall appearance of more than a hint of Marlon Brando in *The Godfather* about him, has advanced and is looking me up and down with an expression which can only be described as distaste. It's as if I had introduced the smell of rotting vegetation, or worse, into this culinary inner sanctum.

"No, thanks; I've just come for a look around." I can see if I walk in a straight line past Signor Corleone, I will be able to have a look at the pool. And that is exactly what I do, but I can feel his gaze following me and pricking my back with poisoned darts.

I wander out onto a terrace where already there are diners, as P.G. Wodehouse would have put it, at the trough. Perhaps I am a *bit* underdressed for the occasion. This seems to be quite a classy restaurant. Smart-casual would seem to be the accustomed attire for the men, certainly not shorts. The women look even more posh – cocktail dresses seem to be *de rigueur*. And here I am in my swimming trunks and *pantoufles*. I snatch off my Panama. I hadn't realised till now that I still had it on. Seconds later, I realise that that was a mistake – that the Panama might have conferred on me the status of some English eccentric – but now I am exposed as some sort of Scottish tramp instead. Since I have already opened my mouth, it's too late to pretend to be English and preserve the pride of my nation, if Signor Corleone and his minions have any ears for accents.

Too late also for the proper use of the swimming trunks: the pool is already closed. Bill was right; it probably did close at six. It looks very nice though: plenty of sunbeds, plenty of space, and a whirlpool as well. Yes, I can see me spending a bit of time here, relaxing with a beer after a hard day's slog down amongst the Roman ruins or on the summit of Vesuvius.

I've seen as much as I want to for the moment. I'll have a shower, a couple of aperitifs, and then it would be very nice to come back here and have our dinner at a table overlooking the pool, watching the sun set behind the palm trees.

I turn to go and meet the uncompromising gaze of Signor Corleone who must be the maître d'. I have a feeling he has never taken his eyes off me ever since I arrived. I smile at him, sweetly. He inclines his head by a fraction which does not register even a flicker on the Richter scale of non-verbal communication. He appears to be transfixed by my *pantoufles,* but tearing his gaze away and meeting my eyes, the corner of his mouth twists in what he possibly imagines is a smile but emerges more as: *Whadda tramp like you doin' in my restaurant, huh? If you think you're gonna be served here dressda like that, you gotta another think comin'.*

I pretend not to understand and pass by as serenely as I can, all the time feeling his eyes stabbing my back like needles in a voodoo doll. If I should cry out in the night with what the people in the room next door might misinterpret as sounds of apparent ecstasy, I will know what it is this time, for – you see – I have previous on this. Once upon a time, when staying with my sister and brother-in-law, I suffered an agonising pain in my chest. I thought I was suffering a heart attack – and could not help but cry out in anguish.

"Shut up! Shut up!" hissed Iona fiercely. "They'll think we are doing it!" They were just on the other side of the wall.

When it happened again, for two pins, she threatened to smother me with a pillow unless I shut up that very second. That is how she came to be known as *La Belle Dame Sans Merci.*

I don't know what it was I was suffering from, but it wasn't a heart attack and I lived to tell the tale to my hosts the following morn. But to this day they still do not believe I was having a near-death experience. The "of course you were, David" (nudge, nudge, wink, wink) sort of sympathy I got was almost as insufferable as the pain in my chest and, of course, I was in the doghouse from you-know-who, the only witness to the truth. Her testimony was discounted. She would say that, wouldn't she?

Should I feel sudden stabbing pains in my heart tonight, I'll know for certain it'll be Signor Corleone dutifully sticking needles into my chest when he comes off duty after having first melted the candles from the dinner tables and moulded them into my likeness. At the inquest, the people in the next apartment will testify they heard sounds of sexual ecstasy in the middle of the night and, just as long she can smother the desire to suffocate me with a pillow first, Iona will collect the life insurance. I don't mind that. It's fair enough: she deserves it, her reward for being married to me all these years.

But it wouldn't be justice. What sticks in my craw is that the verdict – *the deceased died getting it off* – means that the perpetrator of my early demise, the real villain of the piece, Signor Corleone, will be the one who really gets off with it.

4

Drinks Before Dinner

I return to room 374 and report to Iona that dinner will be quite a formal affair. I like that idea. The idea of getting dressed for dinner, I think, makes it a bit more special – makes me feel a bit more on holiday because I am making a special effort, like the effort of dragging myself out of bed in the mornings which, although painful at the time, is usually (in retrospect) a discipline worth the effort in the long run.

I allow Iona to shower first, whilst I take a seat on the balcony and test the temperature of the atmosphere and the gin. The air is pleasantly warm but the gin is still too warm by half – though a warm gin in the hand is better than none at all, and none at all is what Iona will assume I have had when she emerges from the shower, for I have cunningly replaced the gin and the tonic in the fridge. Alert for the sound of the cessation of running water – when it occurs – I swiftly drain my glass, dry it on the bottom of my sheet, then replace it upside down on top of the mini bar in the precise position it had occupied before. I certainly don't wish to be caught red-handed, for although gin and tonic has the appearance of water, *La Belle Dame Sans Merci* would see through me, not to mention the glass, and its alcoholic content. She would never believe I was drinking water on its own.

She emerges swathed in her dressing gown, her hair festooned in a towel, to find me innocently reading the guide-book. I look up with what I hope she will interpret as an expression of vague surprise to find her finished so soon.

"That didn't take you long," I say, to add weight to my subterfuge – and not without a degree of regret, as I had had to down the incriminating last mouthful hastily in what should really have been a couple, at least, of long, appreciative and lingering mouth-swilling swallows. "Did you have a nice shower?"

Like Aunt Polly at the beginning of *Tom Sawyer*, when she called upon the eponymous hero (probably because, like me, he had done something wrong again), I get no answer. She merely sweeps the room with her eyes like a metal detector. Did her nostrils twitch, or did I just imagine it?

"Right, I think I'll have a shower," I announce, even if I am talking to myself.

Even as I speak, Iona is plugging in her hair-dryer and, with the other hand, is reaching for Humphrey the hedgehog hairbrush, which also sees service as a spanking machine on my bum. This is a good sign. It's not what you're thinking – I am not into masochism and Iona even less: she can't bear the idea of torture, though it does not prevent her from giving me a few hard swipes with Humphrey, to make me get up in the morning. No, it means that even with the most leisurely of showers, I will be dried, dusted and dressed before the ritual of the hair-drying is completed – plenty of time to suggest an *apéritif* before dinner, and (if she is in a good mood) another, which means I shall go down to dinner in a very relaxed and ambient state of mind indeed.

Just to make sure, I make my shower a relatively short one, altruistically aware of the fact that Italy is experiencing a bit of a drought at the moment and the desperate need to conserve water. It should also leave sufficient time for that second *apéritif* (if she permits it) before Iona starts clamouring for her food. She doesn't share my view that alcohol *is* food and, when the desire for food comes upon her, she gives in to it instantly. She has absolutely no willpower.

"How about an *apéritif?*" I suggest nonchalantly after I am dressed in my relatively smart (for me) Chinos and short-sleeved shirt.

"All right." She is putting the finishing touches to her coiffure.

We sit on the balcony and drink tepid G&Ts, feeling quite the part: Iona in her crinkle-free, posh or posh/casual black dress, depending whether or not she is flashing her gold jewellery or not. Tonight she is posh. For a moment we can pretend to be rich, sipping our drinks on the veranda before we go down to the sumptuous dinner which cook has prepared for our delectation.

We talk of what we'll do tomorrow. Without having had a chance to speak with the others, it looks like after the walking tour of Sorrento in the morning – too late to do anything else – it'll have to be a relaxing afternoon by the pool, catching some rays and reading a book. A well-deserved rest after the hard work of the previous week. Aaah! This is the life!

"How about another *apéritif?*" I suggest without much hope.

"I should think you've had quite enough already."

I give her a sidelong glance. "What do you mean? This was just a little one." Not quite the truth actually. Hers was the little one; mine was the larger one, though they looked the same in the glass. Being the lion in this relationship it's only right I should have the lion's share, according to the laws of nature.

"Don't tell me you didn't have one while I was in the shower."

Bloody hell, how does she do it? How did she know? Maybe she has sniffed the glass, or maybe she's just bluffing.

"*Quoi? Little moi?*" I may be the lion, the dominant male – only because I am the *only* male in this relationship, admittedly – but lying is not part of my nature. Men may be deceivers ever, as Ophelia put it in such a sexist way, but I will not tell a deliberate lie. I may prevaricate or try to change the subject, or be suddenly smitten with deafness of the most impenetrable kind. On this occasion, however, for no particular reason, I assume an air of injured innocence. I know it is a dead giveaway, and I am deceiving no-one.

Still, miracles do happen sometimes and Iona agrees to more *apéritifs* as long as they are small ones. I wholeheartedly agree. As before: small on the gin for her, small on the tonic for me. That's the beauty of gin – you can't tell the strength by looking at it like you can with a whisky and water. I duck under the steel shutters to go and mix the drinks. If every night is going to be like this and the food is good, this is going to be a most pleasurable second week of our mini Grand Tour.

It's very pleasant to sit on the balcony. Pity there is no sun, though – just a sliver at the back, not big enough for two people to squeeze into. That space is reserved for me. It's another of the reasons we are such a good match, Iona and I. I let her get up first to get the first shower and I preserve her skin from premature wrinkling by sitting in the sunny spots, giving up the shade for her.

By the time the second gin is finished, it's time to descend the stairs and go to dinner. It's a pleasant prospect, and I am suitably mellow. There will be wine, of course, and waiter service, but what I look forward to with the keenest anticipation – because we can't do it in Scotland, or at least very rarely – is to dine alfresco. During the gins I had intimated it would be very pleasant to sit outside, on the terrace, overlooking the pool, and Iona had agreed.

But I had not reckoned with Signor Corleone. Across the vast marble plain he can see us coming and we can see him. I have the advantage over him in that I know who he is, but in my disguise, he, at this distance, probably does not yet recognise me as the tramp who wandered through his restaurant just a few gins ago.

He advances to meet us and hails us: *Buona sera. This way please.* As he looks at me, I can see the light of recognition switching on in his head. I can change my clothes, but no-one in this hotel nor probably, in the whole of Italy, has a face as red as mine.

5

Dinner Disaster

S IGNOR Corleone leads the way into the main restaurant to our right. Like lambs, we follow him, and he pulls out a chair at the table of his choice for Iona, then – from beneath his oxter – he presents a couple of menus with a flourish.

"Drinks?"

"Er... em... house wine."

"Bianco o rosso?"

Iona and I look at each other in mute helplessness. How do we know when we don't even know what we are going to eat yet?

"Er... em... *bianco,"* I say, masterfully taking command of the situation, on the assumption that we may have fish and, in any case, white is Iona's preference. In Sicily, last year, the white house wine had been far superior to the red, so it's possibly the case here too.

"Acqua?"

"Er... si."

"Frizzante o naturale?"

"Um... *frizzante."*

Signor Corleone writes it down in a notebook, gives a slight nod and – with what looks like a manoeuvre bred in a military establishment – turns on his heel and is gone to ensnare the next customers. It's all over in a breathless fraction of a second; so quickly, I can scarcely believe that it's happened. Whatever happened to my alfresco table? How come I let myself be bullied like this? Was it an act of revenge for my former appearance? Had he remembered me looking at the poolside tables and thought: *Right, I'll afixa him.*

I mutter darkly about this regimentation, but am almost instantly mollified by the fact that – although we are under cover – the walls ahead of us and to our left are open panels where, presumably, in the winter, they fit glass panes. But for the moment, they are empty like a mouth with missing teeth: an appropriate simile for a dining room, especially if you're having soup or are an invalid on liquids.

The empty panel ahead of us frames a splendid vista of the bay, at the further end of which the silhouette of Vesuvius shoulders into the sky. It could be a postcard. Naples and its suburbs are beginning to light up: a myriad of firefly lights are beginning to twinkle around the perimeter of the bay like a necklace. Yes, you could go far (apart from outside), I reflect with satisfaction, before you could find a better location in which to dine.

Ah! Here comes the wine already, and brought by the Great Dictator himself. They evidently don't hang about in this place. I am gratified to see that it comes in a bottle, not, as many house wines do, in a carafe. Deftly, he opens it and pours the sample for me to test. I smell it, inhale deeply, and then take a sip. He may recognise me as the tramp who invaded his restaurant earlier, but there's no harm in letting him see that I have done this before. I nod, but do not speak, to signify that the wine is acceptable. Signor Corleone pours and departs. Was that my imagination, or did I detect the faint sound of heels clicking?

As soon as he goes, I read the label. 13%. That's a bit better than the wines we've been having last week. It doesn't come in a nice little bucket with iced water though, like it should, although it is nicely chilled at the moment. Better drink it while it's at its best.

Yes, this wine is not too shabby at all. Very drinkable.

In due course, the waiter comes and we order an *antipasto* and the fish to go with the wine, though I am normally accustomed to putting the horse before the cart, so to speak.

"That's one of the mans I saw earlier," I whisper to Iona once he has gone, bearing away the menus.

She draws me a sharp look. "I mean one of the *waiters* when I reconnoitred earlier." I hope the change of noun will somehow explain away my gaffe. Why *did* I say that? I can't understand it. I've been talking English for half a century, some would say too much.

We are in mid *antipasti* before we realise we have not had our salad. If it had been in the same room, no doubt we would have remembered it, but we were regimented past the table on which it is displayed and then the service had been so fast, we had barely time to draw breath before the waiter materialised to take our order. We have allowed ourselves to be bullied and railroaded all along. I am determined the same thing will not happen tomorrow.

"I don't have a knife," I call to the waiter's back as he leaves.

He returns, wordlessly slides my plate slightly to the side and there it is! My jaw drops in amazement. How come I didn't notice it before he put the plate down? I can feel myself blushing, and daren't meet the basilisk stare of *La Belle Dame Sans Merci*. I don't know if the waiter recognises me as the tramp or not, but the way he just moved the plate to the side without saying anything shows, I think, that *he* must think I am an idiot of the first water. I know for a fact what Iona is thinking. I prattle on in my confusion, saying the first thing that comes into my head in an effort to cover up, to not give her the chance to launch her attack.

When the food comes, since we have ordered the same meal, the same fish, at least the same species, I point out to Iona I don't seem to have a piece of lemon on my fish like she does. Not that I mind at all. She is the lemon lover in the family.

"What's that, then?"

And there, lo and behold, nestling among the shredded lettuce, is something that looks remarkably like a slice of lemon! I'd swear it wasn't there a moment ago, that it's been transmogrified from an onion ring. I am reminded of a *Hornblower* story I read years ago about St Elizabeth of Hungary who, engaged on smuggling bread to the poor, was caught red-handed one day. On being asked what was in her apron, she replied, having been prompted by a vision, "Roses". And no-one was more surprised than her to find that when she opened her apron, that's exactly what it did contain!

Being more of a sinner than a saint, as far as I am concerned, it's just the gods at it again, playing another of their whimsical little jokes on me. It certainly can't be the gin that's to blame. It's the same Spanish brand I always drink.

Meanwhile, *La Belle Dame Sans Merci* is looking at me suspiciously. Three blunders in as many minutes! I am surpassing myself. I can't think of a time when I have made a bigger fool of myself – unless it was at the time when we were at a party, and *La Belle Dame Sans Merci*, who hates the display of flesh between the top of a man's socks and the bottom of his trousers, commanded: *Pull your trousers down!* Ever the obedient servant, I did as I was ordered, all the way down, officiously striving to do my mistress's bidding to the nth degree. Nowadays I am told, *Pull your socks up!* And I do, literally. In the figurative sense of the expression, however, I still have some way to go – especially if tonight's performance is anything to go by.

"How many gins *did* you have?"

"Er... em... just two or three... I'm not very good at counting." I know the joke will not be received with rib-tickling roars of laughter, but I hope it will deflect the question about how big they were. The funny thing is I feel as sober as Judge Jeffreys, yet I'm behaving like a blithering idiot, as if someone had spiked my drink.

"I thought so." There is no satisfaction in her suspicions being confirmed.

There is no further cross-examination, but she certainly is cross. I suspect she suspected from the start that I had had an *apéritif* before the *apéritifs*. I remember how she had raked the room with her eyes like a minesweeper when she came out of the shower. Now she takes charge of the wine bottle, moves it over to her side of the table. Fortunately, I had re-charged my glass before the fish had arrived. It looks like that is going to be my lot. She's quite capable of jabbing a fork in my hand if I made a grab for it.

What I had anticipated being a pleasurable evening is turning into a disaster. It confirms my theory that you should never look forward to anything too much – it just gives the gods a chance to kick you in the teeth.

6

A Little Night Music

I sulkily eye the bottle of wine under the guardianship of *La Belle Dame Sans Merci*, who has her eyes on the *dolci*. She's watching the waiter with undisguised interest as he wheels his trolley amidst the other diners with what looks to me like all sorts of sickly cakes on it, except she would call them *gâteaux*. They hold no interest for me. I am not a sweet person.

"You know, that wine will taste terrible after whatever delicious sweet you're intending to have."

She knows there is wisdom in my words. I know also she's not capable of finishing that bottle on her own. I have not made any other solecisms, have behaved impeccably by the tried and tested method of keeping my mouth firmly shut except to put food in it. And it seems to have worked, because she gives a long-suffering sigh and pours out some wine in equal measures. A lion cub's share is better than none. The main thing is not to let it go to my head. I must be extremely careful not to make any more blunders, then perhaps she'll let me finish the bottle.

Whilst Iona is drooling over the sweet trolley, Tom, Dick and Harriet arrive and are ushered to a table over to our right. Our other fellow travellers from last week, Donald and Helen – the young Scottish couple – are to our left, and look as if they are nearly finished.

Iona chooses sticky toffee pudding and gets tucked in. I can hardly bear to look, and there is scarcely any wine in my glass either. I'm making it last with difficulty, and I don't need a magnifying glass to see it will not last much longer.

Donald and Helen have finished now, and have stopped to exchange pleasantries. Since I am not eating (nor drinking much either) and Iona's mouth is sealed shut at the moment, I hospitably invite them to occupy the two empty chairs so we can discuss possible plans for the week, particularly the trip along the Amalfi coast.

"Would you like some more wine?" I ask Iona, the personification of the solicitous husband. If I'm not much mistaken, Donald and Helen have just embarked on this marriage lark, and this is my chance to give these beginners a lesson on how to remain married for more years than I have fingers and toes by showing them that the secret is to show a caring and attentive attitude towards your other (and better) half.

She shakes her head. Her mouth is full of goo.

"I may as well finish this off then," and reach across. And lo! There is enough for a full glass. All the while, I avoid meeting Iona's eyes.

"So, what's your room like?" Frankly, I couldn't give a damn, but instinct tells me it is a good idea to engage them in conversation, the sooner the better, and hopefully until the wine is finished.

They report it is very nice, with an extra bed in it (as if they would need it) just like ours, only theirs is at the front and overlooks the bay. Ah, hah! Proof, if ever I needed it, that they are on their honeymoon. Why else would they spend extra money on a room with a romantic view? Ironic, as all they should need, as Eliza Doolittle sang, is *a room somewhere.*

Like us, they are teachers. On their salaries, therefore, they cannot be wildly rich, especially being at the bottom of the scale. On the other hand, they are not yet suffering from that unstemmable financial haemorrhage known as children, which no doubt explains how they are able to splash out on the superior room. And quite right too: they may as well while they can, for when those tiny feet start pattering it's like the sound of paper money being shredded.

One thing about teachers is they can't be together before very long before the subject turns to shop talk. It turns out that Donald teaches in a Catholic school and Helen at a Protestant one. That may not seem remarkable, but in the western end of the Central Belt of Scotland, that makes them rather unusual. Normally, it's more a case of never the twain shall meet.

Now that her mouth is freed-up for the moment, Iona tells the story of her mother who taught in a Protestant primary school, which was separated from a Catholic one by a low wall – probably in an idealistic attempt to bring the warring religions together. By growing up together, it was hoped they might form friendships that would o'er leap that small, yet symbolic partition. If that was the intention, the architects of this noble design were literally casting straws to the wind.

In those far-off-remembered days, free milk was distributed to pupils in third-of-a-pint bottles. For the consumption thereof, pupils were provided with gaily-striped straws in a variety of shades. Now here's my point. In the Catholic school, where green was the preferred colour, all the blue ones were left and in the Protestant school where blue was the colour of choice, no-one touched the green ones.

Donald is nodding in agreement. "My uncle had a chemist's shop in a Protestant part of Glasgow," he says, "and he couldn't sell any green toilet paper."

"How bizarre!" I reply. "I would have thought that would have been the very colour he would have sold if they were wiping their ar..."

"Do *you* mind!" *La Belle Dame Sans Merci* rudely cuts in. "Some of us are still eating."

Well one of us is. There is still a mouthful or two of brown pudding left, but Iona pushes it away from her. I can understand that. Brown is a very off-putting colour for food, I always think.

We exchange a few words with Tom, Dick and Harriet as we leave, then take the lift up to our room. It's dull and dark with the metal screen down, prison-like even, so I press the button in the wall and it clanks obediently up to let light into the room. I open the patio door to let some air in too. It would be very pleasant to sit on the balcony, although there is absolutely no chance of a post-prandial gin. I am not stupid or optimistic enough to expect that. Besides, gin is the *apéritif,* cognac is the *digestif.* It's not sour grapes: it just wouldn't be right, drinking gin after a meal, even although it would be sitting outside on a warm, balmy evening on the Mediterranean. I do have *some* culture, despite what Iona thinks.

Bloody hell, what's that? As soon as I open the door, a flood of sound washes in, but even before I had opened it, my senses had been subliminally aware that something was different. Some would call it "music" – I would call it a "bloody racket". The bass booms in that insistent way that basses do and which is impossible to ignore. It throbs through to the heart's core, takes over its rhythm even. I can feel mine beating harder. If there's one thing I can't stand, it's being forced to listen to other people's "music". It's an invasion of privacy, but because you can't see it, it's not deemed as offensive. When someone plays a racket like that, I can't shut it out – it takes over my whole being. I can't concentrate or think of anything else.

I feel so helpless. I'd love to blast back at them Bruch's *Violin Concerto*, see how *they* like *their* privacy being invaded, but firstly, just because *I* adore it, it doesn't mean everyone else in the universe has to enjoy it at precisely the same time as I am. Secondly, I don't carry offensive weapons about with me, such as ghetto blasters or compact radio/CD/tape players with stereophonic sound.

I go out onto the balcony to see where the cacophony is coming from. It's my neighbours to the right. Above the noise of the wailing vocalist with the bellyache, I can hear the voices – young female voices with irritating, elongated southern English vowels. No-one is listening to the "music", except for me and half the hotel within a half-mile radius.

I look over the balcony wall and a couple of floors below me, on the ground floor, a man is standing in the little garden which the ground-floor residents have in lieu of a balcony, looking up to see where the noise is coming from.

"It's not me!" I shout down to him, hoping my next-door neighbours might hear. (Some chance over that racket.) "It's coming from next door. Bloody awful isn't it? It's room number 372 if you want to make a complaint."

He makes a gesture to signify he can't hear what I'm saying and disappears inside.

I try to peer round the dividing wall of the balcony but I can't see anything, only hear the voices. I don't know which

I find the most irritating: their inane chatter, their extended vowels, or the "music". In combination, it's enough to drive me into a lunatic asylum – if they still had them. Now I'd be out in the community at risk from further assaults on my sanity. That's progress.

"Owh nowh, you nevah, did yowh?" The speaker sounds suitably shocked and scandalised, but also deeply impressed. I can't make out the reply. "That was reelly, reelly, ruude of yowh! What did he sigh?" (By which I presume she means the poor sod actually vocalised something, probably in exasperation at her vowels rather than merely expelled air in response to her effrontery.) I can't hear the response, but it's followed by hysterical giggling. I think I can distinguish three separate voices, which is quite possible as presumably there are three beds in their room, like ours.

I can't bear to hear any more. I come in and close the door. The sound is muffled, but now I know it's there, I can't exclude it. If I don't want to hear it, and I certainly don't, I'm going to have to keep this door shut – at least as often as *they* are in their room. And if I want to sit on the balcony, which I most certainly want to, I couldn't – not with that bloody din.

Probably in the entire hotel, accommodating no doubt in excess of 1,000 guests, I have to be the one next to the epicentre of this noise pollution. Just as well we are not Helen and Donald, wanting to sit on the balcony and watch the lights of Naples twinkling across the bay.

Since we don't have a view anyway, I may as well watch the TV. It will drown the boom, boom, boom from next door and maybe, with a bit of luck, there will be one of those quiz shows – the acme of Italian television – where housewives take their clothes off, presumably if they get a question right.

"What are you putting *that* on for?"

If there's one thing *La Belle Dame Sans Merci* can't stand, it's a TV in the bedroom. (Each to our foibles.) She thinks it's the height of decadence. This may be our living room but, since it is also our bedroom, ergo, the TV should not be switched on.

"Just getting a bit of Italian popular culture, dear."

"Huh!" She goes back to her book. "Keep the sound down. And don't call me 'dear'."

7

Last Passenger
to Sorrento

BREAKFAST time is a totally different affair from dinner. Signor Corleone is not on duty, and diners can sit where they want to. We are in luck: there is a table right at the window (if there were any glass in it) affording an uninterrupted view over the shimmering blue waters of the bay towards Naples, with Vesuvius looking hazy and indistinct in the distance.

Immediately below us, we can look down into the gardens and the pergola wreathed in wisteria sending its heavenly scent into the air. Amongst it, a busyness of bees is visiting one flower then another as if searching for the perfect pollen. Beetles as large as my thumb are beetling over glossy leaves of laurel. Oh no, they're not! One monster has just taken flight and performed a low-flying aerobatic display, causing us both to duck before it drones out of the next empty panel to our right. Iona is not so sure she wants to sit here after all, but the view is so splendid, it's worth risking the odd kamikaze beetle landing in our cornflakes.

In the intermediate distance, amongst all the greenery, is the red-tiled roof of a villa, above which rises a square tower with pairs of slim Moorish columns serving as windows on all four sides. I am a sucker for Moorish architecture at the best of times, but this tower, attached to this splendid villa, also enhances the scene, drawing the eye over its red-capped roof to the bay and Vesuvius beyond. It's all quite perfect.

It's self-service, so we can get through breakfast just as quickly or as leisurely as we like. It would be nice to linger, but we have a tour to go on and I have five courses to dispose of first – fruit juice, muesli, fruit, eggs and sausage, croissants and coffee. I'm eating two meals at once. We are on half-board, so in the interests of economy, this is also lunch.

Still plenty of time after we are finished before we go on the tour. No need to hurry, as we heave ourselves out of

A View of the Villa and the Bay

our seats and return to the room to brush our teeth, collect our cameras and other belongings, and head down to the foyer for the rendezvous with our fellow travellers from last week.

Damn! I have just stepped out of the lift when I realise I have left my Panama in the room. It's such a glorious day I'm bound to need it, the natural thatch having thinned to the point that it no longer offers protection from the deadly rays. I dash back to retrieve it, leaving Iona to go on ahead.

When I step out of the lift again, on the ground floor, I expect to see her as well as Tom, Dick and Harriet, and Donald and Helen. I also expect to see Bill and Pat, as we had been told the bus would be picking them up their hotel in the town first. Seems daft to haul them all the way up the hill like the Duke of York's men, only to march them all the way down again – but this is Italy after all, and not for me to reason why.

But the foyer is strangely empty. I know I still have seconds to spare before the appointed time. Not to worry. I expect they are outside absorbing the sunshine. That's what I would have done, had I been early.

I make my way to the exit, only to be rocked back on my heels by the surprising sight of an enormous coach parked outside with its engine running. I had got the impression it was only the nine of us, the nine survivors of last week's Grand Tour, who were to be going on this walking tour of Sorrento.

The door is open and a stout woman is blocking the gangway. She gestures to me, not without a hint of impatience, to get on board. Conditioned to commands from women, I immediately break into a trot.

"Were you told 9 am?" she asks.

"Yes."

"They're always doing that," she tuts irritably. "Should have told you 8:45," she mutters as if the omission of the subject of the sentence, the mysterious and abominated "they", would reclaim a nanosecond of the missing fifteen minutes. OMG! It suddenly occurs to me with horror – have they been waiting for us all that time and I am the last – the very last! She stands aside and I manage to squeeze past her.

The bus is full to capacity. Presumably Iona is here somewhere, as well as the others, but all I can see are eyes looking at me as I make my way up the aisle, scanning for a friendly face in this sea of hostile looks. They don't know it's not my fault; they just think I am some stupid plonker who has kept them waiting all this time.

At last, very near the back, on the right-hand side, I spot Iona and an empty seat beside her. I sink into it gratefully. I am sweating profusely. Nothing to do with the heat; it's the sweat of fear. The bus lurches off and, as we head down the hill, the portly woman begins her commentary.

"Now that we are all here, we are going to the town centre where we will go on a short walking tour of Sorrento. And then you will go to the theatre, where you will meet Karen and her assistants who will be your reps for the week. Karen will tell you about the range of activities available for you."

Not a word about why I was late. In fact, she has made it sound as if I were to blame. If I'm not much mistaken, by her vowels, she's South African. Whatever, she launches into an exposition of the history of Sorrento. There was something about the Sirens and it being founded by the Greeks, or maybe it wasn't. All I heard was the word "Greeks", and the rest was Greek to me because that was all I could make out of what the rotund lady was saying. Even if she has the benefit of a microphone, the sirens behind us are striking up a strident conversation about the endlessly fascinating subject of shopping, and their combined incessant chatter is louder than the guide's amplified voice, try as I might to shut them out.

Am I forever to be pestered by the inane sounds from other people? I'd like to learn a little about the history of the place even if they don't, and I don't give a monkey's turd about the shops – even if it does make me sound like Victor Meldrew.

Inspired by my hero, I twist round in my seat and give them a Gorgon glare: *Would you mind speaking up a bit? I can't quite hear all of your fascinating conversation. I can still hear some irrelevant and fatuous snippets about the origin of and history of this place and as I am desperate, like you, to purchase some see-through lingerie at knock-down prices, I wonder if you would be so kind as to talk a little louder.*

Well, that's what I'd like to say, but I'm just a wimp. I sit there, quietly fuming, furious at the sound of their inanity, furious at myself for not having the courage to tell them to shut up, depressed by the fact that we are billeted next to some teenage girls and I haven't even got the guts to tell them to turn off their dreadful din.

My quick glare has confirmed my suspicions. Podgy and peroxide-blonde mother-and-daughter clones. I bet the younger has tattoos in unmentionable places, not to mention rings that you can only see when she changes her underwear. Maybe the mother has a tattoo, too: I've shopped till I dropped in Sorrento, wittily inscribed over her sagging bosoms. If she hasn't, I expect she has already got the T-shirt.

My hostile look has done nothing to deter the tide of conversation which continues, unabated, to wash over me until we arrive at our destination. Their skins are too thick to take any hints. They probably didn't even notice my drop-dead stare. Actually, they probably did but thought: *What's rattling your cage, wimp-face?*

The journey seems interminable and I know the show will not be over until the fat lady stops speaking. As we pass a small parcel of land bizarrely sprouting a red-brick factory chimney, which would not have been out of place in Lanca-shire, the loquacious twosome miraculously fall silent to get their breath back. That is how we manage to hear this is where we are to go if we wish to catch the complimentary bus back to the hotel.

Up that steep, winding, racing circuit that has no pavement, we most certainly do.

8

Shopping Opportunities in Sorrento

BIZARRELY, the chimney stands in front of what remains of the city walls which date from 1551. You can still see some vestiges of the original Greek walls apparently, but I don't catch where exactly and the Roman walls which replaced them saw Sorrento right through to the Middle Ages. So what we are looking at now are a mere 450 years old. I am a lover of city walls and, although these are impressively thick and tall and solid, tapering at the top like a segment of Toblerone, they are by no means amongst the best city walls I have ever seen. Still, I would have been proud to have built them. I wonder if the patio wall I built will last as long. I don't think so, somehow.

As we drive round a corner, I catch sight of Bill and Pat in the shade of a tree without the city walls but with a guide and a large group of other tourists. Obviously they are not on this bus and not part of the same tour, as we had been led to believe they would be yesterday.

The bus stops and we disembark, giving me the chance to put as much distance as I can between me and the Brabenders. If I never hear the sound of their voices again, it will be too soon. I needn't have worried. Outside the cathedral, as we gather in a tight-knit group around the guide – after her exhortations to come nearer so she doesn't have to shout – my two ex-companions are noticeably absent. Nevertheless, it still proves practically impossible to hear what the portly lady is talking about, because – just as they say about hell, where you can't get near the fire for the ministers – here I can't get near the guide for the number of tourists. We were so lucky last week to have such a small group, just eighteen of us – half this number at least.

As cathedrals go, it's not much of a cathedral; more of a church with pretensions to grandeur. But I prefer it a thousand times to the Duomos of Florence or Siena. It's hard to say which of those two I dislike the most. Florence's exterior is execrable, but its interior is interesting. Siena's exterior is excusable, apart from its campanile, but its interior is intolerable.

I don't know what the interior of this place is like yet as we are not going inside on our tour apparently, but the exterior is pleasingly plain for one of my Calvinist tastes. It dates from the 15th century, and its major attraction seems to be that it contains a 16th century bishop's chair. Very convenient for the peroxide pair who could plonk their ample bottoms there (if they took it in turns) to renew their energies for a further bout of shopping.

My attention wanders to one of my fellow tourists. He's an enormously overweight man, sweating profusely under a Panama hat like mine. The belt of his trousers is cutting his stomach in half, so he appears to have two stomachs, an upper and lower. He's leaning on a walking stick. I have a feeling I've seen him before somewhere. There is something about the way his left eye droops at the corner which reminds me vaguely of one of those character actors you see on TV, whose name you never remember but whom you recollect appearing in the same sort of *rôle*, in his case a sinister one.

The fat lady is singing the praises of some artwork or other which is also inside the cathedral, but I can only hear her with difficulty – not only because of my distance from her, but because of the irritating buzz of Vespas accelerating past us. They aren't even doing it deliberately. It's just what they do.

The campanile, however, does have a pleasant aspect. Free-standing, and set on four arches, it is composed of a pleasing peach-coloured stone with grey brick at the edges, with the columns and arches on the façade picked out in white. Underneath the arches is where public meetings used to be held. The tower was reduced to its present size in the 15th century. Now that our guide happens to mention it, the tower does have a lopped-off sort of look, for the symmetry doesn't appear quite right – it's too short and squat. I like it though, and not just because I am short and squat myself.

Now our guide is leading us down a narrow street where the sun does not penetrate, and we emerge, thankfully, into the sunlight again at the Piazza Tasso, which, judging from all the activity, is the heart of the metropolis. Pavement cafés, crammed with clientele, are a riot of colour.

Meanwhile, on the main street of Sorrento, the Corso Italia – which leads out of it – cars, buses, and Vespas, of course, are running riot amongst the pedestrians, carving a swathe through the motley crowd, forcing them, if they wish to preserve their lives, to hop onto the narrow pavement. It runs as straight as a Roman road (and it probably is) to our left, and continues through the piazza and off to the right. No doubt the Bra-benders are here somewhere.

In the meantime, our guide is bending our ears about the bloke on the statue beside us. He's made of white marble, a cloak flung nonchalantly over his left shoulderb and he looks rather insouciant. Over his skin-tight tights, he's wearing those baggy shorts like pumpkins which you associate with Shakespeare's era. We've approached him from the back and his legs do look rather shapely, especially for a man. You can imagine him thinking: *What do you think of my new baggy breeks? Don't you think they just set off my legs perfectly?* You wouldn't need pockets with these things, just slip your things in at the top. You could keep a lot of stuff in these, if you didn't mind them rattling around as you walked. Going for a jimmy-riddle though, must have been a pain, with those tights underneath.

He is none other than the famous poet Torquato Tasso, Sorrento's most famous son, born in 1544 and so famous they named this piazza after him. So he was a poet and, I confess, I did not know it until this moment. I must have skipped the lecture the day they did Italian medieval poetry.

Now we are heading across the radiant piazza towards the Via San Cesareo, which runs parallel with the Corso Italia. The latter may be wider and the square more square, but this is the real hub of Sorrento, the site of the evening *passeggiata*. It's a medieval street, the middle of the three which parallel the Corso. It is jostling with pedestrians, for it is so narrow that even the hated Vespas are banned and it's purely the preserve of pedestrians. Shopkeepers' stalls and wares line the pavements, further restricting the movement of pedestrians. God knows what it's like during the *passeggiata*.

Here's a stall selling fruit and vegetables, a colourful tapestry of reds and greens and blacks and yellows. The black is olives, deep, deep black – full of what Keats would have called ripeness to the core – and the reds are peaches and to-matoes of various stages of ripeness, whilst the yellow is pro-vided by lemons – naturally. I'm a bit green about vegetables, and there are some species I have never seen before, but I do know that British supermarkets would not touch any of the produce on display here with a bargepole – apart from the olives, perhaps – because they all have blemishes. Not only that, but if they were chocolates, they would be what Thornton's tend to call "misshapes". I like them all the better for that, and have a certain empathy with them. Just because they don't look so good on the outside doesn't mean to say they don't have an inner goodness, just like me.

Here is a clothes shop with garments strung out on chrome rails. I pass them by with only a cursory glance. Clothes hold absolutely no interest for me unless they are skimpy on a desirable damsel, which makes the damsel even more desirable... but then again, it's not really the clothes I'm interested in. I get a vicarious sense of horror, however, from the prices. The ex-pats, of whom there are a sizable number, call this street "The Drain". If they are paying the prices these shops are asking, I can see why.

Further along, a stall is selling pasta. I can hardly be-lieve it. There are pasta shapes of all sizes and colours from great big, fat, thick tubes of penne and rigatoni like something left over from a slaughterhouse, to intricate shapes as delicate as any lace. But my attention is drawn to a pink card on which is written in red capital letters, as if the horrendous clash of colours were symbolic of the tasteless product they are advertising: SEXY PASTA "WILLY AND FEMALE SHAPE" 4,50 EUROS.

Didn't some Victorians think it immoral to have male and female authors sitting next to each other on the shelf? (Unless they happened to be married of course, in which case, it was all right.) Or is that just another myth, like the one about covering up piano legs because they were naked? If they could see this now, they would have an absolute fit – and quite rightly too, for the bag is bulging. They are certainly breeding in there.

I point them out to Iona. "Would you just look at that!"

"Huh! How crude!" and she passes on without showing even the slightest interest. I take it she's not just referring to the standard of calligraphy on the notice. It is crude, but the pasta is cruder. It seems to me a mad, bad idea, as Lady Caroline Lamb almost said of Lord Byron. It's hard to believe, but there's even worse. There are flavoured pastas, would you believe – the point of which, you might say, is just about as useful as a penis on a priest. Of these flavours, surely the most disgusting must be the liquorice.

If there's anything worse than Willy pasta, it must be liquorice Willy pasta. Iona says it's probably squid ink, not liquorice. I'm not sure if that's not worse.

9

Introducing
Mrs Scanty-Panties

NOW we are turning off the Via San Cesareo onto the Via Padre. On the right-hand side, as we enter a crowded little square almost entirely given over to alfresco restaurants, we come across a peculiar building with balustrades and arches on two sides and frescoed walls on the two interior walls. This, says our guide, is the Sedile Dominova where the nobility used to meet to discuss the affairs of the town. We are to note the domed roof of bilious green and vomit-yellow tiles from the XVI century.

Times change, and how! It now serves as a working-men's club, and indeed some old-timers underneath the arches (without subjecting us to the song of that name) are playing dominoes. It is a very good place to be, since, as they engage in their peaceful pastime, it's impossible to see the hideous tiles above their heads. Sorry, proud residents of Sorrento, but to me those tiles look like a job lot from a Victorian public lavatory.

Continuing on our way, we come to a shop with the typically Italian name of "Lucky 13". (How amusing.) Our guide parks us outside whilst she goes inside to fetch the owner, possibly her brother – or perhaps her lover, who knows? Maybe she merely gets commission. What he sells, principally, is a lemon liqueur, Limoncello di Sorrento. This is no surprise to us as we had come across limoncello last October, in Sicily. Iona, whose favourite fruit is the lemon (no comment), was most impressed with it and so was I, since I am generally interested in anything remotely alcoholic, especially anything which might convert *La Belle Dame Sans Merci* to my habit. I thought I had found the Holy Grail and invested in a bottle.

Alas, it is still three-quarters full in the booze cabinet. It seemed to taste much better in Sicily somehow, like the Guinness in Ireland does. And it never had the desired effect I had hoped for. I should have known better, given my usual luck.

The owner tells us he makes it himself from his own lemons. He has little plastic cups and is dishing out samples... only in the throng around him, I am at the back, and what's more, he's got his back to me. Maybe there are only thirteen little plastic cups and that's why it's called the Lucky 13.

The guide says it's time to go, but an assistant of the patron is handing out a business card which has a street-plan with a mighty big arrow on it to show where the shop is located, just in case we are too feeble-minded to find it for ourselves in this small place. Unlike the samples, unsurprisingly, there's a card for everyone. If we come back, offers the owner magnanimously, we will get a tasting, absolutely free, of anything in the shop – for he has other liqueurs, apart from the trademark limoncello.

"Bring your wives with you, gentlemen," he jokes, "so they can make sure you get back to the hotel again!"

That sounds like a good idea to me, only my wife is not like other wives. All the same, maybe we will come back because, if my memory serves me well, this limoncello looks a much deeper lemon than the Sicilian brand. It seems more lemony, though that's probably just colouring. The proof of the pudding is in the alcohol content, which we had not been allowed to see. Well, we'll see when I come back and on that everything depends.

Now we have arrived in the Piazza San Antonio. A cool and leafy square this, with a statue of the saint as its focal point. As I step back to get a better look at it, a Vespa roars past me and sends me scampering back onto the pavement. Because I am admiring the piazza and cursing Vespas, I miss most of the guide's exposition on Saint Anthony where she has gathered the flock around the base of the statue, but I do pick up that he was a hermit and an ascetic. I don't know why he was an ascetic, but he was probably a hermit to get away from those infernal Vespas.

As we troop out of the square, I find myself a few steps behind a woman dressed in black chiffon. You can see right through it, so I can see she has black pants and a black bra. At least she is colour co-ordinated, if her choice is somewhat melancholy, particularly for this hot summer's day. (Does she not know that black absorbs heat?) I wonder why I have not noticed her before, for, to tell the truth, the tour has not been particularly interesting and it has been hard to hear the guide for much of the time, what with bloody Vespas and everything. As I follow her, I can see her buttocks joggling up and down, for the panties are somewhat scanty.

I nudge Iona and point out the phenomenon to her with my eyes. Her eyes turn Viagra hard and she looks daggers at the retreating back – or, more precisely, probably lower down.

"Huh! Who does she think she is?" she hisses under her breath.

I slow my pace so I do not overtake Mrs Scanty-Panties. I must make a point of seeing her face later as I am curious to see what a lady dressed like this looks like. In the meantime, I'll keep her under observation from this perspective.

At last our guide stops on the steps of a church. Facing it, a gaunt statue of a robed man has both arms aloft, antisocially feeding a seagull. She wants us to guess who he is, adding that he's her favourite saint. I guess, but modestly refrain from shouting out that although he bears not the slightest resemblance to the man himself, according to Cimabue's portrait we had seen of him in Assisi, it's easy to tell it's none other than St Francis. He was always one for the birds in the days when he was a young tearaway, before he got religion. She has to

St Francis feeding a seagull

tell us who it is, but she doesn't say why he's her favourite. Perhaps he's also the patron saint of tour guides or plump ladies. I don't know who my favourite saint is – I don't even know that many, but I know Bacchus is my favourite god. I drink to his health every day without fail. It's a bit of a religion with me, in fact.

Still standing on these steps of the XVI century church dedicated to St Francis, our guide tells us that Sorrento is famous for two things in particular and which we should keep an open eye for as we walk around the town – intarsia, which is inlaid woodwork, and also the carving of shells to form cameo brooches and other items of jewellery. That's interesting, as Iona has a birthday soon. As often as not, it coincides with our visit to some foreign place or other. This is good news for me, as since I am usually bereft of ideas, she picks her own present which can also double as a souvenir. The snag is she never gets a surprise when she opens them. She makes me wrap them up so she has something to open on the day, even if it's the very next one. How utterly pointless is that – not to mention a wicked waste of wrapping paper!

Those two items sound promising. Maybe a brooch, or perhaps an intarsia box to keep all the other birthday presents in, like the pearls of great price from Suzhou and the magnificent emerald from Charlotte Amalie in the Virgin Islands.

We move on to the gardens beyond, what's called the Villa Comunale which, despite its name, is not a villa but a public park – Sorrento's largest, as a matter of fact. The gardens are pleasant enough, with splashes of bright red hibiscus adding colour to the cool green oasis, but what's better is the view from the gardens. From here it's only a suicide's leap to the middle of the three marinas which Sorrento boasts, the Marina San Francesco. To the left is the Marina Grande, so called because, according to the rules of Italian logic, it is much smaller than the Marina Piccola to the right, from which all the ferries to Naples, Capri and Ischia depart. It's too hazy to see Ischia today, says our guide, but normally it is possible to do so.

What we can see, however, is a magnificent sweep of the bay. Away to the left at the point of the peninsula, are the remains of a Roman Villa, the Villa of Pollius Felix, Pollius the Happy. It's a walk we should do, the guide says, because from there, it is possible to swim and snorkel. Good enough! I don't care for chlorinated pools much. I much prefer to swim in the sea, where you can rise with the waves and feel their power as they push you to shore. And this has the added advantage that we can take in the ruins of Pollius' Villa at the same time. No wonder he was happy, with a villa situated in such a prime location. Did he, I wonder, nip into the sea for a dip, or did he prefer the luxury of his own baths – for he was bound to have had them, a rich bloke like him.

Looking down on the Marina Piccola, however, it's obvious that Pollius had nabbed the only beach on the peninsula, at least within miles of Sorrento. The cliffs drop sheer to the sea, and far below they have constructed boardwalks and piers and artificial pools which are thronged with people and pleasure craft. These piers are called *stabilmente* and have all the accoutrements of a beach: sun loungers and parasols, except – in place of the sand – they have wooden planks and, as far as I can see, no topless ladies (not that I was particularly looking for them, of course).

Not my idea of fun, this. The loungers are placed side-by-side, cheek by jowl, like sardines, with barely room to step between them and certainly no room to turn like sunflowers, to follow the sun. Bad enough, but imagine being stuck beside someone playing their infernal music all day. Whatever people come to Sorrento for, surely it would not be to do this – and yet the place is teeming with apparently happy punters.

How bizarre, some people's idea of a good time!

10

Sleepy in Sorrento

T HAT'S the second extraordinary thing I've seen since breakfast. It beggars belief that Mrs Scanty-Panties would dress up for a walking tour of Sorrento as if she were going for a strut on the catwalk. I scan our group, seeking her out so I can see what she looks like from the front. Ah, there she is! She's obviously spent some time in front of the mirror making the most of, and trying to improve on, nature.

She's not an uncomely wench for her age – probably fortysomething. She is pretty well-preserved, and her figure is certainly worth showing off – which is exactly what she is doing, though who she is trying to impress (unless it is everybody) it is hard to tell. Somebody should tell her that her accessory spoils the effect somewhat. He's quite stout and bald, with a nose like Julius Caesar. He also looks a lot older than she is, though he probably isn't. She should really think about changing him if she wants to be the coolest cat in Sorrento. Needless to say, I am not even thinking of applying for the position.

Iona must have seen me looking at her, for: "I hate her! I really hate her!" I hear her growling under her breath as we troop off towards the theatre where our tour is to end and where we are to meet Karen, our rep.

I look at her, surprised at the strength of her feelings. "Why? What has she done to you?"

"Dressed like that, for an occasion like this! It's ridiculous!"

"*Chacun à son goût,*" I reply tolerantly, for I am a very mellow sort of fellow and little annoys me apart from people with rings through their noses and someone else's "music" played full blast when I want some peace and quiet. And bloody Vespas, of course. But everybody hates them, don't they? Oh, and I nearly forgot – people who wear baseball hats back to front, and people who drop litter in the street and who chew gum incessantly except when they are spitting it out on the pavement.

La Belle Dame Sans Merci is usually quite tolerant too, unless it is one of my sins of omission like failing to put the cork back in the malt whisky bottle, or not having done the ironing properly, or a sin of commission, like opening another bottle of Chilean Cabernet Sauvignon, or leaving the toilet seat up, or some other arcane domestic law. I think her rant must have something to do with Mrs Scanty-Panties looking cucumber cool whilst she herself is looking like a peeled prawn after this walk in the heat of a Sorrento sun. With her fair skin and galaxy of freckles scattered across her nose like a cascade from a box of cornflakes, she was born for Scottish climes. It was never intended for her to travel to hot centres of ancient civilisations like Rome and Egypt.

It must be all over now, the tour, because the fat lady has stopped singing the praises of Sorrento and has decanted us on the Terrace of the Teatro Tasso where we are to be treated to a welcome drink. Hey, this is more like it! We can have either chilled Italian sparkling wine or orange juice. Hmm! Which will I choose? I line up for my glass, whilst I make my mind up. It's baking out here. After a massive struggle, I've come to a decision. A glass or two of chilled sparkling wine is just what I need on a day like this, but how do I get two or more from the waiter or, more significantly, past *La Belle Dame Sans Merci?*

I take my glass and stroll over to the far end of the terrace where I can watch people coming in. Iona has met up with Tom, Dick and Harriet, and is nursing an orange juice. There's no sign of Mrs Scanty-Panties. Maybe her mascara will melt in this intense heat, so she's stayed in the theatre. I know just how intense it is, because when I take my Panama off for a moment, the sun felt as if it were trepanning a hole through the centre of my scalp.

Ah, there's Bill and Pat. It looks as if their tour has just finished. I leave my empty glass on a nearby table and go over to greet them, picking up a glass of Spumante Muscato on the way. It's probably only about 9%. Still, much lighter and more refreshing than orange juice.

We wander over to where Iona and the others are, and presently are joined by Donald and Helen. Phew, it certainly is roasting out here – and there is not an inch of shade. They decide they'll go in, out of the heat, but I decide to stay outside and get some rays. And while I'm waiting, I may as well recharge my glass because I can see some other people are getting refills. Just my luck – the bottle runs dry as the waiter is pouring for the person in front of me, but it's only a minor hiccup – he scuttles away to procure another bottle.

A little later, the place is full of abandoned glasses and the crowd is thinning out. The other waiter is beginning to clear up. No more bottles will be opened. I suppose I may as well go in and join the others after I finish this glass. Hmm! Not too bad, this stuff, even if it doesn't pack much of a punch.

The theatre is lovely and cool, with plush blue seats. I have no difficulty in spotting my companions in the middle of the centre row. They have kept a seat for me beside Iona. There is obviously a show here in the evenings, for the stage is half-set with columns and lights, huge globes, suspended from the flies, but not lit at the moment. In the background, I can make out some bulbs in an arch spelling out SORRENTO and beneath that, MUSICAL. It will be a night of Neapolitan song: 'O Sole Mio' and 'Torna a Surriento', some strumming on the mandolin and some dancing. Not for me, that sort of thing. Variety may be the spice of life, but to sit through a variety show would be more like a life sentence to me. I'm sure they are very good, whoever they are, but it's just not my sort of thing.

At last Karen comes to the podium and gives us some tips on finding our way around the town. Iona has a map and is following it intently. I can see her twisting the map to follow what Karen is saying. That's the good thing about being married to an ex-geography teacher – she's interested in maps and has a very good sense of direction (usually), and since she's the one who decides what we are going to see and since wheresoever she goeth, so doth I, there's no point in me taxing my brain with listening to Karen's exposition. All I need to know is the way to the Lucky 13, and I think I'd be able to find that easily.

I slip off my shoes, stretch out my legs and let my feet breathe. Aaah! That's better! I lean back in my seat. This is really quite comfortable. I feel my head nodding. I can still hear Karen, no need to watch her as well, so I'll just rest my eyes for the moment. Except when I close them, I see Mrs Scanty-Panties' buttocks jiggling in front of me. How bizarre is that! I shake my head to clear the image and force my eyes to focus on Karen.

She is telling us about all the exciting tours we can go on this week. The one to Ischia sounds very interesting. You get a tour of the island which includes a visit to Casamicciola Terme where Ibsen wrote Peer Gynt. I am a bit of an Ibsen fan, so it would be interesting to see that, but I have to confess I prefer Grieg's music to the play. But better than that, it is a volcanic island and has hot springs. Now, if there's one thing I like, it is bathing in hot springs. I'd like to go on this tour and whisper so in Iona's shell-like. She has a sheet with all the attractions printed out and points to the price. What! My jaw drops.

"What's that in real money?" I whisper, as the price is in euros and I am a bit numerically challenged to say the least. I have an awful feeling it is going to be a lot.

"£48."

"What? Each?" Her silence speaks volumes. "I don't think I fancy it," I tell her. After all, we've got to economise. Because of a strike by BA we had to pay £320 extra to get here – with no guarantee that we'll recoup the money from our travel insurance.

Karen moves on to describe the next attraction, but since the seven of us are supposed to be hiring a taxi to see the Amalfi coast and Vesuvius and Herculaneum, and Iona has it all written down anyway, I give in to an irresistible urge to close my eyes. I stretch out my legs and tip my Panama over my face.

It's a funny thing how I can't sleep in a bed, yet here I am in the Teatro Tasso in Sorrento and I can hardly keep my eyes open. Karen's voice is so soothing. It's drifting in and out of my head, like the sound of waves lapping on the shore of a desert island...

I feel myself jerking, my body twitching in a spasm. I really think I must have been asleep. How remarkable! Certainly I haven't a clue about anything that Karen has been saying, but apparently she has stopped now and it has been the applause which marked the end of her talk that interrupted my slumbers.

We must go and organise our private tour, but there are queues and queues of people ahead of us wanting to sign up for the Teatro Tasso show and other attractions. I leave the others to do that and wander out onto the terrace. As I suspected, the table covered with the crisp white napery and the Spumante Muscato, along with the glasses, has long since disappeared, but the sun is still beaming down with a blistering intensity.

By the time I get back, the queue has diminished considerably and we are next in line once the people in front have finished their tiresome and seemingly endless questions and transactions. Yes, Karen can fix it – a tour of the Amalfi coast by minibus. She just needs to know which day and how many there are of us. That's a problem. We are one too many, or one too short. The minibus seats six and we are nine, so we need two buses but they won't go unless there's a minimum of five in each bus. However, Karen is confident she'll be able to persuade another couple to join us. After all, it's cheaper per person than the coach tour and we can stop in places the coach can't – and we can stay just as long as we like at each location.

"So we call the shots?" I ask.

"Yes," Karen assures us.

"And what about the route?"

"Well, they'll have ideas where to take you and the drivers speak English, so they'll give you a commentary and answer any questions."

Whichever way you look at it, it sounds good, but one of the best things about it is we don't have to get up at the crack of dawn to go on the coach tour – we can leave at a more civilised 9 o'clock or something like that. We sign up for it, for Wednesday. €45 per couple.

"Don't worry about finding another couple," says Karen, as a parting shot. "I'll find someone to go with you."

I'm not in the least worried about that, but what *is* worrying me is I'll miss the next bus back to the hotel. Because it is a Sunday, there is only a skeleton service, and if I'm not careful I'll be stranded in the town all afternoon being dragged round the shops by Iona when I want to get some rays by the pool. After that she is going back to Bill and Pat's hotel, where Pat is going to lend her a swimming costume as she has a spare and Iona had forgotten hers. Swimming is not one of her priorities on holiday. The others are staying in town too, to have lunch and wander about. I don't need lunch. Breakfast was lunch too.

"What time's the last bus?" I ask Iona.

She consults the little card we were given with the schedules on it.

"12:45."

I look at my watch. "Right, I am offski." If I leave now, and don't get lost, I should make it to the bus stop in time. "See you later."

I don't waste time in fond farewells.

11

Alone in Sorrento

I STEP out of the cool shade of the Theatre into the sizzling Sorrento sunlight. Right, now: which way? I feel a momentary twinge of panic. I reckon I can't afford the time to make a wrong decision, as the time is tight enough as it is. I've got a reasonably good sense of direction though, I think, and this is not a big place, so I should stumble upon Tasso Square before too long and after that it should be easy. My instinct is to turn to the left, so that's what I do – and to my relief, in a few minutes, I spot old Baggy Breeks over there on his pedestal. I slacken my pace, panic over. I'm on the right road, so all I need to do now is follow the Corso Italia and then turn up to the left somewhere after the cathedral and I should come to it.

There's the cathedral. I turn up the Via Sersali and emerge into the Piazza Antiche Mura. Yes, there are the walls. So if I turn right, I should catch sight of the phallic factory chimney before too long. Yes, there it is! It's very helpful having an erection like this in the town so you can get your bearings. I congratulate myself on my navigation. There's no bus though, and no other people waiting, which is strange as it should be due to leave in just two or three minutes. I was expecting just to step on board and be whisked away more or less at once. I couldn't have missed it, could I? Impossible. It wouldn't leave early; late maybe, but never early. Not in Italy.

I wait. And wait. At least I am getting some rays here, on my arms and legs, if not on my manly chest, though it is getting to be a bit more like a woman's these days.

Because there's nothing else to do, I study my surroundings. There are some dingy flats across the road with balconies crowded with an overflow of household detritus and some limp washing. A muscular man in a singlet is leaning on his balcony, smoking a cigarette, looking at me, looking at him. I don't like the look of him, so I look away and watch for the bus coming instead, but still there's no sign of it. It should be leaving now and it's not even here yet, nor are any would-be passengers. The horrible feeling I have that something is not right is becoming, with each passing second, ever more of a certainty.

Suddenly a hair-raising scream emanates from the block of flats across the road, followed by a woman screeching at the top of her voice, which – in turn – is followed by the sound of something breaking, like a plate or crockery smashing and all the time, the invective continues unabated without even a pause for breath. A vase, I suspect, has been thrown, rather than accidentally damaged – probably aimed at someone's head.

Instinctively, I look up at the block of flats. Muscular Man is still serenely smoking, leaning as languidly as before on the rail of his balcony, looking down on me in the most unnerving way. It's hard to say where the sound is coming from, but certainly not from him. I should say it's from the flat above, but there is nothing to see.

Just as suddenly as it started, the screaming ceases and all is silent again. There have been no other sounds from the mystery flat, no male voice pleading for mercy, no desperate leap from the balcony to avoid the wrath of Her-Indoors. Is it such a regular occurrence that it merits no response from Muscular Man? Or did I just imagine it, as Keats nearly might have put it: *Was it a vision, or a waking dream?/ Fled is that almighty scream.*

I think I may well be in a waking nightmare. There is still no sign of the bus and no other passengers. There is no sign of Muscular Man either. Maybe he has finished his fag and his wife is letting him come back in now, or else he has decided he doesn't fancy me after all, or – even worse – what if he does, and he's already on his way down to speak to me? It has happened to me before, waiting at a bus stop, when I was a student. I had hair down to my shoulders then, as was the fashion. There was an old man also waiting for the bus, eyeing me with curiosity. At last he spoke: *Are you ane o' they homosexuals, then?* He put the stress on the last syllable, making it sound like two: u-als. He wasn't being judgemental. He just wanted to know. So I told him.

Ah, hah! Here, at last, are two people coming, looking like possible passengers for the Monte Somma bus, but strolling, like they have no idea they are late for it, but with a bit of Irish luck, might still catch it. Sure enough, they stop, and sure enough they are Irish. If his ginger hair and freckles and green football top with the shamrock on it were not enough evidence for Sherlock Addison to leap to the foregone conclusion, as soon as he asked me if the bus had left, his accent put it beyond any doubt. And I tell him without any doubt that the bus had never arrived, as I had been here well before the departure time.

"Ah, well," he says with the phlegmatic patience of his race, "we'll just have to stay in the town then."

"That's just what I was hoping not to do," I mutter glumly. "There's not another bus for bloody hours now."

"You can catch a public bus up to the hotel."

"Can you?" I say with sudden interest. "Where from?" I add ungrammatically in my eagerness.

"At the train station."

That has to be right. It's the very place where you would catch a bus. "Where's the station?"

"Go to Tasso Square, turn right onto the Corso, then take the first right and I think it's the first off to the left after that. You'll see it, anyway."

I thank him – only there's one small problem. I haven't any money. Iona does not normally trust me with it in case I lose it, and I didn't think I would need any anyway since it was supposed to be a complimentary bus. Embarrassed, I explain my predicament to my new friend. He digs in his pocket and fishes out a €1 coin.

"Thanks very much. I'll let you have it back. I'm sure I'll see you around the hotel."

"Don't be daft," he says and turns to go.

"Just a minute, er... which bus is it?"

"The blue bus."

"Er... right, the blue bus. Well, thanks again."

"Not at all." My Irish friend and his speechless wife stroll off towards the town again.

Is it because it's a blue bus that they're walking back to town, like the children in the primary Catholic school I told you about earlier? It's the direction I have to go too, but it would just be too embarrassing to walk along with them and in any case, I bet the silent wife is just dying to say: *What kind of an eejit is it who comes to town without any money?*

I had wanted to say: *Has the blue bus not got a number?* A blue bus sounds a bit vague, but I sensed that the Irishman wanted to be on his way and I didn't want to annoy him, since he had been so kind. In any case, I felt that any more questions would confirm his wife's opinion of me.

As they reach the corner, the wife looks back before they disappear from sight. Right now she's probably saying: *The fecking eejit is still standing there looking as lost as a monk in a convent, so he is.*

The block of flats across the road is silent now, and appears completely deserted. I have an intense feeling of loneliness. Although I know it is hopeless, I hang about, hoping that the bus – like an angel on wheels – may suddenly materialise and deliver me from having to undertake the blue bus journey. I think, if I see Iona in the town as I head for the station, I'll just say I missed the bus and will pretend I've changed my mind about staying in the town.

At last I think it is safe to go without bumping into my Celtic friends. I take the Corso Italia, with its narrow pavement, out of the Piazza Tasso, to the right, just as directed, and then the Via Marziale which broadens out as it climbs up the hill. Is this right? Then to the left, I see a street, at the far end of which is something which looks like it could be the station. And it is! And there, in front of it, is a blue bus, its engine running. I go round to the front of it to see where it's going: S. AGATA. It doesn't mean anything to me.

There is also an orange bus and a green bus which, no doubt, my Celtic friends would be relieved to see but there is only one blue bus to choose from, which is heartening. It says SITA on the side so, all right then, if the Italians do it by colours rather than numbers, I'll have a seata on the blua bus and hopefully I'll be back at the hotel before too long.

The first thing I'm going to do is have a shower, for this forced march through the streets of Sorrento has left me hot and sticky. Then I'm going to have a nice cold beer, and then I'm going to have a swim, and then I'm going to have a nice long sunbathe. Ah! That sounds like paradise.

12

Into the Unknown

I EXCHANGE my euro for a ticket from the driver and sit down on the right, about half way back. The bus is practically empty. Phew! It's nice to get a seat, but it's as hot as Hades in here. There doesn't seem to be any air-conditioning and, in any case, the door is open. Without warning, as if he's just forgotten something, the bus driver gets up and leaves. I watch to see where he's going, but he's only heading off to talk to his mates. I remember when that happened on a bus in Rome last week, and one of the passengers had to go and haul the driver away from his pals and make him drive the bus. I hope this is not going to be a repeat of that performance.

Passengers arrive in dribs and drabs and take their seats. One of our driver's mates gets into his bus and drives away, then another, but our driver is having too good a time apparently as I can see him laughing and joking, as if he had all the time in the world. Timetable, what timetable? The sweat is running down my neck, and I can feel rivulets of it trickling between my bosoms.

I'm beginning to fantasise about that beer now. I can see the can with its gold lettering and there are drops of condensation on it, and I can hear the fizz as I peel back the ring-pull and smell the hoppy aroma. If I'd not missed the free bus, I could be drinking it at this precise minute.

Across the passage, a young bloke – attired in a bandana and Bermuda shorts and a T-shirt with red-and-white vertical stripes, and who had been sitting with his girlfriend – gets up and goes to stand outside. I wish I could do that. It's like the Black Hole of Calcutta in here, but I'm scared to give up my seat as I'm sure to lose it as the bus is filling up now and I don't want to have to stand all the way to the hotel. Besides, if the colour of my oxters is anything to go by, my shorts will be betraying signs of dampness which might be misinterpreted. I sit where I am and sweat it out. Is that why no-one chooses to sit beside me?

But at last a party of backpackers arrives and a young girl is forced to sit beside me, resting her rucksack on thighs as brown as berries and as thick as road rollers. She sits with her back to me and engages in a spirited conversation with her friends across the passage and behind. They appear to be French: *Some friends you are! It's no fun being stuck next to this sweaty old prune.* They laugh uproariously. She doesn't know I can understand French better than I can speak it.

At last the bus driver appears to be coming. Oh, no he's not. He's thought of something else witty to say to his mates and has turned back. Now the bus is practically full, the heat is even more intolerable than before. If he doesn't come soon, I'll swear I'll go and drag him away myself, even although I can scarcely string two words of Italian together.

But at last he does come, in an unhurried sort of way, and swings into his seat. The girl who belongs to the bandana youth is waving frantically at him to climb aboard – and with good reason too, for the driver takes off at once. No doubt he has to make up for lost time. But what about all those fares? I suppose it makes his life easier if he doesn't have to bother with the tiresome effort of collecting them and giving change and all that nonsense when he could be having a good time with his mates instead. For its part, the bus company wonders why, with all those tourists, they are not making a profit. And if only I had known, I could have saved myself the humiliation of begging from the Irishman.

The bus makes its way through the town. We're heading in the right direction at least, past the factory chimney, and at last we begin to climb the hill. I recognise the Marina Grande far below on the right and the Hotel Bristol on the left. I remember noticing that, because two people from Iona's church had stayed there earlier this year.

The bus chugs on, upward and onwards. But wait a minute! Surely it is going downhill now? I don't remember that, but maybe it has to go down before it goes up again. I was probably seething at the Bra-benders at the time and didn't notice. We are going uphill again, but surely I should have arrived at the hotel by now, yet there is no sign of it.

The bus stops at a camping ground. Don't remember seeing that before. Passengers pile off, including my companion who has sat with her back to me throughout the entire journey, keeping up her cheery conversation with her companions. I don't mind. I don't fancy her much either.

The camping site is down a shady avenue. I can't see any tents, but it looks as if there would be plenty shade in which to pitch one. All the same, I am glad I am not camping there, that I have a comfortable hotel to go back to – if only I can get to it.

"*Bonne chance avec le camping!*" I say to my departing companion who is hefting her backpack onto her shoulder. "*Quelle chaleur formidable! N'est ce pas?*"

She looks at me with a flicker of astonishment, but doesn't make any other response. She'll know I can speak French, and will wonder how much I've understood of their merry conversation. I leave that thought with her as she steps out of the bus and out of my life forever.

Now that the backpackers have gone, the bus is singularly empty and silent. Bandana youth and girlfriend have also gone. In fact, as I look round the bus at the few passengers remaining, I confidently conclude there is not a single tourist amongst them. The growing feeling of unease that I have had for some time now, strengthened when we passed the camping ground, has become a rock-hard certainty now. I am on the wrong bus. Presumably I am heading for Sant'Agata but where it is and how long it will take us to get there, I have absolutely no idea.

I am furious with myself. Why didn't I just stay in the town with Iona? At this rate, she will be back at the hotel long before me. Suppressing a wave of panic, I reason that when we get to Sant'Agata, all I need to do is stay on the bus as it's the terminus. It'll take me back to Sorrento and probably by that time, the free bus to the hotel will be running again. I'll have lost some time, that's all, apart from a little dignity in front of the Irish. Then panic washes over me again as I remember I've no money and since it's the terminus, there probably won't be any mates for the driver to talk to...

We are climbing higher now through countryside and sparse little villages. Sorrento must be far below. At least I am seeing a part of the country that most tourists probably never do. There are only half-a-dozen of us left now.

78

The driver has stopped on a straight bit of road and gone into what looks like a depot, because there are three or four buses parked there. He goes into a shed, which I presume is actually an office. There is nothing else to do but sit and wait. I resent this waste of time. When I think about all the time I spent waiting at the station and now this, that right now I should be sitting at the pool soaking up the rays and the beer – I feel sick.

I make up my mind, when the driver comes back, I'll try to find out how far we have to go and how long I may have to wait in Sant'Agata before we come back again. I move down to the seat behind the driver, conscious of the curious eyes of the locals on me. I look so out of place.

Before he has time to sit down, I accost the driver in my most fluent Italian.

"Hotel Monte Somma?"

"Hotel Monte Somma?" He shakes his head at me and spouts a torrent of Italian. I know from the intimation of his voice that he is asking me a question, but all I can do is look blank. For the second time in half-an-hour, I feel like a blithering idiot. I wish I hadn't asked. Apparently he doesn't speak English (why should he?), and I am no further forward. Oh, well, I'll just have to wait and see what happens.

The driver gives me up as a hopeless case and pulls away. I don't know if it's the heat or the stress, but I am sweating even more profusely than before. When is this nightmare going to end?

Ah, this looks like a bigger sort of place; probably we have arrived at Sant'Agata at last. The beginning of the end of the nightmare is in sight. The driver stops at a crossroads and turning round, gives me another few rounds of Italian, gesturing along the road to his left, and operating the pneumatic door at the same time. It's clear he intends me to get off.

Get off? But why? I look at him in dismay and disbelief. Can he really mean it? Why did I have to open my big mouth? If I had just sat there quietly, it would have been all right, I would have got back to Sorrento eventually, I suppose. But I don't have the Italian to tell him I want to stay put.

There is an impatient toot from a car behind. This is not even a proper bus stop. Clearly the driver has every intention I should get off and the way he is looking at me, the quicker the better, if I don't mind – can't I see I'm holding up the traffic, and he's late already? I can also feel the eyes of the passengers boring into my back at this unscheduled stop. Whatever the future holds, it has to be better than the present. What was it Shakespeare said in *Henry IV Part 2*: *Past and to come seems best; things present worst*. Getting off the bus now seems the only possible solution to my present predicament.

The bus draws away and turns off to the right. No one else alights. What am I going to do now? My gaze is drawn to a bus at the other side of the road in a small piazza. It has its engine running and is pointing down the hill, the way I want to go. Could this be my saviour? I scamper across the road before it disappears like a mirage.

The driver, like the last one, is young, dark-haired, and dressed in a short-sleeved blue shirt which seems to be the badge of all his trade. He's also wearing sunglasses, which give him a sinister sort of air. He and the other could be clones. In that case, he won't be able to speak English either. I wish I could say: *Does this bus go to...* but all I can say, like an idiot, is: "Hotel Monte Somma?"

He shakes his head. "Nostra Verde," he says and points to his right along the road.

"Nostra Verde?"

"*Si. Si.* Nostra Verde," he nods and indicates the road again.

"Nostra Verde?" What the hell is Nostra Verde? I've heard of the Cosa Nostra and I know that *verde* is green. Perhaps it's the youth movement of the Mafia, though what he imagines a wrinkly like me would want with that organisation beats me. Maybe the Hotel Monte Somma is the headquarters in this region, where they meet for a working dinner and complain about how Signor Corleone marshals them into seats they don't want to sit in and demands they choose the wine before they've seen the menu.

"*Si. Si.* Nostra Verde." We could keep this up all day. He is nodding at me as if I were a congenital idiot, each nod urging me to retreat down the steps of his bus. He thinks I'm probably harmless, but he's smiling at me to keep on my good side, because, as it is written on page three of the bus driver's handbook: *In the event of an insane person trying to board your bus (he will probably be dressed in swimming trunks and a Panama hat) do nothing to antagonise him as he may turn violent.*

"Nostra Verde. Grazie," and I back off – literally and metaphorically – down the steps, nodding back to him as if we were Japanese, and indeed, that's just what we might have been speaking for all the sense it makes to me.

The doors shut with a pneumatic hiss and the bus disappears across the road and down the hill. Bloody hell! That's the way I want to go! I check an impulse to run after it, knowing it's hopeless. It is a forlorn sight, watching it disappear down the hill like that. Perhaps if I'd said "Sorrento" I might well be on it now.

I stand and gaze after the retreating bus, feeling like the loneliest person on the planet. Far away down to my right, a woman in a brown dress is crossing the street, the only sign of life. A café is behind me, but seems to be closed. Even the birds seem to be having a siesta. I'm stranded high in the hills above Sorrento in what appears to be a deserted village.

What am I going to do? I can't think of even a single thing.

13

Stranded in Sant' Agata

JUST then, up the hill, comes a blue bus. It looks just like the one that took me to this hellhole. Surely it will be going back to Sorrento! It's stopping across the road. I race across. No need to hurry; it's disgorging passengers.

At last it is empty and I prepare to step on board, but before I can set foot on the first step – "Nostra Verde!" says the driver, and points down the road ahead. With a shock of recognition, despite his sunglasses, I realise it is the same driver who brought me here. It's no surprise at all that he should recognise me as the mad foreigner who wants to go to the Hotel Monte Somma.

Anyway, he's not going to let me on his bus, that's for sure. He's already hissed his doors shut and now the bus is empty, he drives off. To my utter disbelief, he turns and goes back down the hill again! I want to tear out my hair in frustration, to yell at him: *That's the way I want to go, you bloody moron! I don't want to go to Nostra Verde!*

I cross the road again. The disgorged passengers, about a dozen of them, are all standing on the porch of the café, waiting. For the café to open, or another bus? Maybe that will be my bus.

Time passes. So does the occasional car. A dog barks somewhere out of sight. A cat strolls unhurriedly across the road, looking neither to left nor right. No road sense. Or else it knows perfectly well that there will not be another bus for hours. I stand by myself, staring down the hill. Time passes...

Ah, here's a bus coming up the hill, a green one this time. I watch to see what the group in the shade of the café porch is doing. Not much. Just standing, waiting. Right, that's what I'll do too.

The bus reaches the crossroads, crosses to where we are standing, and reverses into a space in front of the café with its nose pointing down the hill. This could be hopeful – if only I had some money. No chance of me sneaking aboard amongst this little lot of passengers.

The driver opens the door and I realise with a start that it is the same driver again, the one who had just driven the blue bus down the hill minutes before, the one who seems determined I should go to Nostra Verde, whatever that is. He hasn't been gone long so I deduce he has not gone as far as Sorrento but only to the shed-like depot where he has swapped his blue bus for this one. Don't tell me he didn't like the colour.

I'm in the prime position to get on the bus first, but I am hesitant.

"Nostra Verde!" repeats the driver. It sounds as if he's irritated, or maybe he thinks I'm deaf. Wait a minute; maybe Nostra Verde is swearing! It sounds a bit like it, the way he is saying it now, and – since I am dressed all in green – maybe all the time these clone bus drivers have been telling me in impolite terms: *Piss off, you little green git!* Which is all I want to do, really: get out of here, if only one of them would please take me.

The passengers push past me. I am cowed. I dare not try to get on and, just as I suspected it would, the bus crosses the road and takes off down the hill towards Sorrento. I want to weep with frustration, rant with rage. What's it all about? Why did the driver decant his passengers here only to pick them up in a different-coloured bus, presumably to bear them to Sorrento and why, oh why in the name of the wee man, will he not take me? If I live to be a hundred, never in a million years, will I ever understand Italian logic.

The street is hot, dusty and empty. My throat is dry. I gotta get outta this place, if it's the last thing I ever do, sang The Animals in the Sixties. I have a song for every occasion, though I never felt less like singing in my life. I hate Sant'Agata. I never wanted to be here, but – now I am – how do I get out of it with no money, should I ever manage to find a bus driver who will let me on board? I suppose I could walk back the way the buses won't take me, but it's absolutely miles and miles and would take hours and in this heat... No! There has to be a better way. But God knows what it is.

The one clue I have is that the drivers seem to be insistent I walk down what appears to be the main street to the right. There's nothing else I can think of doing, so I may as well do that. Maybe I'll see a sign to Nostra Verde, or I'll be given a sign. I could pray to St Anthony, whom – I heard the fat lady say this morning – is the patron saint of lost things. Except I am not a Catholic, let alone religious. In any case, I am not lost. I know precisely where I am, and I just want to get the hell out of it. I'm not too much up on my saints, but I bet St Agatha is the patron saint of bloody-minded bus drivers. I set off down the empty street, but with more of a shuffle than a spring in my step.

At the corner I come across a greengrocer's shop with a green awning and trays of fruit on display. I can hear some sort of activity going on inside and, in a few moments, a man arrives on a scooter and goes inside. After a time, he emerges with a bulging polythene bag, starts up his scooter and – once the faint puttering of his exhaust is swallowed up by the distance – silence falls again and this sleepy town resorts to its state of afternoon somnolence.

Across the road, sitting on a wall, an old man is sitting in the shade, watching life go by. I can see up and down the entire street, and there's not a living soul to be seen. It's like in *High Noon* when Gary Cooper singlehandedly took on the outlaws. For a mad moment, I wonder if it's worth going across to accost him, but dismiss the idea almost as soon as it sprang to mind. He looks the sort of old-timer who was born here and who has not been further than the grocer's shop in his life. He reminds me very much of the person I chanced to encounter many years ago while driving through Tennessee. I had stopped to ask for directions, not having seen any signs to anywhere.

"Where does this road go?" I asked.

"The supermarket," replied he without the slightest irony.

"But where does it go to after the supermarket?" I pursued, patiently.

"Don't know," he shrugged. "Ain't been further than the supermarket."

And with that, he shambled off before I asked him any more tiresome questions. It was a foreign country. They inbreed them differently there.

Time passes, like night-time in Dylan Thomas's Llareggub, which, though it looks Welsh, is actually Buggerall backwards – and that's all that's happening here. Although I like the sunshine and the heat, it's not an atmosphere conducive to appreciation.

I am not going to go round the bend in the literal sense of the word (though if I don't get out of this place soon, I can't guarantee it in the figurative sense), for Sant'Agata peters out a few hundred yards further on and from this point I can watch for the approach of any buses. Yet where I am seems an unlikely place to catch a bus. There is no sign of a bus stop, no sign of anyone else waiting.

The owner of the shop comes out and appears to be counting his produce. Maybe he has been watching me from inside, suspecting me of loitering with intent of pinching his peaches. He gives me a Sheriff-of-Nottingham sort of look and disappears inside: *I'm watching you, Robin Hood, so don't try knocking anything off my stall to give to the poor.*

"Salve!" The speaker is a man who has appeared from nowhere, possibly out of the house on whose wall the old man is seated and whom he is greeting.

"Salve!" replies the old man. It's incredible, just like out of my Latin book at school! They are actually talking Latin! I hated it to the heart's core because I didn't see the point of learning a dead language. How was I to know, some forty years later in the heights above Sorrento, I would need it to ask where the next ox-cart leaves for Nostra Verde and when?

Giving that conversation up as a non-starter, I make my way back along the way I have come. There is an AGIP filling station and a small public park and then, the sign I was looking for – only ironically, I wasn't really looking for it at all when I found it.

Maybe I've calmed down a bit, perhaps I was panicking – I don't know why I didn't see it before, but here is the bus stop! No doubt about it. It's got a picture of a bus on it and it says FERMATA with SITA in larger letters beneath. There can be no doubt about it. I touch it and it's there, so it must be real.

There is a board with the times of the buses. There it is – Nostra Verde! And it seems the next one is not until 2:50. Good grief, it's only 2:05 now. What a waste of an afternoon! Iona will have been back at the hotel for ages now and so would I have been, if only I had stayed with her. But at least I have found the bus stop now. There's just the slight matter of getting on the bus without any money to pay the fare.

14

Another Chance Encounter

A S I stand red-faced and loitering, contemplating the timetables, I am joined by a couple who have also come to study them. Relief washes over me as, from their accents, I immediately know they come from Liverpool and they are seeking the same bus as me. Unity is strength, especially in adversity.

They are staying in Sorrento and even know my hotel, having seen it on the way up. There's even a bus stop, just outside it! I feel like jumping for joy. And with some people to talk to, the wait for the bus will not seem so interminable either. All of a sudden, my fortunes have changed. The gods have stopped toying with me evidently, and shown some mercy at last.

It seems my new friends are in Sorrento for their daughter's wedding and, on a whim, had decided to take the bus up here, just to see what it was like, to while away the time before THE day, which is tomorrow.

"Oh, is she marrying an Italian then?"

"No, she's running away."

The father, seeing the look of puzzlement on my face, continues: "It was going to be £80 a head for the wedding and there's so many relations we would have had to invite, even before we invited our friends, she decided to get married in Sorrento instead."

What a nice daughter! I hope, when the time comes for my own daughter to tie the matrimonial noose – I mean knot – she will be as considerate, though no doubt this alternative wedding is still going to make a considerable dent in his pocket. Daughters are a bit of a liability. I had taken out an insurance policy against this eventuality, estimating when I would be smitten by this financial catastrophe, but time passed and since it showed no signs of happening in the immediate future, when the policy matured, instead of reinvesting it, I bought a car instead. (What's wrong with her? Does she not get her good looks from me?) I may, and probably will, live to regret that decision.

I confide this to the Scousers and also how I came to be here, though I miss out the bit about my Irish benefactor. I don't want them to think I am begging, but I do happen to mention that never mind paying for a wedding, I haven't even got the bus fare back to my hotel. The mother of the bride opens her handbag and proffers me a blue ticket.

"No! No! I couldn't possibly! I wasn't suggesting... I mean I hope you didn't think..."

"Here, take it," she insists. "It's a spare."

"Oh, well, in that case! Thank you very much. Thanks very much indeed!"

So now everything is all right! I no longer need to fall upon the mercy of the bus driver to give me a free ride. All I need now is the bus to go with the ticket. I can hardly believe my problems are disappearing so easily, like snow off a dyke in Scotland in June. I feel positively light-headed with the relief of it all.

Just then, a blue bus pulls up across the road. Is that it? If so, it is early and not from the direction we were expecting. But perhaps it has to turn round. We go over to investigate.

"Hotel Monte Somma?"

The driver shakes his head. "Nostra Verde."

I have a sense of déjà-vu. He points across the road to where we were standing. "Nostra Verde," he says again, adding, "ten minutes."

We thank him, but don't walk back to the stop as there is shade where we are and my new friends have had enough of standing in the sun. The bus departs, leaving a residue of diesel fumes behind, and – amazingly – another couple joins us.

He is wearing one of those cotton vests which have huge cut-away holes at the shoulders so only a thin strip of material joins them altogether at the back. He has shorts which are too long by half, emphasising a pair of bandy legs with bulging calves knotted with unsightly varicose veins. He is sandal-shod without socks, so he's not a complete eyesore. On his left bulging bicep he boasts a tattoo and his skull, shaved down to the wood, glints in the sun. His equally lovely wife, not to be outdone, has her own tattoo on a freckled upper arm so thick I would never accept an arm-wrestling contest with her, as the defeat would just be too humiliating.

They are Scottish and are looking for the same bus as us. This is getting to be a regular little ex-patriot colony. I wonder where they have been all this time whilst I had been doing my Gary Cooper act. Had they been watching me from behind curtained windows all this time?

The Scousers tell them about their daughter's wedding tomorrow and I chip in that at that time, I hope to be climbing Vesuvius.

"We were there yesterday," says the pride of Scotland's manhood.

"Oh, really? What's it like? I mean, how easy is it to climb?"

"Not bad," he replies. "Your shoes get full of ash, but you can hire a walking stick to help you. And you know, the funny thing is you don't pay till you return the stick! The hillside is littered with sticks which people have thrown away on the way down!"

"That'll be all the Scots!" I suggest, laughing at my own joke.

My compatriots suddenly stiffen and fix me with an outraged stare which instantly wipes the smile from my face. Oops! After all, I was making a joke at my own expense, just as much as theirs. Maybe it's the way I told it. Perhaps they don't realise I'm a fellow Scot. My accent often puzzles new acquaintances. When I am asked where I come from, I turn it into a guessing game and many people suggest I'm Welsh or Irish. Perhaps that's what has happened here, but to explain would be to make an issue of it and it seems better to let it pass as a bad joke.

"I think I'll go over and wait at the bus stop, just in case it's early," I say to break the awkward silence. "If you'd like to wait in the shade... I'll give you a wave if I see it coming."

Nobody says anything and nobody follows me, only the hostile looks of the Scots: *Little Irish nyaff, walking around dressed like a leprechaun. Just who does he think he is?*

I complete my ostracism from across the street, staring up and down the road, willing my deliverance to come. The thought of no bus arriving, of being stranded with my fellow Scots, seems a worse fate now than when I presumed I was alone. I am conscious of them looking at me, talking about me as I stand in the full strength of the sun, confirming their opinion of me that I'm a nutter.

"I even had to give him a bus ticket," Mrs Scouse is probably saying. "He's up here without a ticket and without any money." They are nodding. Undoubtedly insane and should not be allowed out alone.

"Maybe he's got sunstroke." This from Mrs Scotland, who, taking my red face into consideration, is more charitable than Mrs Scouse.

The bus is late. Somehow I knew it would be, but at last I see one coming up the hill towards the crossroads. I indicate to my ex-companions they should cross the street but they seem to prefer to keep in the shade or out of my company, or both.

Please, God, let it be the bus! And it is! I can read Nostra Verde picked out in orange dots on the screen above the driver's head. I wave more energetically at my companions, who, now they can see my salvation stopped at the crossroads and signalling it is going to turn in our direction, are prepared to believe me – this truly is the bus we want.

I don't believe it! The driver is the very same who had brought me up here all those hours ago! "Nostra Verde," is what he actually says, but what he is actually saying with his eyes is: I told you that this is the bus you need. (But you didn't tell me that it wouldn't be till 3:05 in the afternoon though, did you? And why didn't you take me back to Sorrento with you in the first place? Surely you must have known that depositing me in town would have been faster by far than hanging around this God-forsaken place for three hours?) Just my luck to arrive at siesta time. What a waste of your life spending it in bed – sleeping.

We are the only passengers. The Scousers and the Scots look as if they have been life-long friends, chatting amicably across the passageway. I sit at the front on my own on the lookout for the hotel coming up, glad of the excuse to keep me occupied and to cover up the uncomfortable feeling I can't shake off that I'm *persona non grata* with my compatriots.

I wouldn't say it was worth it, not all the stress and time I've spent, but the view is splendid as we sweep down the hill towards Sorrento, through lush vegetation which parts from time to time to afford views of scattered hillside settlements and panoramic views of the bay with Sorrento nestling at the cliffs far below.

The bus is slowing down. The driver knows where I want to go. Just as well. We would have passed it before I realised it was coming and I would have had to toil back up the hill in the merciless sunshine.

"Thanks again for the ticket," I call to the Scousers before I go down the steps. "Enjoy the wedding!" To my fellow Scots: "It never gets as hot as this back in Falkirk, does it? Enjoy your holiday!" It's unlikely they are from my hometown but I don't expect many Irish eejits have heard of it. And if I sound like an idiot at least they might think I'm a Scottish idiot and not a racist.

I'd rather be an idiot than a racist – yes I would, yes I surely would. It should give them something to ponder anyway. Hopefully our paths will never cross again.

15

Another Sort of Stress

AS the bus pulls away, I look at my watch. 3:15. Three-and-a half-hours it has taken me to get back from the town! At least the sun is still out. Instead of going into the hotel, I decide to walk round to the swimming pool first to see how busy it is, to see if there are any sunbeds left or if they are all occupied by German towels.

It's all right – there are plenty of beds, and the pool is in full sun. All my weariness seems to drain out of me as I make my way through the foyer to the lift and that cold can of beer and, just for contrast, that warm shower.

Uh! Uh! Even as I round the bend towards my room, I can hear it, the bloody racket from next door. That's just typical of the gods. They lull you into a false sense of happiness, then the next minute, they dash you onto the rocks of despair – just like the Sirens, who the fat lady told us, came from Sorrento.

I slip my credit-card key in the slot, my feeling of relief at being back somewhat tempered by the jolting reminder of the fiendish din from next door. All day I'd never given them a moment's thought.

Iona is sitting on the bed, reading a book. She'd probably be outside on the balcony if it were not for the noise. The sun has already gone from a large part of it.

"Where have you been?" She asks in a tone of wonderment, as well she might. "I couldn't see you at the pool and then I noticed your swimming trunks were still here."

I have a pair of swimming trunks that I reserve for their proper purpose, for poolside wear only, grey with lemon piping from my lemon-and-grey period in the early Eighties and still going strong since they are so seldom worn, and short, to afford the maximum decent exposure to the sun.

I go straight to the mini-bar and unzip a beer. Normally I would never contemplate such a thing at mini-bar prices, but it's only an Amstel. I'm bound to find a replacement later in a supermarket.

"What a bloody afternoon I have had!" I announce, putting on the agony in case she objects to the beer. When I've finished telling her, every nut and bolt of the tragic tale, I ask: "When did you get back?"

"Ages ago."

I knew she would have. "But how did you get back?"

"I walked."

"What! It's miles!"

"No, it's not. Not that far."

"How long did it take you?"

"About half an hour."

"You're joking!" But I know she's not. If she could do it in that time, up that hill, in that heat then I bet I could do it in twenty, if not fifteen. Three hours wasted! Obviously I had totally misjudged how far it was. Maybe having to listen to the Bra-benders had made it seem a lot longer than it actually was. It's all relative. Einstein was right. He said something about time bending through space. If only I had known, then I would have walked and spared myself all that stress.

"Bloody hell! I don't believe it!" *I hope you enjoyed that, ye gods.* Anyway I'm back now and I'm going to put it behind me. "I'm going for a shower and then I'm going for a swim. You coming?"

By the time I come out, Iona has changed into Pat's borrowed cossie. She and Bill weren't happy about her walking up that hill alone in that heat. Save the sympathy. If only they had known what was happening to me!

It seems a bit of a waste of time and effort to dry myself as I'll be getting wet again in a few minutes anyway, so I do just enough to stop dripping all over the carpet. I'm in a hurry to get down to the pool and ease away the stresses of the day. For the purposes of concealment, I put a beer in Iona's little rucksack. The din is still emanating from next door. Iona agrees it is terrible. That's another change.

* * *

I am feeling much more mellow now. I have swum and been in the whirlpool. I have read some more of my book, got some rays and drunk my beer, keeping it under my Panama to keep it out of the sun, but mainly from the eyes of the pool police who seem to have nothing better to do other than go around straightening sunbeds until they are all perfectly parallel like someone afflicted with Obsessive Compulsive Disorder. Probably if you got into difficulties, you would make their day as you would be giving them something to do to relieve the tedium. Since there is a bar at the far side of the pool from where we are, I expect part of their duties is to watch for people drinking their own beer, instead of the hotel's at rip-off prices.

Suddenly there is a splash and high-pitched screaming and laughing. I look up from my book. There's no mistaking those accents: "Yowh little bitch! Wait till I get yowh!" One of the girls is floundering in the water, squeezing the water out of her hair and eyes, whilst her two friends are doubled over with mirth. Apparently they have thrown her into the pool and unfortunately for the pool police, she can swim, so they are not needed.

Now the other two dive in and bomb her. More shrieks, more gales of laughter after they pop up to the surface again. Before they came, people were swimming with varying degrees of effort, up and down, minding their own business. Now, fled is the peace, fled is the tranquillity. THEY have arrived.

I watch them as they emerge. Hmm! They represent the three degrees of attractiveness. The one in the white bikini looks rather pretty. It sets off her long black hair. The one in the red is passable, preferably in an on-the-other-side-of-the-street sort of a way, but the one in the black is the one I would have got if my pals and I had gone out on a threesome. For it is written that every attractive girl has an ugly friend who goes everywhere with her – and that's the one I end up with.

They go to their sunbeds at the far side of the pool. Have they brought their infernal music with them too? Apparently not – at least I can't hear it, and I'm sure I would have if they had. They've probably left it on in their room so I can enjoy it, just in case I should go back before them.

"I'm going up now to get changed," Iona announces. Her idea of a good time is not sitting in the sun for prolonged periods, and Pat's costume never even got so much as a drop of water on it. "Don't be much longer. I'm hungry and I want to have an early dinner."

"I'm not hungry."

"Well, you're stupid." She gathers up her stuff. "Don't be much longer," she repeats, which she needs to do since I am pretty thick, apparently.

I don't see that not being hungry makes me unintelligent but maybe that's because I'm too stupid to think of the connection, but as I lie on the sunbed, I get to thinking maybe this is the best time to go. There might still be some sun on the balcony and I can sit out and have my *apéritifs* in peace and quiet – with a bit of luck.

I take the stairs up to the room and, on the way, stop to see what today's menu is. It's a buffet. Signor Corleone won't be so busy, maybe not on duty at all, and we'll be able to sit where we like.

The silence as I approach the room is music to my ears. They have not left their ghetto blaster on, and there is still some sun on the balcony if I squeeze into that slice of sunlight over by the rail. Iona is still in the bathroom. I'll just have a quick G&T before she comes out.

I look over the balcony, glass in hand, letting the sun's rays beat on my back. There's still a lot of power in it. Ah, there's the man on the ground floor whom I saw before. I give him a wave, and he waves back.

"It's nice without that bloody racket isn't it?" I call down.

"Yes, very nice!" he replies, but he doesn't sound convincing. He won't hear it as much as me of course. He disappears inside as Iona appears, like a *deus ex machina*, taking me by surprise, her hair turban-wrapped in a towel.

"What are you doing?"

"Just talking to that man downstairs."

Of course there's nobody to see now, making it seem as if I'd been talking to myself or just making it up.

"No, I mean what's that in your hand?"

I look at it as if it had just bitten me. "Bloody hell, how did that get there?"

She is not amused. "I'm not sitting up here while you get afloat on *apéritifs*. I want to go for my food. I haven't had anything since breakfast, let me remind you."

"Yes, yes, of course. But it's still a little early and there's still some sun on the balcony, and while you're doing your hair, I'll just finish this." She should have had a couple of beers. Beer is food.

"Right, but no more."

She goes in to do what she has to do.

I know when I'm beaten. Good job I had made it a large one. It's been a fraught day, the worst we've had since this holiday began, and I had some stressful – not to say embarrassing – moments last week on our tour.

Over the sound of the blast from the hair-dryer, I drink to a less stressful and more successful day tomorrow.

16

Setting Out for Ercolano

AT breakfast, two of the Three Degrees are sitting together, behind us – the ugly one and the pretty one, but the third is sitting with a couple over at the window. Probably her parents. Better be careful if I am going to make any complaints; I will probably have to reckon with them, too. It's not the father so much – it's the mother. I don't know what her husband thinks of her, but she terrifies me. I wouldn't care to undergo the third degree with *her*. It's amazing how well the girl turned out, considering.

I don't realise it at first, but at an adjacent table is Mrs Scanty-Panties. Strangely enough, it is her husband, Bill, I recognise first because of his huge beak. She's not wearing her see-through clothes this morning, which is probably why I didn't spot her straight away. I don't know what she's going to do today, but it looks as if she may be going to the opera even although it's only 8:30 in the morning.

She's still in black though, this time wearing a halter-neck top, deeply slashed to display her cleavage. They're not the biggest couple of swells in the world but there's enough to be interesting and I admit the dress is very elegant. The strange thing is she is facing *into* the room, although she has a seat beside the blank windows that frame the sweeping curve of the bay where Vesuvius hoists itself heavenward in a couple of uneven peaks. Imagine sitting with your back to that heavenly view! Perhaps she thinks we would prefer to look at her twin peaks, so to speak. I point her out to Iona, who hasn't yet seen her.

It was a mistake.

"Huh! Just look at her, showing off again! No wonder she looks like that if *that's* all she has for breakfast."

It's true. None of the scrambled eggs and sausages for her – nor the muesli, nor the croissants, and certainly not the Danish pastries. To give her the benefit of the doubt, perhaps the waiter has already cleared away the dirty dishes, but I don't think so because Bill's appear to still be there. She's daintily eating a slice of toast with a black coffee (I presume) and, if she could, *La Belle Dame Sans Merci* would cheerfully make it choke her. I have rarely seen her so vituperative towards another person before. I find it quite amusing. For a laugh, I might have pretended to fancy her, only I value my life too much.

Ah, there's my friend Stan just come in. Not really him, of course, because he lives in the United States and you'd easily tell them apart if they stood side by side, but they're definitely the same idea. It's amazing how often God repeats his ideas for faces. Think of George V of Great Britain and Nicholas II of Russia, for instance. On the other hand, when you stop and think of all the billions of people there are in the world, I suppose it's not really all that surprising. It just goes to show that, unlike Cleopatra, who, according to Shakespeare, had an *infinite variety* all by herself, there is not an infinite variety of people. I look like George W. Bush myself, though naturally I do not draw people's attention to this, although I do get a number of queer looks.

Of course that might just be because of my unique dress sense. Today, for example, I am gaily attired in my yellow outfit. My green ensemble got rather sweaty yesterday with all the stress and the heat of the occasion.

Iona and I don't see eye to eye about my yellow matching set, and I have to admit the Speedos are rather startling. I would have preferred a more muted tone myself, if the truth be known, but my chain stores only carry a limited stock and I have to make do with whatever the widow of the deceased donates. The previous owner of these must have been a young bloke who had had a tragic accident: an older person would not have been attracted to such a lurid shade unless he was colour blind.

La Belle Dame Sans Merci had bought me a horrible new black pair from a real shop, but which I refused to wear as they were so gloomy – never mind expensive.

"Well, it's your funeral," she had said, "if people laugh at you."

"I wouldn't be seen dead in those deadly black ones," I had wittily rejoined, but she didn't even smile and took them back for a refund.

Time to go and get ready now breakfast is over. Whilst I was stranded at Sant'Agata yesterday, Iona had been networking. We, by which I mean us and the rest of the gang, are going to catch the 9:37 train to Ercolano, the stopping-off point for the ascent of Vesuvius. A bus will take us pretty much most of the way to the top, though we don't have much of a clue where it leaves from or when, though we'll find out,

I'm sure. But first we have to catch the free bus down to Sorrento, then walk along to the station. At least I know where *that* is, so not everything was a waste of time yesterday.

On the way down, I look to see where I could have gone wrong. I think I can see what happened. There is a fork in the road to the left which goes downhill. That must have been where the bus went instead of continuing up the hill. Pity my Irish friends hadn't told me I had to get off there. Perhaps they didn't realise I had only just arrived and didn't know my way about. Or maybe they assumed I had a brain.

There's the factory chimney. What! There already! Iona is right – it's not nearly as far as I had thought after all. It had seemed so long on the way down yesterday, but then again I had been under stress, like the Bra-benders' brassieres. So far on this leg of the holiday, only two days into it, I seem to have been under little else. And I had thought it was going to be much more relaxing than last week!

When it comes, the carriages of the train are covered in graffiti. It's hard to tell if it's modern art or vandals. Certainly the carriages don't look very new, and the graffiti suits them in a rough, tough, you're-going-to-be-mugged sort of a way. Still, it was a brave decision by the tourist board of Sorrento to adopt this design – if they did. At least it doesn't leave the vandals any room to operate.

The only air conditioning is the windows, the type with chrome rails that you pull down. For the entire length of the train, they are pulled down as far as they can go – which is to say, half-way down. The seats are hard and plastic. This is not going to be the most luxurious journey in the world, evidently. Not to worry. It's not going to last too long, so the seats won't get that much harder.

We're due to arrive in Ercolano at 10:25, so that means that it will take... er... let me see... After a few minutes, I can't be bothered doing it, as the take-away number is bigger than the one above and too complicated. Arithmetic is not my strong point.

Ercolano is the second-last stop on the *Circumvesuviana*, the last being Naples. We'll probably go there this week sometime, just to go to the museum, to see the treasures of Pompeii, as well as revisit Pompeii itself – the stop before Ercolano.

It's a funny thing, but the Italian name seems to emasculate Hercules, after whom the city was named. I mean, if he can't even say his aitches, how can you really take him seriously? The poor beggar had to labour very hard to become a god, unlike the Roman emperors who had nothing more to do to achieve the godhead than merely expire. His speech impediment reminds me of my American friends who say *'erbs* for "herbs" and *crik* for "creek" – and most bizarrely of all, they *flay* a fish when they intend to do nothing more serious that fillet it, though I suppose if you are a fish, it's still a pretty serious business.

If you give it the French pronunciation, I suppose you can just about see where they're coming from.

17

Trouble with a Dutchman

WE'VE stopped. But we've barely started! We're running to time. Maybe the myth about Mussolini making the trains run on time is true after all. Mind you, Sant'Agnello is only two minutes down the line, so if you start at that end of the line on time, as we did, it would be pretty hard not to be.

We're picking up speed now. The next stop should be Vico Equense and we're rattling along, the wind from the open carriages whipping our hair and making speech impossible unless you shout over the noise of the clacking rails. When we stop – bang on time – at Vico Equense, Pat, who is facing me but at the other side of the passage, says, "I'm sitting on your side."

I see what she means. She is on the sunny side, whilst I am in the shade. I was notorious last week for walking in the sun whilst all sensible people kept to the shade. She's looking very hot and bothered.

"Do you want to change?" I ask gallantly, springing up. "I don't mind."

For some reason, I happen to look down at my empty seat. To my horror, "springing up" was *le mot juste*, as the French say, for it is soaking wet – for even on this shady side of the carriage, it is so hot I have sprung a leak. It's only sweat. I wipe off as much as I can with my hand. I hope Pat thinks I'm just dusting it out of politeness.

When she does take my place, if she does feel anything, she doesn't show any reaction. Perhaps she's too polite. So am I. I can't help but notice her behind has left behind its own damp imprint. There are two kidney-shaped stains where both buttocks have been. It's a bit early in our relationship to be exchanging body fluids I would have thought. I sit down beside Bill, too polite to wipe the sweat away in front of him.

Castellammare di Stabia – so long they shortened it to C/mare – and we're still bang on time. The next stop is Pompeii and, as expected, there is a mass exodus for the *Scavi*. We arrive at Ercolano on time, and just in time for me to finish regaling Bill with my adventure of yesterday. I can tell that Iona is subjecting Pat to the same story, only she finishes it a lot sooner than me – but then of course, she was not there and can't provide the same amount of detail as I can to make it such a riveting story. Funnily enough, I catch Bill trying to stifle a yawn. He must have had a bad night.

As soon as we leave the station, we are mugged by taxi touts. They will take us up Vesuvius, wait an hour and bring us back. All that for €8 – each. It sounds good to me and it sounds good to the others too. The bus, wherever it is, would be cheaper, but this will be a lot quicker and an hour on the volcano should be long enough. There's a snag though, the same as that for our proposed Amalfi trip. The others are already on their way in another taxi – Helen and Donald and Tom, Dick and Harriet, but Bill, Pat, Iona and I are one short. The wheels of the bus will not go round until we have another passenger.

It's not long, however, before we do acquire another person to make up the numbers. He has straw-coloured hair with a straggly, scruffy beard and is wearing a battered hat and a denim shirt with dark patches under the oxters. He seems to be a serious photographer, because he has an SLR strung round his neck and a bag which is probably full of different lenses. From his accent, I deduce he's Dutch.

He engages in lengthy negotiations with the driver about the length of time we have at the top, but at last climbs aboard muttering something incomprehensible (but probably Dutch swear words) and, having taken his seat, occupies himself with fiddling in his bag.

We climb steadily through the narrow streets and lanes of Ercolano till, eventually, we leave the outskirts of the town behind and start climbing, by a tortuous road, the open slopes of Vesuvius.

The Dutchman sticks his head out the widow and snaps away as each hairpin bend swings him away from the hillside and affords him a view of the diminishing town and the bay. It's hard to see why he needs to take so many, and from a moving vehicle too. Surely the view from the top will be better anyway?

I think I have figured it out. He is going Dutch on this holiday with his wife. He paid to go on this trip whilst she paid the price of staying at home to look after the kids and this is her quid pro quo: *And here is a view looking down Mount Vesuvius as we were going up... and here is another. It's just the same, only it is 20 meters higher up and here is another one, just like it, but it's another 30 meters higher up than that.* She's not going to miss a thing.

The driver stops in a car park so teeming with vehicles it is difficult to find a place to park. He tells us we are to remember the registration number of the minibus so we will be able to find it again and we *must* be back within an hour, or he will leave without us. This sends the Dutchman into a paroxysm of incoherent spluttering. It's not nearly long enough as far as he is concerned. Well, it probably isn't for him if he is going to be taking a photograph every two minutes. The driver is unflustered and just shakes his shoulders phlegmatically. Perhaps he's pretending not to understand; it's all double Dutch to him, although he is probably thinking there is only one of *him,* thank God.

I reckon the driver's got it co-ordinated to match the trains. Once he's dumped us, he'll be back down in time to catch the next trainload of tourists and back up in time to take the previous lot down again. Nice work if you can get it, not too stressful, offering this shuttle service. He could probably do it backwards, like Ginger Rogers did what Fred Astaire did, and if he doesn't get a place to turn, probably that's just what he'll do.

Because he's nearest the door, none of us can leave the bus until the Dutchman finishes his protest, but at last he gives up and complains to me, who is first off behind him, about how unreasonable the arrangement is. I agree. I always think it's best to agree with disagreeable Dutchmen. I tell him I imagine how the system works and suggest he might be able to catch a later bus back, provided there's room. He grunts something ungrateful like: *Thank you very much for your bright idea, canary brain,* before he stomps off up the volcano.

The car park is surrounded on all sides by a sea of flowering broom which is emitting the most heavenly scent of coconut. I breathe in great lungsful of it. If the gods live on air, this would be their ambrosia. It seems a perfect place to join them, ceasing to breathe in this scented air, just as Keats, listening to his nightingale, felt like slipping into *easeful death*. I feel if I were to wander amongst those violent yellow flowers in my yellow outfit, I could just melt into them and fade away.

And if I changed my mind about joining the gods, I could always, for a laugh, leap out on tourists and give them a fright, then disappear into the broom again and give birth to the legend of the mysterious "Yellow Man of the Mountain". I imagine the gods would take their hat off to me for devising such a merry scheme and I'd get brownie points when I did go to heaven.

We have to go to the top on foot, I am happy to say. A funicular to the crater would be no fun at all, making it far too easy. A rustic wooden fence pens us in and the trail snakes alarmingly steeply ahead. It looks high and it looks far, and maybe the Dutchman was right. Maybe he's been here before, maybe he missed a shot of the crater from a particular angle and knows just how long it takes to get up and down. By the time we make it to the top, it might be time to set off for the bottom again, leaving hardly any time to peer into the crater. He looked fit too, as if he could make it in pretty good time. But then, we won't be spending nearly so much time taking snaps.

Off we set. The ground is cindery and slippery and my feet tend to sink into it and little bits of ash keep finding their way into my sandals, just as the Scot I met yesterday had said, so I have to stop every so often and shake them out. But that is good because I can stop for breath to take in the view until the thumping in my heart returns to normal.

It's spectacular, Naples and its suburbs, with the bay sweeping round in a broad arc. Unfortunately it's spoiled by a pall of pollution, mauve and dense, hanging over it – almost like a fog. I can also see just how densely populated the entire area is. With 3 million souls, it is the largest conurbation in southern Italy. Should Vesuvius erupt, the death toll could be horrendous. Despite the early warning, would people believe it? Would they leave their homes and possessions to possible looters? Would there be enough time to get all the people out? And where to? Where *would* be safe?

It's only a matter of time before Vesuvius does what active volcanoes do...

18

Vesuvius and the Mad Hatter

TIME to go on. Iona has caught up, pink and perspiring, clutching her hat which threatens to fly off in sudden gusts of wind which swirl around us without warning. She wants to rest awhile, so I continue the ascent alone, now I have my wind back.

I come across a shop and a turnstile with a lot of people milling about: people who have come down and people queuing to go up after they've visited the shop. Of course, Iona can't pass a shop without stopping to buy something she doesn't need. But not this time – all she's interested in is a drink. I could murder a pint myself.

She has murder on her mind too – murdering her pint-sized husband who has forged on ahead with the water bottle, leaving her to die of thirst. Wordlessly, she stretches out her hand and I only need to take one look at her face to know what she wants. She's incapable of speech at the moment but, after she has had a slug from the life-sustaining water bottle, I know this form of low-life is for it.

"Thank you! Thank you very much! Leaving me without any water! Thank you very much! It was very kind of you, I must say."

"I'm sorry. I am a burden to you and a beast of burden besides." Then, seeing her face darken, "I just didn't stop to think," I add contritely, doffing my Panama.

Fortunately for me, too many people are looking on for me to be ritually humiliated in public. We go into the shop to buy more water for me to carry, as the bottle I've been humphing around is already a bit warm. The cooler it's encased in doesn't work at all. It certainly doesn't cool tempers.

We pass through the turnstile and stick together as we climb to the summit, just in case Iona should need another slug of water.

I don't know what my compatriot yesterday was blethering about. I don't see any sign of sticks for sale or any abandoned ones, nor did I see any on the way up, but there is another tourist trap just before you reach the rim of the crater, where you can buy some cute little frogs and other little critters which have nothing to do with volcanoes, except they are made of lava. I may be a mite cynical, but I wouldn't mind betting they were made in Hawaii.

Iona buys a postcard, not that she'll send it to anybody. (At least I'll save on the stamp.) Does she realise what €2 is in real money – for a postcard! But, to be fair to Iona, this is no ordinary postcard. It was taken from a plane, in 1944, of Vesuvius in action. No wonder it was so expensive – it was taken nearly 60 years ago.

The crater is deep and the edge is jagged. I suppose if you made a film of it, you could call it *The Jagged Edge*. Through gaps in encrusted lava, you can see the bottom of the crater, and at the other side, the remains of the funicular rail-

way which was aban-
doned after the 1944
eruption and never re-
built, left to rust quietly
away. Rust to dust.
Ashes to ashes.

Over to my left,
precariously balanced on
the lip of the crater, is
something that looks as
if it has landed from outer space. It's like the sort
of satellite we send to
the moon, all aerials and
antennae glinting scien-
tifically-silver in the sun.

Crater of Vesuvius

And if we didn't know
where we really were, we could easily imagine that's where
we were. What they are really, are sensors placed by volcan-
ologists to listen into the volcano in order to give warning of
an impending eruption: *I'm coming! I'm coming! I'm coming! I
can't stop! Whoosh!*

The path ahead is pretty rugged and the rim is really
ragged, so it's not surprising we should not be allowed to go
right around the crater. In fact, it's been a bit too rocky and
difficult a path for Iona with her slippery, flat shoes so she
decides to turn back. But not me – I want to go as far I can go.
My mother often said I was the "bloody limit", and she could
be right because sandals are not the best of footwear for this
expedition. When I get to the end of the path, I notice I have
cut a toe. If Stendhal had written a book about my feet, he
would have called it *The Red and the Black*: black with ash-

dust, except where the blood has carved a path through it like a rivulet of molten lava.

It's time I got out of here, not that I think Vesuvius is in any imminent danger of erupting, but I know someone who will if I miss that taxi or keep people waiting. Far below, I can identify Tom and Dick by their bare backs, since they have stripped to their waists in order to catch a tan. There is no sign of Harriet. In fact, I wonder if she has even embarked on the expedition at all, in this sweltering heat, over this soft ground. Nor is there any sign of our Dutchman who had forged ahead for the multitudinous photographs, the taking thereof.

I set off in pursuit and it's not long before I catch up with them, bloody foot notwithstanding. Apparently they had been to the extremity of the path like me. The rest – who, like Iona, hadn't made it that far – are out of sight. I say "bye" to Tom and Dick and leave them behind in a cloud of ash. I pass through the turnstile and can see Iona further below with Bill and Pat.

The ash is deep and I scoot past them like a skier. He, who was last, shall be first back to the taxi if it kills me and it nearly does as my sandal-skis skid on the ash and I almost turn base over apex. I don't know why I get these crazy ideas in my head sometimes, I just do.

I'm not the first as it happens, because Donald and Helen are there, but they're not in our taxi, so I suppose they don't really count. As it turns out, I'm in plenty of time for the taxi, and so are the others, but when it's time to go, there's no sign of our Dutchman. I hadn't seen him but, since I was passing so many people, I may easily have gone flying past him and never noticed him.

We're all sitting in the taxi and the driver is manoeuvring amidst the ranks of parked vehicles so he can go down the mountain head-first instead of having to reverse all the way down, when the missing Dutchman appears as if by magic at the passenger door. He doesn't look out of breath, doesn't look as if he's been busting a gut to get here. Where has he been? Lurking about, watching us, waiting till the last possible minute to get his money's worth?

As soon as he's ensconced in the seat beside the driver, he begins haranguing him about how ridiculous it is that we should be going down so soon. Wisely, I think, the driver seems to have developed sudden deafness and says nothing. Having made his protest, the Dutchman reverts to sulk mode but is soon engaged in his photography again: *This is one I took before, only on the way down this time.*

When we get back to the station, we pay our dues and leave. The Dutchman is still in conversation with the taxi driver as we leave the forecourt behind and follow the brown *Scavi* sign down the hill. It's one of life's annoying little unfinished stories. We'll never know what happened. Did he walk off in a rage, did he negotiate a reduction, or did he stump up after being threatened with the police?

It's lunchtime and, although there is no reason why we should do so, as we are walking round Herculaneum independently, we decide to – or it just happens – we all end up at the same restaurant within sight of the excavations. The difference is that poor Iona has to sit outside whilst the others go inside in search of air-conditioning. I'm not a completely bad person though – she has a seat in the shade, whilst I sit in full sun. The good thing about sitting outside, in my view, apart from being in the fresh air, is you can see what's going on in the street.

I'm not here for the beer alone – I wouldn't be allowed to be. I don't like a big meal in the middle of the day; it tends to make me want to go to sleep. We share an *insalata mista* and a calzone, and – of course – you have to have the *coperto* as well. There is a bread mountain in Italy, and every tourist has to do his or her duty.

Near the end of the street, some poor bloke is trying to start a motor scooter sort of thing – a sort of hybrid between a scooter and a motorbike. He's standing on the pedal, jumping on it even, turning it round to face downhill, running with it and jumping on the pedal but it doesn't matter what he does, it just won't fire: *Start you little, bastard! Start!* Eventually, he comes up the street past us, pushing it, sweating, swearing. I haven't got the Italian for it, but – even if I had – would I have said: *Hey, Giovanni, have you checked the petrol?* I wonder if he'd thought of that. At least his misfortune is our good luck, and we don't have to suffer the fumes and the noise from his irritating engine. Not as irritating as *he* finds it though.

And what the heck is this? I've never seen its like before. It's a young chap making a spectacle of himself wearing a banana leaf as an impromptu hat, anchored in place by his specs. As a hat, it's effective enough: the sun wouldn't penetrate the leaf's thickness and it covers the back of the neck too, and depending at how jaunty an angle you wear it, it could also shade the eyes. Not only that, it's flexible – you could roll it up and put it in your suitcase, like I roll up my Panama. Probably you would have to rub baby oil or something into it to keep it supple, but if you couldn't be bothered, you could just pick up another one.

It maybe doesn't look very elegant, but to tell you the truth, I've seen a lot worse at some weddings and some mothers-of-the-bride would be well advised to take a leaf out of his tree, if you pardon the expression, since bananas grow on plants, not trees, as I expect you know. And if you don't wear specs, I suppose you could always fix a bit of string or elastic to the sides and strap it under your chin to hold it in place.

The others emerge from the restaurant complaining it was not air-conditioned and, even worse, was hotter still due to the heat from the kitchen. They look as if they had emerged from a sauna rather than an eatery. Not only that, but they missed all the entertainment. Iona, on the other hand, has had fresh air and entertainment, which just goes to show you, I am not always wrong.

We, not they, are the more rested and refreshed, ready to explore Herculaneum, the entrance to which we can see from here and to which we now make our way down the hill.

19

Introduction to Herculaneum

A T the entrance to the *Scavi*, whilst Iona and the others queue up to pay, I notice a room off to the left of the entrance with a whole lot of literature about Herculaneum, including a little maroon booklet called *A Brief Guide to Herculaneum*. Perfect. If we use this as our guide, it should give us the highlights. There's nobody there, nothing to say if they're free or not – certainly no price on the cover, but presumably printed in their thousands for visitors, the use of. With nobody to ask, I help myself to one. When the others see my prize, they want to know where I got it and pick up a copy for themselves. So I have another use on this holiday. I hope it's not on how to be a thief.

Unlike Pompeii where we walked *up* to it, Herculaneum is approached from the top and entered by descending a massive ramp. Iona and I stop next to a beautiful pink oleander bush in full bloom and look down on a panoramic view over what has been excavated of the city so far. Narrow, straight streets laid out in a grid

Looking Down on Herculaneum

pattern, it's much smaller than Pompeii. Scholars reckon it was home to about four thousand souls.

It nestles in a pit with the new town of Herculaneum scarily close to the edge. In fact, one house has a massive, great crack running down it and – what's more – it looks as if it is inhabited. Living life on the edge, literally.

The old town was covered in boiling mud up to 82 feet deep, which solidified to form a tuffaceous crust on which the new city of Resina was built. Thus Herculaneum was lost until rediscovered again in the early 18th century, when the construction of a grand villa began.

Never in their wildest dreams could the inhabitants have dreamt their city would rise, like a phoenix from the ashes, nearly two millennia later. On the day it died, the 24th August 79 AD, their dreams were the stuff of waking nightmares – ironically the day of the Vulcanalia, when the Romans celebrated the feast of Vulcan, the god of fire. Don't tell me the gods weren't having a laugh.

It's like looking down on a kind of oasis. There are one or two isolated palms, sprays of green in a drab, monochrome-grey landscape, as if the houses themselves were made out of the tufa which had entombed them for so many centuries, or – by some sort of osmosis – had taken on that drab colour.

By the time we've taken all this in, the others have moved on and are well ahead. That suits me. It's not that I'm anti-social, it's just I'd prefer to walk round the ruins on our own. We can move at our own pace and wander where we will. We don't need to follow the booklet if we don't want to, but can move off at a tangent if something interesting catches the eye. We are also armed with that magnificent guidebook with the transparencies that we had bought in Pompeii and which, fortunately, also has a section on Herculaneum. Worth its weight in gold for the information it provides, it does get quite heavy after a while, lugging it around in this intense heat. Iona will tell you. She's in charge of it.

At the moment we are looking down on the barrel arches which, in antiquity, were the warehouses which gave out onto the shore, now more than half-a-mile away after Vesuvius dumped thousands of tons of débris there. Here, they dug out nearly three hundred skeletons of the poor souls who had been sheltering there.

It was not the hot mud that entombed these poor devils that killed them, but the deadly pyroclastic gas. At 500° Centigrade, it burned the skin off their bodies and boiled their brains. Too horrible to contemplate, but at least it must have been swift. Despite the sun beating us to death, or maybe because of it, a cold shiver runs down my spine at the thought.

As we enter the street which the archaeologists have unimaginatively called "Cardo III", the first house we come to, on our left, is the House of Aristides, not that it's much of a house any more. Iona has the map and the guidebook as well as the little booklet I liberated,

Overview of Herculaneum

from which she relays the information. This is a very sensible arrangement, as it means we don't have to pass the books backwards and forwards all the time. It also means she has to carry them and I don't have to bother. It's a good arrangement for Iona too, since – as she is reading to me – I can't go haring off with the water. That is my use. Aquarius is not my star sign, but it may as well be, since being the water bearer seems to be my principal use on this holiday.

Iona tucks the map under her oxter and searches for the House of Aristides in the booklet. At last she finds it. According to the rules of Italian logic, this is not number one in the guide, but third from last.

Whilst Iona finds a spot in the shade, I wander off to find a place in the sun, but still within earshot, whilst she gives me the reading. She tells me this house is named after a statue found there, wrongly identified as being that of the famous Athenian politician, whereas, in fact, it is a statue of that extremely well-known Athenian emperor, Aeschines. How they could have made such an obvious mistake beggars belief, but there it is and the house, having come down in the world, found it impossible to recover from this demotion and the name stuck, like solidified boiling mud.

Iona has moved further away to stand in front of a wall where the red plaster has worn away so it's possible to see that the wall behind it is constructed of square tiles standing on their points to form a diamond pattern.

The Romans called it *opus reticulatum.* That looks deco-
rative enough to me – almost a shame to plaster over it.

Off to my left, I spot a middle-aged couple marvelling at Iona beginning to cook in the heat and turning a
pinker shade of prawn by the minute. And because we
are so far apart now, she is apparently reading aloud to
herself. Wordlessly they look at each other saying: *Poor
woman, the sun has obviously gone to her head. Mad!
Quite mad! Poor thing!* Iona, happily, is too busy reading and looking at what she's reading about, to notice
any of this unvoiced conversation. I catch their eye, put
on a sympathetic expression and shrug as if to say: *I
know. It's a shame. But what can you do?* She should, of
course, have worn a hat.

They move off and so does Iona, but I stay in the
sun, sitting on a wall enjoying the sight of a rectangular
strip of grass much more lusciously green than seems
possible in this grey and dusty landscape. Three palm
trees in the middle provide a touch of the exotic and the
whole rectangle is delineated by a trim box-hedge. And
this little oasis is itself enclosed by a colonnade of pure-
white pillars with red tiles capping them off. It seems to
me a most idyllic spot to spend some time in solitude and
contemplation, like Wordsworth.

Actually, what I'm contemplating is a lot more
prosaic. I'm betting the middle-aged couple look back to
see if I have any connection with the mad woman. After
all, we look a pair in a sort of way, although I look more
like a lemon in my outfit. Sure enough, after a while they

An Oasis Amongst the Ashes

do, and there I am, sitting on the wall and there goes Iona, strolling on ahead, studying the map and reading aloud from the booklet for the benefit of my ears, but – from their point of view – apparently muttering to herself. Actually she may not be reading from the book at all, but cursing Italian logic as she tries to figure out precisely where we are. If that is the case, I'm glad she is out of sound also.

When I catch up with her, she is at the House of the Skeleton. It is the fate of these houses to be named after the most prominent feature found when they were excavated. Unfortunately that's what was found here – the remains of a body, or rather a skeleton, on the upper floor. The actual bones of the poor unfortunate have long since been removed, perhaps re-interred in a drawer in the archaeological museum at Naples, but what does remain are some splendid mosaics.

Above a semi-circular alcove with brown frescoes too faded and too far away to see clearly, but whose central panel seems to glow with a curious luminosity, there is a frieze in vibrant turquoise and blue. The contrast is startling, those colours looking so fresh and new. Could they possibly have been restored? And yet I suspect not. They are protected by an overhanging foot-or-two of roof and I don't suppose it rains much here, despite the evidence of the luxuriant grass at the House of Aristides.

Two of the mosaics depict half-man (definitely not woman), half-serpent creatures floating about in an oc-

Frieze in the House of the Skeleton

A Vision in Yellow Rests in the Sun

topus-ink black sea whilst in the middle, a reclining figure, presumably Neptune, appears to be feeding a seal in a sea of azure blue. Strange that our attention is not drawn to it in the booklet.

I would take it home and install it in our bathroom if I could. The subject matter would be appropriate and the colours would match our colour scheme perfectly.

20

An Unexpected Encounter in the Baths

NOW we are standing in one of the fast-food shops or *thermopolia*. Terracotta jars or *dolia* are set into a marble counter, with only their rims showing, as neatly finished off as any sink or hob in a modern kitchen. The Romans, apparently, were accustomed to having lunch out. These were the takeaways, the McDonalds of their day, and – like them – you could also eat in the back room if you wanted. The most popular dish was not a *Mac Maximus* but *garum,* an evil-smelling sauce made from fermented fish guts, which reputedly had aphrodisiac qualities. That said, it's hard to imagine *garum*-guzzling geezers rushing back to the villa in the middle of the afternoon intent on ripping off their wives' *tunicas* (or, more likely, other people's wives' *tunicas*) and being welcomed with open arms – or anything else for that matter. *By Jupiter, your breath's foul – I*

Thermopolia

mean fishy, and that's what my husband will think if he comes back and catches you here at this time of day.

And they didn't just have fast food shops; they had pubs too – so who can doubt that the Romans were civilised, even if they did have crucifixions and blood-baths in amphitheatres and thought them so amusing they called them "Games"? We're in one of the pubs now, which has a painting of a ship and some graffiti too, amongst which is a quote from Diogenes – that arch-cynic whom people came to look and laugh at because he lived in a barrel and thus gave birth to the phrase a "barrel of laughs".

I have to trust the guidebook here. Apparently the graffiti says: *Diogenes, the cynic, on seeing a woman being swept away by a river, exclaimed: "Let one ill be car-*

ried away by another!" I wonder what mad, brave fool wrote that? An educated bloke, plainly, well-up on his Greek culture and up a creek without a paddle if any woman got to hear about what he'd written. I imagine he'd been rejected by some dame, came to the pub, had a few pints to drown his sorrows – though what he really wanted to do was drown *her* – and vented his frustration by writing on the wall instead, as you do. It just goes to show 2,000 years later and in some ways we've not evolved at all.

Everybody knows about the Romans and their baths, and that's where we are off to now – the men's baths. Unlike those in Pompeii which were heaving with humanity, here it is empty and it's good to plonk my bum in the changing room where countless bare Roman bums have been before, take the weight off my feet, slip them out of my sandals and let them get some air.

"Just look at your feet!" Iona exclaims in horror.

They have been up and down Vesuvius, and the ash and sweat and blood have combined to form an encrustation thick enough to plant potatoes and indeed there *is* some vegetation sticking to my sole! I must admit I am rather shocked at the state of them myself.

"Well, that's why I've come to the baths."

Iona gets up in exasperation. Was it the joke that was bad, or do my feet smell as bad as they look? In any case, she wanders off before someone comes along and links us together. She should worry, going around reading and talking to herself like that.

I check out my other foot and look at them wonderingly. I wonder if they are dirty enough to win a dirty-foot contest as one of my bucolic cousins once did after a ploughing match, much to his mother's undying shame.

"Hello!"

I can't see the speaker against the light. I can just make out that it is male and he's wearing shorts and he's short and stocky.

"Er... hello." I self-consciously slip my feet back into my sandals and stand up. Whoever he is, I hope he hasn't noticed them. Now I can see his face I recognise it, but can't think who he is. He seems to be accompanied by a trio of females – presumably his wife and two daughters, who look as if they could be in their early twenties but who also look as if they are in a hurry to get out of here, as if they were ashamed to be seen in the company of this tramp their father has engaged in conversation.

"Are you having a good time?"

"Yes. Yes. Thank you." (Who the hell is he?)

"And are you?"

"Yes, thank you."

He is just about to turn away, when I add: "Is the noise bothering you?" For now, in the nick of time, I have suddenly realised who he is. He is the man in the apartment below me with whom I've had the brief conversation about the Three Degrees.

"The noise?"

"Yes. The noise from the radio next door to me."

"No. I don't hear it at all."

What! Can he really mean that? I suppose it is two floors below and along a bit, but I would have thought he could have heard it easily.

"Oh well, that's good." That's what I say but in reality I am disappointed. There is no hope of roping him in as an ally against the noise pollution, then. I had been hoping for some support to show I was not just some intolerant crank spoiling other people's fun – that their bloody noise was an invasion, not only of my space and happiness, but other people's too. Now it seems, if the noise persists, I'll have to tackle the girls alone. If the truth be told, I feel a tad nervous about such a confrontation. I have had enough dealings with the young to expect their more-than-likely response would be to call me a boring old fart and turn the volume up louder.

And with that, the conversation with my new friend is at an end. We have nothing further in common at the moment, and I can tell he is eager to be off after his family. I have learned he is Dutch, though. They are ubiquitous, the Dutch. You see their distinctive yellow number plates everywhere. On the tour last week, we had been isolated from other nationalities, more or less; now I have met a couple of Dutch people in as many hours.

We continue our tour of the baths. I notice the shelves where the bathers stored their clothes and, on the floor, the black-and-white mosaic of a triton with some sea creatures which time has buckled so it looks, appropriately enough, as if they were all floating on a massive wave. The grooved roof above, although it looks like a WWII Nissen hut (a similarity furthered by vast areas of rust-coloured patches), is actually, as I had discovered in Pompeii, a device which kept the condensation from dripping on the punters.

Cunning devils, these Romans.

21

At Home with the Romans

HIGH in the *opus reticulatum* wall of the House of Two Atriums (there's posh!), a terracotta face is gazing down at the heads of those about to enter. Iona says it was to ward off the evil eye. It is certainly giving me a most distasteful look: *Hey you! Yes you, yellow belly. You're not coming into my house with feet like that, so clear off!*

According to the booklet, it is a Gorgon mask, but to me it looks too human – and I wouldn't mind betting it had been modelled on the owner's mother-in-law, the scariest woman he knew. Only he told her (with forked tongue) it was a mark of respect and she could visit any time she wanted and stay as long as she liked – which she probably did anyway, without his say-so.

At the College of the Augustali, we meet up with the rest of the gang who, seemingly, have still stuck together. Tom and Dick are topless, as they were on Vesuvius. I'd like to get some rays myself, but it doesn't seem seemly to go about a town and people's houses half-naked. Besides, I might be mistaken for an ugly, under-developed woman and might be arrested for indecency.

I'd certainly not be mistaken for the caretaker of this place, poor devil, whose skeleton was found lying on the bed of his room. They've left him here in a bed of grey ash, an apology of a skeleton, so little remaining you would scarcely recognise it as human remains at all.

The College or Boarding School, established by wealthy freedmen who had made good, the *nouveau riche* of the day, is a huge rectangular area with blind arches and four columns which support a rectangular opening in the roof. In a room off to the left, there is a

College of the Augustali

Fresco of Hercules, Juno and Minerva

small room with frescoes which are in remarkably good condition. These depict scenes from the life of Hercules after whom Herculaneum was named, unsurprisingly enough. One shows his arrival in Olympus accompanied by Jupiter, Juno and Minerva. Jupiter is a bit hard to recognise, however, as he appears as a rainbow – the gods move in mysterious ways – and there is a massive crack running diagonally right through the fresco which spares Iona's blushes but is just where it would have hurt Hercules the most.

Not to worry, though; there is another one beside it showing everything, and depicting Hercules' battle with Achelous, the god of all water and all the rivers of the world were his sinews. They were fighting over a princess named Deianira. Hercules was winning the combat, being so strong and manly, so Achelous, being godly, turned himself into a serpent. Hercules just laughed and pointed out he had been killing snakes since he was in his pram. Achelous changed tactics and form, this time into a wild bull and charged our hero but Hercules snapped off one of his horns. After that, Achelous gave up the battle for the princess. He wasn't feeling so horny any more.

The horn was picked up by a goddess called Plenty, who ordered that it be filled with all the fruits of the harvest, and so it came to be known as Cornucopia, the Horn of Plenty. Meanwhile, having lost much of his powers, Achelous was confined to the river that bears his name today, thereby creating a great deal of prime agricultural land to keep the Horn topped up.

As for Hercules, a fat lot of good winning the hand of the lady did him. Jealous of his many infidelities, Deainira smeared the blood of Nessus, the Centaur, on Hercules' fetching lion-skin shirt. That's the thanks he got for shooting Nessus with a poisoned arrow when he attempted to have his wicked way with her. The itching and burning drove Hercules so crazy he immolated himself on his own funeral pyre but he got his reward in heaven so it all concluded happily in the end.

Our book with the transparencies shows this drab place, which obviously had been ravished by fire, transformed into a lavish, luxurious-looking five-star residence with frescoes and red wainscoting to match the sumptuous red of the couches where couples recline, partaking of the fare served by slaves. One is bearing a flagon of wine, while another bears a platter on his shoulder on which is the head of some poor animal – probably intended by the artist to be a boar, but which, at first glance, looks like a large member of the feline family on account of what appear to be whiskers, but is actually some sort of vegetation sprouting out from behind it. Still, there is no accounting for taste – and the Romans were catholic in theirs, even more than the Gauls, whose modern descendants, the French, notoriously eat everything (but who, as far as I know, draw the line at eating the head of an oversized kitty).

The couples reclining on the couches are of the same sex, apart from a bearded bloke and a redhead who appear to be getting on very well together in the background. If this was the Roman idea of a boarding school, forget your Harrow and Eton – the eating may indeed be harrowing if the fare on that platter is anything to go by, but I think the décor and furniture is in incredibly good taste and, if I had lived then and my parents had decided to get rid of me by sending me off to boarding school (as well they might), I wouldn't have declined. I could have reclined here with the best of them.

The more of the Roman world I see, the more the Romans of two millennia ago seem, or at least some of them, to have lived a life much more luxurious than mine. I remember going to a new housing estate to see the show houses and returning to my own humble abode and thinking what a slum I lived in. As I tour these houses now, I get much the same feeling, the difference being that with the Romans, each house has its own individual style and character, unlike the clones they build for us today. Here, at the House of the Tuscan Colonnade for example, the house was apparently remodelled to incorporate an adjacent house, a bit like knocking two semis into one, only your average semi doesn't have colonnades or mosaics on the floors, or murals as fittings for that matter. Like this for example – a seated Maenad and Pan acting the goat with a couple of women.

The House of the Beautiful Courtyard, on the other hand, has dispensed with what I thought was the indispensable atrium, in favour of the aforementioned interior courtyard. Just because you call it beautiful, that doesn't make it so, any more than being called "Addison" makes me a dyslexic Adonis. It seems that in a later stage of its life, this house was also a boarding school. This is definitely the one that my parents would have sent me to, not the Hall of the Augustals.

Perhaps it looked better in its heyday when the paint and the frescoes were fresh. Now it looks like the stairwell of an inner-city high-rise block of flats, with peeling dark-red paint and plaster. And – as if to confirm this unappetising impression – in a back room, is a gruesome display. Entombed in a glass case are two, or possibly three, skeletons. Like chameleons, they are as grey as the lunar-landscape dust in which they lie. It's hard to tell exactly how many there are as they are all jumbled up together.

So, here they are, sleeping throughout eternity to-gether. Maybe, before the eruption, he had said he'd of-fer a sacrifice to the gods if only he could get to sleep with these two ladies. And now he is. It's funny how your dreams can sometimes come true, but not always in the way you expect. But that's the way the gods operate. They have a wicked sense of humour.

In glass cases on the back wall, it is a relief to see, after such a grisly sight, a thing of beauty indeed. In fact, three marble reliefs – in the centre, a pair of charging horses, their legs and hooves as delicately and intricately carved as if they were real, and next to them, on the right, a headless youth with every muscle of his six-pack proudly on display. On the other hand, he is not in the least well-endowed but is naked and unashamed, for a flowing garment of some description is nonchalantly folded over his left arm. Of course, being headless, he has no need to feel embarrassed.

Still, that's probably also him, like a cartoon strip, in the relief on the other side of the charging horses, ap-parently about to be mown down by them. His left hand is placed insouciantly on his hip, while the garment aforesaid has been whipped away from his body towards those thundering hooves by an apparently violent wind. He shows no fear, quelling the horses with a haughty look, confident they will stop before they trample him into a pulp – and you can see they are already braking.

Next is the House of the Wooden Partition, so-called because of the device used to separate the *ta-*

blinum from the atrium, and which, incredibly, has survived. The side rooms were used as shops, and if you have been worrying about how the Romans managed to have such creaseless togas, well, here is the answer – a Roman iron. Actually, it looks more like a wine press, and the *lanarius* (literally a wool-worker), who operated it, lived in two small rooms above the vestibule. Which just goes to show you that not everyone lived in a magnificent house.

The House of the Deer is so-named because of the statues of two stags, amongst others, found in the garden and now in the museum in Naples, while the Trellis House looks surprisingly Elizabethan and to me instantly

The Trellis House

identifiable from the two storeys jutting out over the pavement. I think it's been in just about every TV programme I have ever seen on Herculaneum. In actual fact, it's a much more humble building than it looks, made of tufa and wood with reed laths. Not so much a house but a tenement. It was the skyscraper of its day, and the sort of place where I would have lived.

But the star of them all, for me the most desirable address in Herculaneum, has to be the House of Neptune and Amphitrite, so-called because of its magnificent mosaic. It's not those two figures though, but the colourful fan design above them and the broad design running down the sides which immediately draw the eye with their startlingly-vivid blues and reds. The mosaic depicts the god of the sea abducting Amphitrite, having seen her sporting with the Nereids, or sea nymphs. If you're a god you can do that sort of thing, have whomever you fancy. I suppose it's still the same today, if you've got the looks of a Greek god (or enough money) – women just fall at your feet. I wouldn't know.

Having said that, Amphitrite doesn't look that upset about being abducted. She seems like an upwardly-mobile sort of a person and they both seem to be waving farewell to an audience prior to their ascent to Olympus. Anyway, like a Victorian novel, it all ended happily, for Neptune made an honest woman of her. Reader, he married her.

In the House of Neptune and Amphitrite

This room is the summer *triclinium*, or dining room, if you please. Imagine having a room for all seasons: *You're sleeping in the winter bedroom tonight, Sextus. I've got a headache.* On the wall adjacent to this is another mosaic, not so well-preserved, but also decorated with shells. In a niche stands a little fountain. This, says the guidebook, is the *nymphaeum*. As it does not say what a *nymphaeum* is, I imagine it's where the nymphs were kept and the master of the house nipped along to play with them from time to time, especially if the atmosphere in the house was a little bit frosty. Actually, if the truth be told, perhaps Sextus *was* nipping along to the *nymphaeum* just a bit too frequently, and that's why he was relegated to the winter bedroom.

Talking of nymphs, since we are just opposite the women's baths, we may as well have a peep. It's smaller than the men's, but better preserved – all those cosmetics, all the care they took of their bodies, has evidently rubbed off on the building. The mosaics on the floors, for instance, are in much better condition. There is one of a triton surrounded by sea creatures, and much less interestingly, another with a geometric design. The shelves where the ladies placed their clothes are still there, and so is the tub they would have soaked in. I would have liked to have sat in it, even if it has no water, and even more regrettably, no ladies, just for the feeling of what it might have felt like to be there – but the bath is roped off and we are clearly just meant to use our imagination.

My feet are tired and even dustier than before, if that were possible, and a look at the watch confirms it is time we were heading back up the hill to the station. What foolish thought was it that made me think we might get round this site in half a day – actually not even half of that? There is still so much we haven't seen, for example, the *Pistrinum* of Sex Patulcus Felix.

According to our booklet, Patulcus Felix was a *pistor*, which contrary to what you may be thinking, means he earned a crust as a baker. This was the bakery, and they called it after him because of a signet ring they found here which had his name on it. He was not necessarily the owner: he might just have been a punter.

And guess what else they found there? Two stucco phalluses! Just think about it for a moment. In an age where most of the plebs couldn't read, couldn't go to the cinema, couldn't afford – or weren't interested in – the high-class stuff at the theatre, but who could go, free, to see death and destruction at the amphitheatre, where else could you go, on your night off, for a bit of enter-tainment? The brothel, obviously. And how would you know where it was if you couldn't read and were too embarrassed to ask, unless it was two massive phalluses sticking up in front of your nose, pointing the way?

Scholars say they were there to ward off the evil eye. Who do they think they are kidding? I think it was the bordello disguised as a bakery.

And where are you off to, Sextus Insanitus?

Just off to the baker's, dear. I fancy a couple of rolls.

22

Seeing Double, and Some Italian Logic

WE have not seen our friends since the College of the Augustali and there is no sign of them either in the old town, or the new, as we make our way back to the station. Probably they have left long before us. We increase our pace and press on, afraid we will miss the train. They run every half-hour and, if we catch this one, that will give us twenty minutes to board the courtesy bus back to the hotel. I desperately want to catch it. If there's one thing I *don't* want to do, it's to get on the wrong bus or even get on the right bus but get off at the wrong place – though that is less likely to happen since Iona is in charge of me.

It's a dangerous thing, even to think it, in case the gods get wind of my plans and screw me up, like they did yesterday. It's my dearest wish to get back, and in this order – have a beer, wash the dust and blood and vegetation from my feet, have a swim, catch some rays, and have another beer to toast the sun going to its watery bed. As it is, even if things go smoothly, it's still going to be more than an hour before I can realise that heartfelt desire as the journey takes three-quarters of an hour alone, never mind the walk to the factory chimney, though once there, the bus journey takes only a matter of minutes – as I had discovered to my cost yesterday.

At the station, I am surprised to see no sign of our friends. In fact, the platform is deserted, apart from one solitary who is the spitting image of one of my brothers-in-law. Funny that. The second example today of one of those burps God has when He repeats Himself, or is too tired to think up a new idea, because it's Saturday night and He's had a hard week creating and He's looking forward to His day of rest.

What's different about this occasion is that I really thought my brother-in-law must be unique; there couldn't possibly be another like him. That after God saw what He had done, he would think He could do better and broke the mould. Yet here he is, the living proof He didn't! If you put the two of them together, and you will have to take my word for it, you couldn't tell them apart. Whether they have the same personality or not, if he's an exact clone, I'll never know.

I am struck by a sudden thought. What if everyone in the world has a clone and we only bump, by accident, into the one of someone we know? What if it's a test – the one who leads the better life lives on? Or maybe that's the one who dies and goes to heaven, that living on Earth is a stage you have to go through until you get it right. I know it's not an original idea. One of these days I hope I will find out if it's true or not. Of all the things to die of, I think ignorance really must be the worst thing.

We buy our tickets and know we must validate them, but first we have to track down the machine that does so. Just as well we have plenty of time, as it takes ages to locate it. There do not appear to be any on the platform and we hadn't seen any on the train itself (which would be a good idea), and ever since I had an unhappy episode with the bus police in Nice, I am paranoid about validating my ticket.

I sit in the sun and curse the Italian lack of logic while Iona decides to go back down the stairs to search for the machine there. In a few moments, back she comes waving them triumphantly in the air. The machine had been right where we had bought the tickets – it was amazing we hadn't bumped into it when we turned round from buying them at the kiosk. The system appears to be that you buy your ticket then immediately stick it in a machine to show you've bought it, as if having it in your hand – with the time and date stamped on it – wasn't enough evidence. Strange but true!

And *still* the train does not come. This is an experience I am unaccustomed to. I absolutely hate hanging about and prefer to arrive as close to the moment of departure as possible. Still, it is pleasant enough sitting here in the sun, though modesty prevents me from exposing my bosoms to the sun as I could have done if I had been at the pool.

At last, along come Tom, Dick and Harriet, stripped to the waist as usual (with the exception of Harriet). Bill and Pat are with them. Presumably they have been together all afternoon. Finally, along come Donald and Helen, both looking hot and flustered.

"Where's the validating machine?" Donald has a hunted sort of look in his eyes. His eyes are scanning the platform for the machine, while his tone makes "validating" sound like a swearword.

"Downstairs, by the ticket office," Iona tells him.

He looks at her carefully for a moment before deciding Iona is not the sort of person to make practical jokes. I can read Donald's lips as he expresses an uncomplimentary opinion on the logic of the Italian railway system before he scurries down the stairs, clutching his tickets. He'd better be quick. It's 16:55 and the train is due at 16:58 – and probably will be on time, if the outward journey was anything to go by. Actually, he makes it in plenty of time, what I call a minute before departure.

The train is not very crowded. I wouldn't have been surprised if I had a carriage to myself, as the colour of my feet should be an effective deterrent from any prospective companions alert enough to notice them. I don't think there's any smell; it's just I would have thought no one would willingly choose to sit anywhere near me. There is, however, an antidote: the air-conditioning system, which – as before – is operating at full stretch, the windows wide open, allowing in a welcome draught of warm air but also the noisy clack-clack of the wheels over the rails.

In actual fact, Iona and I do have travelling companions: a young Canadian couple sitting opposite us. As the train rattles its way along the coast, we shout at each other as Pompeii, Castellammare, Vico Equense, and Sant'Agnello all slip past, until finally, we arrive and are decamped in Sorrento.

The crowd begins to disperse, mainly down the street straight ahead, as we linger to say goodbye to our Canadian acquaintances in a normal tone of voice for once.

"Are you *still* here?" Donald grins as he and Helen pass by, his tone conveying mock surprise. His face is still red, but it's due now more to sunburn than from the effort of catching the train. "It's just I saw someone with a yellow shirt and shorts and wearing a Panama hat, going down that street there," he explains, pointing it out.

Impossible! Is he winding me up? When I look down the street at the retreating backs of the passengers, there is no sign of my sartorial double. Can it really be true? Can there really be another person as well-dressed as me strolling the streets of Sorrento?

Actually, perhaps it's not such a surprise. I've been here a couple of days now. Obviously I've been spotted and my outfit has been admired. It must have been difficult to procure the Panama and probably, whoever he is, had had to go to Naples to root it out, though the exact shade of the yellow of my shorts must have been just as elusive. It's quite flattering really.

The others announce their intention to go shopping in Sorrento. My intention is to go for a swim, so I need to head for the free bus. I am glad to hear Iona does not intend to join them but to join me in the pool, on condition I wash my feet first. We take the short cut, such as it is, and head up to the left towards the bus which I hope *will* be here this time.

For the second time that day, we are in plenty of time. The bus is already there (thank God!) by the factory chimney and we are allowed on board, which is why I have time to notice as we sit and wait, what I have failed to notice before – the logic (or rather the opposite) of the numbering of the bus seats.

I am sitting in seat number one, appropriately enough for the sartorial leader of Sorrento, but Iona, next to me, is in number 18 and we are sitting in the middle of the bus. Across the passage are 20 and 14; in front of us are 12 and 22. I suppose there is a kind of logic to that, if I could work it out, but how do you explain that the seats in front of 20 and 14 are 16 and 17? We can't see the numbers of the seats directly in front of them because of the bulky passengers occupying them. What could they be?

I point this out to Iona, and we spend the journey in a delightful discussion of what the numbers could possibly be. Iona guesses 15 and 13. I think number 2 has to be near me somewhere, so I go for that and... what? It could be practically anything, but I pick 13 as I usually have bad luck so it's unlikely to be right.

And do you know what? As we file down the passage and make a point of looking at the numbers – we were both wrong, though one of us had one of the numbers right. Work it out – if you can! Answers on a postcard, please.

It just goes to show that as far as I am concerned, Italian logic will always defy rational interpretation.

23

High Jinks and Lofty Thoughts

BACK at the hotel, the sun is still shining brightly and I'm smiling too as there is no sound from next door – but that is probably because they are at the pool.

I don't bother washing me, just my feet. The rest of me is going to get washed in the pool, after all. No point in expending any unnecessary effort, and I am in a hurry to get out there before the pool closes.

There are plenty of empty sunbeds. I pick one a couple away from a French lady, who happens to be topless. It's as good as any. Well, I suppose she may not be French, just reading a book in French, but she looks French and the Scots and the French have always been good friends – especially against the common enemy, the English, and perhaps I'll get into conversation with her in due course. Better than being near my English neighbours, the Three Degrees, that's for sure. I can see then away over to the right, sunning themselves and being remarkably quiet.

After a swim, and by the time she has dried off in the sun, Iona has had enough and starts getting her things together.

"I'm going to go and put some food on."

"Eh?" Is she going to smother herself in chocolate or something more Italian; male and female-shape pasta perhaps? Perhaps a lemon *gelato*, though I would have thought that would have been a trifle chilly. Besides, if it is her plan I should lick it off, you might have thought she would have done me the favour of choosing black cherry flavour.

"You know perfectly well what I mean. I mean I am going to put some clothes on," she says irritably.

"Hmm."

"Don't be too long. I want my food."

I knew all along she has been thinking of food. And it's not as if we had skipped lunch today, like we do some days, yet here she is still thinking of food. I seldom think of it myself, but I can think of lots of other things as I sit here looking at the ladies sunbathing or splashing in the pool. I notice that the French lady has covered up. The temperature must be dropping, though I can't say I've noticed.

After I have had another swim and saved the effort of drying myself by letting the towel beneath me and the sun above me do their work, I'm struck by a sudden thought. I'm thinking if I want to have some *apéritifs* in the sun, I'd better start making tracks to the balcony.

Suddenly a disturbance breaks out at the other side of the pool.

"Yowh cheek-eye cow!"

I look over to where one of the Three Degrees, the pretty one, is sitting up, clutching her bikini top. Apparently her friend had tried to rip it off whilst she was lying on her front, unsuspecting. They have been too quiet for too long. Glad of the excuse for some action, she and the other one grab the would-be rip off merchant and a wrestling match follows on the edge of the pool, followed by an almighty splash as two of them over-balance and topple into the pool. When they bob to the surface, screwing the water out of their eyes, the third – who was left high and dry – dive-bombs them, drenching them again, to say nothing of their immediate neighbours. Just as well they were wet already.

Of all the people in the entire hotel, these are undoubtedly the most noisy and disruptive, and I have ended up next to them. Well, that's just my luck and I hope you are satisfied, ye gods. I expect you are laughing merrily in heaven just like they are, but I'm not staying to hear any more. With a bit of luck, I'll be able to have my *apéritifs* in peace without the accompaniment of the cacophonic "music" from next door, though it fills my heart with dread to think that, high on this excitement, they may come straight back to the apartment to continue their high jinks.

Showered but not dried, and swathed in a blue towel, I make my way out onto the balcony and manhandle the table into the corner where there will be a quarter of an hour or so of sun before it is obscured by the trees. Quicker than you can say "gin", I have poured out a couple – a double for me and one for Iona, and still the Three Degrees have not yet returned. This is more like it.

By the time I have started my second, stronger gin, though the sun has gone down, they still have not come back up and I can enjoy the activity of just thinking how nice the gin is and how much nicer it is without the girls from next door. I pass the benefits of my musings on to Iona, who is sitting stitching, stitching, stitching – in her own way at peace with the world.

"Oh, for heaven's sake, you are obsessed with those girls!" She seems to jab the needle more pointedly into the material. "Go and put some clothes on!"

On the bus back to the hotel, I had expressed the hope they would be down at the pool, had commented that there appeared to be no noise as we approached the room, had pointed them out to Iona across the crowded poolside and now, because they were not next door, I had brought them up again. Maybe she's right. They do seem to have got under my skin rather.

It's time I got out of this damp towel in case the dye comes out and dyes my bum as blue as a baboon's. And just as the colours should be fast, that's what I'd better be. I get dressed, as I suspect Iona's irritability has much to do with impatience to be at her *food*. If she'd only drink more gin, she'd probably be less snippy. Take me for instance. I'm feeling a lot happier now. Those girls aren't so bad really. They are just young and exuberant; they're growing up, full of the joys of life. I have no objection to that – just as long as they enjoy their lives as far away from me as possible.

I sigh and stroll over to the balcony with my glass in my hand. When I look down, there is my Dutchman in his garden again. I raise my glass and call down to him.

"Did you have a nice time in Herculaneum?"

"Yes, it was splendid! And you?"

"Yes, very good! In fact, I preferred it to Pompeii. More compact. Have you been to Pompeii yet?"

"Yes, we were there yesterday. Very interesting!"

"Yes, it was." I can't think what to say next. "Well, enjoy the rest of your holiday."

"Yes, you too!"

And with this, I curtail the conversation as I disappear from his view. It's good to make distant friendships, but I mustn't make such a nuisance of myself that he becomes too scared to go out to his garden for fear of being accosted by me.

There are to be fireworks tonight at the Marina Grande. We could go down to the port or we could just stay here and watch them from the roof. The problem is they are not due to begin until midnight, and in Italian time that means it could be God knows how much later than that since it's got nothing to do with the railways. Iona is not too keen on going out at that time of night. She has no problem with getting up in the morning, but needs to go to bed early – unlike me, who can stay up all night but who can't get up in the morning. So, before we go down to the restaurant, we go up to the roof to see if, from there, we are in sight of the port.

We aren't, but I reckon we should still get a good view of the fireworks – perhaps even better from this distance, and with the lights reflected in the water, we might get a more global view of the pyrotechnics. We decide we'll come up here at midnight to see what it's like anyway, rather than walking all the way down there and all the way back up the hill again.

"If I'm still awake," adds Iona.

We are the only ones up here – us, the last remaining rays of the day, and scores of sunbeds around the perimeter, some still in sunlight. This looks all right. It must be what they mean by "wall-to-wall sunshine". I am cheered by a sudden thought. If the girls and their racket get too much to bear, I could always come up here with my *apéritif* and get some more sunshine into the bargain. Or I might sit on the wall with my glass and admire the view, for it really is stupendous – from the blue of the bay, speckled with white sails, to the sheer cliffs where the green of the trees clothes the hillside. Sprinkled here and there are clusters of orange roofs with the white of the houses gleaming as if not to be outdone by the whiteness of the sails on the boats.

Yes, I could be in my element up here, I reflect happily. What was it that fella Omar Khayyám said? *A loafer bed, a slug of wine (to which I'm not averse) and view.* Something like that. It sounds perfect to me anyway. Who could ask for anything more?

24

The Trouble with Figs

WITH these thoughts I am feeling a very mellow sort of fellow as we make our descent to dinner. But now it is Iona's turn to be the malcontent.

"I hope *she* is not there," she mutters.

Naturally she means Mrs Scanty-Panties.

"Really, you are getting quite obsessed about that woman!" I cannot resist this riposte to her unreasonable reaction to my hostility towards the girls. Why *does* she hate *her* so much? It's totally irrational.

Of course Iona should never have uttered those words. I can only think she doesn't know, like I do, how the gods like to have a laugh at our expense. I suppose they could have read her mind, at any rate, and arranged what happened next anyway. As we reach the ground floor, the lift parts to reveal, not Mrs Scanty-Panties, but Tom, Dick and Harriet on their way to the dining room.

We fall into step and conversation with them and as we approach Signor Corleone, the maître d', he advances to head us off, and – assuming we are together – shepherds us off to the area at the far side of the pool where the tables for more than four diners are located. Behind his back, we look at each other helplessly. No-one has the courage to explain to him that we are not together; no one has the boldness either to say: *Look, we'd rather be on our own.*

Actually, I don't mind. I'm not one of these romantic people who enjoy intimate candle-lit dinners with my wife alone, though I must admit I am fond of a candle on the table. Actually, I once ate a candle, though I wasn't very fond of it. It was my first birthday party, as a guest, and I was six.

"Now remember to behave yourself and eat everything that is put on your plate," cautioned my mother before I left.

I knew she would have ways of finding out afterwards if I had or not, and it was the fear of her long arm when the birthday-boy's mother placed one of those little, thin birthday-cake candles on our plates, that I dutifully began gnawing my way through this delicacy. It tasted rather nasty, but I had obediently consumed most of it before our hostess noticed and explained it was not for eating, instead intended to be taken home as a souvenir. Well, how was I to know? Orders is orders, especially when you are scared of your mum.

So that is how we came to be dining in an area we would not normally be in and that is how, as soon as I sit down, who should I see – sitting straight across from me – but none other than Mrs Scanty-Panties, dressed elegantly in black, with see-through, fine-net sleeves and a silver necklace flashing at her, oh so slender, swan-like white neck. For all I know, it could be the very same outfit in which she had paraded her backside in Sorrento. It looks rather like it, but she would have to stand up for me to confirm it, and – since it is waiter service – there doesn't seem to be much likelihood of that. It's a bit of a bummer, you might say.

"Look who's over there," I indicate the most-hated to Iona with a nod in her direction.

Iona freezes. From where she was about to sit down next to me, she would have been able to see Mrs Scanty-Panties perfectly. She sends a look across the tables at her unwitting enemy, which – if she had noticed it – would have been cold enough to have brought goose bumps to those slender white arms gleaming palely through the diaphanous sleeves.

"Would you mind changing places with me?" Iona addresses Harriet in a tone which leaves no doubt that the question is rhetorical.

Harriet, who was just about to plonk her plump posterior on that chair which would have presented her back to Mrs Scanty-Panties, looks at Iona in astonishment.

"Yes, all right," she agrees bemusedly.

Iona feels it incumbent upon her to explain. Harriet, it seems, had not noticed her on the orientation walk of Sorrento and if *he* had, Tom deems it politic not to admit it. It's no good asking Dick – he's not yet reached the age of distraction from computers, digital cameras and e-mails. Although had he been following right behind her, his eyes must have been practically at eye-level with those two wobbling spheres. If he *did* see them, he probably did not realize their global significance.

Harriet is wearing an opaque brown dress. Good choice! Only, if I'd a tan like that, I think I'd have worn something lighter to show it up more. But how did she get so brown so quickly? I've been exposed to just as much sun as her, yet she's already as brown as a walnut.

"I don't know," she chuckles, in response to my question. "They say I've got Spanish blood in me, from the Armada, when it was wrecked off the Cornish coast. I don't know why it is – I just have to get the slightest touch of sun and I go brown as a berry."

Actually, I have a friend called Frank – Frank McSherry – who also claims to have an ancestor from the Armada. You can imagine going around advertising your origins, boasting you were named after an alcoholic Spanish beverage known as "Jerez", was possibly not the cleverest of ideas in the years after 1588. Thus they cunningly changed their name to the much more politically correct (and Irish) McSherry, so people would never guess where their roots were – until they gave the game away by effortlessly getting a tan instead of going through the lobster stage first.

To be honest, I believe every word Frank told me, for does his daughter not speak Spanish like a native – and where does she get that from, if it's not in the blood? However, having said that, I'd like to plant Frank in full sunlight to test if he does go as brown as Harriet, because whenever I visit him, he only offers me my national drink and never sherry – which, of course, is the national drink of his ancestors. And thank God for that, too. I got drunk on it once and I've never touched it again since, though I do keep it in the house, for the use of others, like an Eskimo's wife.

As we study the menu, I regale Harriet with my Frank story. She is suitably impressed. She really is very easy to get on with. She seems to have forgiven me for the little solecism I made in Florence last week. That's definitely not going to happen again. I'm going to be really, really good, be on my best behaviour this time around.

We order a red wine, not the house wine for the sake of appearances, and Tom orders a white. If Harriet drinks as little as she did the last time we shared a meal, at the Villa Borghese in Florence, there could be some extra glasses in it for me. It was remarkably good timing of mine, I reflect, to land on the ground floor just as the lift was disgorging Tom, Dick and Harriet.

Now we are at the dessert stage and I haven't put so much as a little toe wrong, never mind a foot. But little did I know that hubris was just about to appear over the horizon.

To my astonishment, for his sweet, Dick orders a bowl of green figs which he sets about with gusto. Tom and Harriet express no surprise, seem to treat this as perfectly normal behaviour. I suspect this is a regular occurrence. But is the child regular, that's what I'd like to know. I also want to know if he could spare one.

"Do you mind if I have one of your figs?" I ask the boy crouched over his bowl of fruit as keenly as Oliver Twist did over his bowl of gruel.

He probably is not too keen on the idea of losing one of his precious figs but he wordlessly slides his bowl over to me and his expression registers not a flicker of regret. He's been well brought-up.

"Thanks." I pick up the sacrificial victim by its stalk and plop it on its fat, round, bottom in front of Iona. "Why don't you present this to your friend over there? Then you could say: *I don't care a fig for your fat bottom!* Ha! Ha! Ha!"

When I recover from the sharpness and hilarity of my own wit, it is to observe that Tom and Harriet have controlled their mirth and are smiling in what looks suspiciously like rictus. Dick is looking plainly bewildered. He's wondering to what end, to what higher purpose, was this fig unnaturally sacrificed? And what of Iona, *La Belle Dame Sans Merci?* What does she think of my little pleasantry? Predictably, not a lot.

Dick is such a nice boy I don't want him to think his fig was going to waste by being merely a visual aid, which, if I'm honest, seems to have fallen rather flat as a method of getting my point over. I had forgotten, in my desire to play the comedian, that no-one in present company would get the joke. In an attempt to retrieve the situation, I lift the noble fruit by its stalk, let it dangle above my lips before I tilt my head back and bite into its fat, juicy-fleshed bottom. I can just picture the rich Romans of old doing this as they languished on their couches – with the exception of Augustus, who famously plucked one from a tree which his charming wife Livia had previously painted with poison. All of them, to make sure there was no mistake.

You may be surprised to hear this, but this is the first time I have attempted to eat a fig in this style – and it shows. A thick, brown mucus is dribbling down my chin but worse, to my absolute horror, Harriet is brushing her chest with her napkin and when she removes it, I can see a big brown stain darkening its pristine whiteness.

From the gladness of only a few moments ago, when I had been inwardly congratulating myself on my easy ability to get on famously with almost perfect strangers, I am instantly reduced to abject depression, although Harriet accepts my profuse apologies graciously while Tom, who might justly have given me a piece of his mind, says nothing at all. Perhaps he might have said something if Iona hadn't got in first with her tongue-lashing.

What can I do except repeat my apologies? It's just too embarrassing to stay and continue what has, up to now, been a congenial evening. Time to make a sharp exit, in fact. We take our leave and wish them a pleasant evening. Tom and Harriet respond in the politest of terms, but God knows what they'll say about me later when Dick is out of earshot in case his tender ears are exposed to expletives for the first time.

Signor Corleone is lying in wait and expresses the hope we have enjoyed our meal, and we say that we have. It's all sycophancy. What if, when it's their turn to leave, Harriet replies: *No, it was perfectly awful. How dare you put us with these awful people whom we hardly know! And just look at my dress! Expect a bill for the dry-cleaning in the near future!*

Well said, Harriet. It *was* all his fault after all. He was the one who put us together. If he hadn't done that – if Iona and I had been on our own – there would have been no Mrs Scanty-Panties and no figs, and Harriet might have considered me a reasonably normal sort of human being, instead of a boor and a fool.

25

Full of Sound and Fury

AHEAD of us is an enormous expanse of marble floor before we reach the lift or the stairs and which we cross in silence, but ahead of me I know lies the wrath of the best-beloved. I know I will have to face the music, whether or not the girls are at home. Unfortunately I know they are: I can hear their radio faintly as soon as we round the corner, growing increasingly louder as we approach our door.

"You really made an exhibition of yourself, didn't you?" Iona says as soon as we are behind closed doors, but her tone is not as severe as I had feared.

"It was an accident. It could have happened to any-body."

"Huh! It's *you* who's the accident. You're a walking disaster."

"I wish that bloody radio would have an accident."

I crank up the metal screen just high enough to duck beneath, open the glass doors and go out onto the balcony, hopefully to dodge any further recriminations. Sound floods in from next door, as I knew it would. I can see the top of their patio doors which are open so the whole complex can get the benefit of their diabolical music, except it doesn't – it's only us. They also have their balcony light on, but their voices are from inside the apartment, competing with the radio – which, ironically, I bet, hardly impinges on their consciousness. I try to peer round the dividing wall, but it is too thick. If I had been able to catch their eye, I might have asked them politely to turn the din down.

I look over the balcony but, down below, the apartments are in darkness and there is no sign of my Dutchman. Not much chance of anyone else complaining, then. I'll either have to do it myself or go up to the roof. I close the doors and the shutters and shut out the sound. It's like being in a prison. I can't help but hear the sound of "music" seeping through the walls. It's worse in the bathroom. I close the door and shut it in. I can't even put on the television and drown it out because of Iona's thing about TVs in bedrooms. She's already got her stitching out.

I sit down and open my book, but it's useless. Iona is unconcernedly, blissfully stitching away. The silence, apart from the noise from next door, is getting on my nerves. It seems to get louder in my head, like the tell-tale heart in Poe's story. I throw down my book and get abruptly to my feet.

"Where are you going?" Iona looks up in surprise.

"I'm going up to the roof." How can I complain to the Three Degrees when it doesn't seem to bother Iona, yet I bitterly resent that I can't sit outside in the fresh, warm air. You can't do that very often in Scotland and now, thanks to them, I can't in Italy either.

"But it's ages to the fireworks yet."

"I know, but I can't stand that bloody racket next door."

She looks at me and shakes her head sadly.

172

It's quiet up on the roof. It's deserted, apart from a couple of smoochers. Good grief! Is there no end to the things being sent to try me? I look away before I feel sick and direct my gaze down to the bay twinkling with lights. I console myself with the thought that the view is much better here than from my balcony. I lie down on a sunbed and stare at the stars.

And as I lie there, out of the dark-blue sky, an idea suddenly strikes me. Yes, that's what I'll do! I'll come up here before the show begins, lie on a bed and marvel at the wonder of the universe before the puny effort of Man's pyrotechnics begins. Besides, God's are a lot less noisy and less ephemeral by far.

* * *

Time passes. It's practically pitch-black up here but brilliant for stargazing. The roof is beginning to fill up with people. I seem to be the only person on my own. Iona has decided not to come, even although we have no agenda tomorrow and we can more or less get up when we like within the dictates of breakfast times. Her last request was for me to open the patio doors. It certainly was very hot and stuffy in our room.

The water in the bay is "wine-dark", in Homer's famous phrase, except where a boat writes a phosphorescent wake on its inky-black surface. A huge cruise-liner, lit up like a forest of Christmas trees, with a necklace of diamonds strung bow to stern, noses out to sea. It's too far away to read its name, though if I had thought to take the binoculars, I should have been able to read it. Meanwhile, down below, the villa has the Italianate tower lit-up, and if anything, it looks even more attractive by night than by day.

Come on! Come on! I've been up here ages now, and I'm beginning to feel cold. Then, suddenly, out of the darkness – with an earth-shattering bang – the show begins. From this height, we look down on the fireworks which are being liberated from a couple of boats moored offshore. There is so much sound and smoke, sometimes coloured crimson, that one could be forgiven for thinking the boats are shelling us and we are watching some bloody conflict – if it were not for the bursts of kaleidoscopic colours which set the sky alight and which drift harmlessly to earth, or rather sea, in a myriad of sparks.

The show lasts for twenty minutes or so, some of which I record on my camcorder for Iona to see later, though it won't be the same as being there in person. As I head towards the stairs, someone ahead of me opens the door and the light from the corridor spills on to the faces of a cluster of people nearby. I recognise them as my Dutchman and family. They are too busy talking to notice me and in any case, my face is still in darkness. I decide to pretend I have not noticed them and slip past them and through the door. It could have been another embarrassing conversation: *Did you enjoy the fireworks?... Yes, they were splendid... And you?... Yes, I thought they were excellent. Well, goodnight... I hope you have a good night too.*

When I get back to the apartment and creep in, as quiet as a mouse, it is to discover Iona in a state of fear and alarm.

"What is it? What's the matter?" I ask, concerned.

She is literally shaking.

"That noise! I got such a bloody fright! I still haven't got over it. I was fast asleep and it woke me up!"

"Bitches! Well, that does it. I'm going to speak to them tomorrow. They're not playing it now anyway, thank God!"

"What are you talking about? Can you not think of anything apart from those bloody girls next door? I'm talking about the fireworks. I thought World War III had started."

"Oh! Oh, I see! The fireworks!" Yes they were very loud, especially the one that announced the performance and of course the patio door was open. I reflect upon this for a moment. "When *did* they put off the radio, by the way?"

I can hear Iona's breath hiss as she takes a sharp intake of breath. "Do you want your hair pulled out by the roots, do you? Do you want your toes stomped on until they are pulp?"

"Er... no, dear."

"Well, for the love of Mike, will you *please* stop going on about those bloody girls! Good night!" And she turns over in bed with an air of finality and puts the pillow over her head.

"Yes, dear. Good night dear." But I doubt if she heard me as I spoke in a very chastised tone.

And to the Three Degrees I mutter under my breath, like Hamlet: *Good night, ladies; good night, sweet ladies; good night, good night.*

Huh! That'll be right! I wish I could put a rocket under their tails and blast them off into space where they would never bother me again, but the truth is, as I crawl meekly into bed, I realise what I already know – I'm too much of a wimp to even speak to my friendly Dutchman, let alone give the enemy a rocket.

26

A Little Nature Study

I DID not go gentle into that good night. Perhaps that's why I didn't sleep – raging, raging, not at the dying of the light but at them next door – but I don't think so. I had been well-warned to stop thinking about the Three Degrees of Pulchritude next door –so of course I did. I am too feart of my wife not to do so.

In the darkness I squint at my watch. Because of the metal shutters, it's as dark as Hades in here, but I can see bright light through the little rectangular holes which tells me it is a bright and sunny day outside, just as I expected. The light casts an intriguing pattern on the wall behind my head like starlight which gives me sufficient light to read the time on my watch. 9 am, but after my sleepless night, it feels more like the middle of the night.

The sound to which my ears had been unconsciously aware of suddenly ceases. It was the sound of running water. Damn! That means Iona is in the shower and very soon will emerge and make me get up. I turn my back to the bathroom door and put my head under the sheet. I'll pretend to be asleep – that should be good for another few seconds before she threatens to attack me with Humphrey the hedgehog hairbrush.

"Get up!" says *La Belle Dame Sans Merci*. I can hear her padding over to the dressing table and moving things about on it. I lie doggo.

"I said, get up!" She sounds in angry mood.

Before I have time to clutch it, a moment later, she seizes the sheet and whips it off me. Perhaps she's had a bad night too after her rude awakening. I make a vain attempt to snatch the thin covering back, but it's too late, it's down at my ankles.

"Bloody hell! What did you do that for? I was asleep – and I didn't sleep all night either," I add grumpily, struggling onto my elbows and wondering if I could make a sudden lunge for the sheet but dismiss the idea almost instantaneously, first-ly because it would take far too much effort and even if I did make it, she would just wrest it off me again. I know when I am beaten. I may as well get up.

"It's not as if we're going anywhere today," I protest, ill-humouredly. "I don't see the point of getting up at the crack of dawn when you haven't slept all night and when we've not got to go anywhere." God, how I hate mornings, especially after a bad night.

"We've got to go for breakfast."

No wonder I call her *La Belle Dame Sans Merci*. She cares not a jot for my exhausted condition. She is ensconced in front of the mirror and further conversation is impossible as the hair-dryer roars into life. There's no point in suggesting I could skip breakfast. She wouldn't wear it, even if she could hear me. It's another of her little foibles. She says we need our protein, and by God, she's determined we're going to have it.

I suppose we have paid for it, right enough. Besides, it is lunch as well.

I hobble off to the bathroom. My ankles are always weak first thing in the morning. I wipe enough condensation off the mirror to be able to see my reflection. My God! What a sight! Little piggy eyes stare back at me. They are as small as the bags under them are big. Not a pretty sight. I knew I needed more sleep. If only you could get protein from that, what a wonderful world it would be!

On the bright side, I'll look better after a shower when my hair, at least, is tamed and lying flat, looking less like Polly the Parrot's. And I can always sleep on the sunbed, for, in the absence of any other plans, that's what I plan to do today although I'm sure Iona will have other ideas. She'll never be content to sit around the pool all morning, let alone all day.

Down in the dining room, there are plenty of tables to choose from. Presumably the early birds have already had their breakfast, which means there may be a problem in finding a sunbed, but the good news is that the best table in the house is free, right at the front, by the picture window that frames the blue waters of the bay with Vesuvius brooding sulkily to the left. That smouldering mountain is so indistinct today it's almost as if we were looking at it through cheesecloth, but the sun is high in a cloudless sky, slashing a shimmering phosphorescent line through the water so bright that mine eyes dazzle.

For some reason I can't explain, before sitting down, I have a compunction to lean over the sill to see what I can see below. On the wisteria is the biggest bee I have ever seen, busily going about its business, flitting from bloom to bloom. As I watch, a lizard, clinging to the wall, startled by my approach, scuttles away to safety, though it was never in the slightest danger. That's nature for you. The busy bee and the lazy lizard. Two different types. One always on the move, the other only when he has to, and quickly at that. Just like Iona and me. She's the bee; I'm the lizard. She likes to be up and about; I like to soak up the sun and move in my own good time but preferably not in a startled way.

As expected, the poolside is very crowded, but amazingly, we still have our pick of sunbeds. Where could everyone be? Perhaps they are off on a tour, or perhaps they have gone shopping. I'd never have thought shopping could have had such a beneficial use, but if that's the reason why there are so many free beds, then, for once in my life, I heartily approve of it.

When it comes to choosing a sunbed, we have different needs, Iona and me. I, the lizard, naturally need a place in full sun, and which will remain so all day. Iona needs one which has a parasol and preferably, a little table so she can put all her sewing stuff on it. It seems we are in luck: we can have one which suits us both. But why I should want one which will be in the sun all day when I won't be able to use it for more than an hour or two, defies logic. That's as much as Iona will be able to tolerate, and neither will I for that matter.

I slap on the sun cream. Well, not quite, it's more a case of persuading it to crawl out the bottle by giving it a good thump on the bottom, like La Belle Dame Sans Merci getting me out of bed in the morning. It's getting a bit low. If we are going to be doing as much sunbathing as I hope, I'm going to have to buy a new bottle. There's still enough for today though, especially if I can sneak out a knife with a serrated edge from the dining room and saw it open to get the last drop out. It's not that I'm mean. What I mean is, I really hate any type of waste.

I settle down to write my postcards. It's a good idea this, these visors which the sunbeds have which you can arrange to shade your face but which leaves your body exposed to the rays. It would be nice to get my face brown, but it just gets redder, like a piece of raw beef. I hope I can get browner before Iona gets totally browned off.

She settles under her parasol. She's wearing shorts and a T-shirt. Shorts, shirt and sewing and she's sorted for an hour or so at the pool. The three S's. Other people come to the Mediterranean for three S's of a different kind. I don't.

I have postcards to write but there's plenty of time to do that, so meanwhile I have a look at the people round the pool. You can tell the Brits by their pale skins or red sunburn. More precisely, they are probably Scots or Irish. The English, particularly the southern English, are topping up their tans, but the brown bodies belong, I imagine, to the Germans or the French, or possibly the Dutch, or Scandinavians.

It's easy to confirm the nationalities because all you have to do is look at the books they are reading, for if they never read a book during the rest of the year, practically everyone takes one to the beach or the pool, even if it does turn out to be ballast in the end. Not that I can see the book titles from here of course, but I bet if I were to predict the nationality from the faces then go round and check them out, I'd be right.

A lady is walking past just now. French I would say. Tall, slim, brunette, probably about thirty-five. She must have left her book on the sunbed, so I can't tell for sure, but that rich tan was never built up in a week, even two weeks, so she's most certainly southern European. The curious thing is her bikini top is dangling from her long, slim fingers, which, I have time to notice, have pink nails to match. Why is she doing that I wonder, giving herself this burden to carry? Maybe she went shopping for a couple of melons but they were sold out so she is coming back empty-handed, so to speak.

On closer inspection, however, I think it was probably a pair of large peaches she was intending to put in her carrier bag. Must keep my eye on her to see where she is going. I'll stroll past later on and see if I can see what she's reading. I'd like to put my nationality-guessing skills to the test.

"Just look at that," says Iona.

It's all right, I am. But I'd better pretend I wasn't.

"What?"

"That man over there." She wouldn't be looking at what I was, naturally.

"Where?"

She nods in the general direction. "That man over there, doing the exercises."

Down to our right, a man is doing bending exercises, holding on to the pole of the parasol for support. He doesn't exactly look the type who does body-building exercises, developing his muscles. If anything, he's rather scrawny. Although he looks a bit old for it now, perhaps he was a ballet dancer once upon an age, but like smoking, can't kick the habit and can still do a *pas de bas* with the best of them.

Now he has shown the way, perhaps some of the ladies around the pool might copy him and use the parasol pole for their own particular style of dancing. I don't know where I get these ridiculous fantasies from. It's never going to happen in my wildest dreams.

Which reminds me – where did my topless lady go? I've been distracted and she's disappeared. She must have found a sunbed and lain down for a rest after the strain of carrying her top about. It will make her more difficult to find, but as long as she is not lying face down, I should recognise her all right.

27

Making a Rash Decision, and a Find

AH well, the entertainment's over. Down to the work; down to the postcards.

Well, that's that done at last. Still too early to go for a swim – I'm not hot enough yet to cool off in the pool. Nothing else for it. I'll just have to resort to reading my book. I'm not enjoying it at all. It's heavy going but, no matter how hard it is, I never give up on a book – I keep on going to the bitter end. The way I look at it is that the poor author has probably sweated blood over it; the least I can do is sit in the sunshine by the pool and merely perspire as I read the mortal words.

Time passes. Iona has had enough of stitching and reading and even I have had enough of lying on the sunbed, and certainly enough of the novel from hell. I really can't understand people whose idea of a good holiday is to do this all day, every day for a week – or in extreme cases, even two on the trot.

I've had a dip and let the sun dry me off, but I know from past experience I should really go back to the apartment and dry myself properly. This lesson I learned in Lourdes, thirty years ago, when after a day spent wandering about the town and the holy shrine under a blistering French sun, I decided to cool down by having a holy bath. With your permission, gentle reader, I will regale you with the following little tale.

I stood in a queue, dressed only in a flowing white gown, and watched increasingly nervously as two burly men took the victims by the upper arms and totally immersed them in a tank. It wasn't so much the ducking that was making me nervous – it was the ritual. Without exception, although I couldn't see clearly, I could tell by the way the gown was twitching, the bathers were making the sign of the cross before being plunged under the water. Too late, I realised you were supposed to be a Catholic for a start, and for another, suffering from some ailment or other, which the restorative powers of the waters were, hopefully, going to cure.

I was suffering from ignorance at best; insanity at worst. Besides, I was there under false pretences. I regard all religions as a form of superstition and each to their own beliefs, but I was brought up as a Protestant. Nervousness gave way to panic as I realised I didn't have a clue as to how to do the sign of the cross. Which comes first; the warp or the weave so to speak?

Desperately, I tried to see what those in front of me were doing, but when it came to my turn, I was none the wiser. I executed a cross so rapidly I hoped my captors couldn't be sure I'd done it in the correct order or not. And although I had been expecting it, it still came as a shock to find myself tipped back into the water. I gasped with surprise and swallowed a pint of water where scores of bare bums had been before me, then – just as suddenly – I was back on my feet again and a figurine of what I presume was either Mary or Bernadette, was thrust into my face. Clearly I was meant to kiss it. At the precise moment of that Judas kiss I could imagine my Protestant forebears in the north-east of Scotland birling in their graves at a speed fit enough to send shock tremors through the earth.

I certainly paid for my misdeed, for not having arrived with the intention of having a holy bath, I had not brought a towel, and – none being provided – I was obliged to put my clothes on top of my wet body. The clothes soon dried off in the baking sun, but where the sun does not shine, those parts remained damp.

By the time we got back to Bayonne, where we were staying, I had a severe case of nappy rash. Which just goes to show you what a rash decision it was to have a holy bath when you don't need to be cured of anything – except it did cure me of the notion I could encourage my congenital laziness by drip-drying.

On the other hand, I was lucky, considering the quantity of untreated holy water I had ingested, that no-one in front of me, apparently, had been suffering from diarrhoea – for the only ill-effect I suffered from afterwards was a dire rear... for days.

No, it's time to go back to the apartment and dry myself thoroughly, so I tell Iona I'll be following her shortly. I'll just finish this chapter first. I just can't put a bad book down. It's another of my little eccentricities (which annoys *La Belle Dame Sans Merci* intensely), that we can't go anywhere until I've finished a chapter. She, who can apparently stop reading a book at any place, any time, any sentence, doesn't seem to realise a chapter is a natural break and that's why the author put them there, because that's where you're meant to stop.

At last the dreary chapter is over. I stand up. The towel I've been lying on is quite damp. I may as well let the hot sun do its work and dry my swimming trunks off a bit more by taking the long way round the pool and, while I'm at it, I'll just check out to see if my assessment of Peaches' nationality proves correct.

The sun is beating my back mercilessly as I circumnavigate the pool. I can practically see the steam coming off my trunks. Ah, there she is, glistening bronzely, and my luck is in as I can see she is propped up on her sunbed, reading, though I am too far away at the moment to be able to read the title which will reveal all. There is no sign of her shopping basket, but a lighted cigarette is clamped between her nicely-manicured, pink nails. Perhaps that was what she had been fetching – a packet of fags, though where on earth she was carrying them, I can't imagine.

Her novel has a lurid cover and a conveniently bold and large title written in French, so that – unlike the Starship *Enterprise* – I don't have to boldly go closer and risk having my own enterprise being misunderstood as perving. It is comforting to know that although I do not possess many skills, my ability to hazard a guess at the nationality of ladies by their skin tone alone is up to scratch. Some sort of instinct, however, tells me not to boast of my skill to my trouble and strife and so I return – apparently as useless as ever – to the room.

For once there is silence from next door. God knows where the Three Degrees are. They were certainly not by the pool. I would have heard them, never mind seen them, had they been there. I suppose it's too much to hope their holiday is over and they have gone home, taking their infernal machine with them. But I know I don't get that lucky – at this very moment, they are probably buying more CDs even more unmelodious than before.

Dried and nappy-rash safe, I have slipped into the canary-yellow swimming trunks and packed my actual swimming pair in Iona's rucksack, just in case I decide to go for a dip. We have decided we are going to walk down to Cap Sorrento, get a bit of Roman culture, check out the villa of Felix Pollius and, you never know, we might have a swim afterwards.

Out of the gates of the hotel and to the left, is the road which I now know is called "Nostra Verde" – not, I have to say, one of the safest roads in Italy, since there is no pavement but plenty of blind bends in this land where pedestrians are at risk from being mowed down by speeding traffic at the best of times.

However, not long after we set off on this venture, my eye is caught by a burnt-orange plastic bottle lying on the grass by the side of the road. If it's what I think, it's just what I need. The cap is missing and sand is sticking to the viscous white liquid which has trickled out of the hole at the top.

I pick it up. It's only factor 8. I'd prefer 15, but finders can't be choosers. As far as sun cream is concerned, it seems a fact of life that the higher the factor, the higher the price seems to be – but which is nothing at all in my case, and just at the right time too. For once the gods are smiling on me.

"What do you think you're doing?" *La Belle Dame Sans Merci* wants to know, seeing me picking up the litter.

When I explain, she says nothing. She can't argue with the logic, but throws me a look and marches down Nostra Verde as if we weren't together. I don't see what harm there is in giving a good home to something which other people don't want.

I snap off a piece of ivy trailing down a wall and, as I follow her, I stuff the stalk into the hole to plug up the leak. Imagine throwing the bottle away because of a trivial thing like that. It feels practically full. There should easily be enough to last me for the rest of this week and, if I wrap it in a plastic bag, I see no reason why it shouldn't be good for a decent number of holidays yet, considering how little sunbathing I actually do.

It's a relief to get off that road with the traffic whizzing past us by inches. In Iona's opinion, we owe our safety entirely to the fact I am wearing the violent-yellow swimming trunks, as they are so horrendous it's little wonder the oncoming motorists give us a body swerve.

Which just goes to show you I do have a use on this holiday, and I'll not be cast aside like a broken bottle of sun cream. Not yet anyway.

28

On Being Considered a Moron

THIS is more like it; more like my type of Italy. No traffic, and where the silence is almost tangible – just the buzz of the occasional insect, perhaps a bee flitting on to the next clump of bougainvillea and this lane winding between somnolent houses which, having forgotten to set their alarm clocks, doze on, since siesta time should surely be over by now. But this is Italy. Funny how it is either frenetically busy or completely comatose. There seems to be no middle way.

For us, however, there is a path down to the right, which – the sign says – will take us down to the beach. The sign is a family coming towards us, beach towels slung over their shoulders, plainly on their way back from a morning spent at the shore. This indeed proves to be the case for, from far below us, comes the sound of shouting and laughter. A handful of people are in a sheltered lagoon, access to which appears to be through a tunnel in the massive cliffs which provide protection from the onslaught of the waves. Some are in the water; others, like seals, are perched on rough ledges on the cliff. It reminds me of Doris Lessing's short story *Through the Tunnel*, only that tunnel had to be negotiated under water.

Steps take us down to the rocks and the remains of Felix Pollius' villa. You can see something had been here – once. Now, apart from a barrel-vaulted ceiling which may or may not have once been the cellars, but are now a repository for rubbish, there is little evidence there had once been lavish accommodation built on these ragged rocks. There is no sign of any ragged rascal either, just a handful of bathers – sunbathers toasting themselves on the smoothest rocks, for a stiff breeze is sending waves crashing to shore, making swimming impossible.

So much for the Roman villa and the swimming, but perhaps there is a more sheltered "beach" further round and at least we can stave off boredom by taking a walk along the cliffs – along the boardwalk, naturally. This part, where we are now, is built on slender stilts of pine trunks, weathered white, taking us high across a little cove in which some bathers are bobbing like corks. Although choppy, the water is broken by a massive rock at the entrance offering the bathers some protection from being smashed into the rough rocks over which they must have clambered to enter the water. Not the most inviting of places to go for a swim, nor the most comfortable of places for sunbathing either. We'll walk further round and see what other possibilities there are.

Under the boardwalk, down by the sea, I sing mainly to myself as we make our way over the boards. A song for every occasion. *Under the boardwalk. Dum de dum. Under the boardwalk. Boardwalk.* Unfortunately I can't remember any more words and it's a very long boardwalk. "Board" may be the name for the walk, but "bored" is the word *La Belle Dame Sans Merci* has for this repetitive strain of mine.

"Can't you 'sing' anything else, for God's sake? If you must 'sing' at all."

I can't see the inverted commas, but I'm sure they are there.

The boardwalk ends in a flight of steep steps which leads to a café at the top. There has not been anywhere suitable for swimming so far, but here at least are some flat rocks which might be suitable for sunbathers as long as they disregard the hardness of the rocks and the stiffness of the breeze.

We don't climb the steps to the café. Instead, we leave the path and pick our way over the rocks to where the sea, assisted by the wind, comes crashing and foaming into shore. We stand gazing at it for a while, our towels tucked under our oxters, then make our way over to a long, flat, finger of rock projecting further out to sea and which forms, on one side, a natural edge to a pool, while the other side is bordered by rocks as rough as this is smooth. The pool itself is a cauldron of foaming water. It's impossible to say how deep it is or what rocks lie below. It is fascinating watching it bubbling and boiling like that. We marvel at the power of nature. On a calm day, this might be an ideal place to swim, but today it is totally out of the question. Only a lunatic would attempt to swim in there.

Under the boardwalk in Sorrento

We turn to go and can't help but notice a young woman in a white blouse and tight, red jeans gesticulating at us as she comes striding towards us across the flat rock.

"Don't swim in there!" she is shouting.

"Swim? Swim!" I don't need to shout back as we are by now within speaking distance. Why, the very idea is preposterous!

"I was watching you from up there," she turns to indicate the café at the top of the steep steps. "I thought you were going to go for a swim." Perhaps she owns the café. I can tell from her accent she's Italian. But how did she know we speak English, not German for example?

"No, no, we'd no intention of swimming," I reassure her. Perhaps from her viewpoint we did look as if we were about to take the plunge and commit suicide instead of just contemplating the scene.

"Very dangerous," she says, and then as if she is still not convinced we are not completely insane, she adds, "You might drown."

"Yes, yes!" I agree. "We were only looking at the water. We're not going to swim."

"Good." She looks convinced at last. "Goodbye." And she turns to go.

"Goodbye. And thanks!" Thank you for assuming we haven't the brains of a gnat between us and the trouble you've taken to come all this way to warn us not to go swimming in that. We follow the bright red twin globes of her buttocks back to the boardwalk where she takes short, tight steps up to the café, while we return the way we have come, not having entirely given up the idea of a swim somewhere else.

To reach the secluded bay, we'd have to swim through the tunnel. I'm a self-taught swimmer and not a very strong one. In Doris Lessing's story it was a rite of passage to swim through the tunnel and, as far as I am concerned, I severely doubt if I could make it all the way through the passage (to say nothing of back again) without anything to hold on to while I stopped for a rest. What if I got so far in and found the walls were too smooth to proffer a handhold? In any case, there are no waves in the bay – it's just a giant open-air pool without a wave machine. I might as well be in the pool at the hotel. No, if we are to have a swim at all in the sea, it will have to be here, at this end of the tunnel.

We clamber down the rocks, and in order not to cause offence to any possible onlookers, seek a suitable place where Iona can undertake the changing-into-the-swimming-costume manoeuvres, being mindful of the cliffs behind us where she might be overlooked. As for me, it's easy under a towel.

Ah, this looks a likely spot; not too far from the water, where a cleft in the rocks affords a certain amount of privacy, far enough removed from the sight of even the most sharp-sighted of other bathers. Someone has been here before, evidently. I pounce on the evidence with delight. Isn't life strange? This morning I had practically no sun cream and now I am wallowing in the stuff. For here is another bottle, practically full and which some careless sunbather (and perhaps sea bather) has forgotten, for unlike the other bottle, there is nothing wrong with this one.

Except there is something wrong with it. It's not sun cream at all, but sun oil. Not the stuff that protects, but fries.

"No. No, you don't! Put it down at once!"

She's right, of course, but there's no need to adopt a tone as if I could catch some foul contagion just by touching it. I put it back where I found it for the next person to pick up and promote their skin cancer.

I am not as stupid as I look.

29

A Chapter of Accidents

I T'S not easy picking our way over the rocks, but I make it first and slip into the water in one of those moments which at first takes your breath away, yet – once you're submerged – doesn't feel so bad. Not enough to make you cry out in pain certainly, yet nevertheless, that's just what Iona's doing.

"What's the matter? It's not that cold!"

"It's not the water, you idiot!" Right enough, she's only immersed up to her ankles. "I've cut my foot. I'm not going any further." The lady's already turning back.

She can turn if she wants to, but a few minutes later – when I turn, but only to look back – I can see her still clambering over the rocks, using her hands to help her. All that effort of her changing into her swimsuit just for that! It looks as if it's been another of my less-than-successful ideas, and no doubt I'll be in trouble again when I get back to shore. Ah well, I'll face that music later. In the meantime, I'm going to make sure I make the effort of having put on my real swimming trunks worthwhile by having a long swim. I think I'll head out as far as the massive rock at the entrance to the cove, then I'll turn back. I've no idea how deep the water is, but I do know I am out of my depth and I know my limitations.

It's amazingly hard, swimming against the tide. I'm not making a lot of progress. Two strokes forward and one back, but it's good fun and invigorating meeting the waves head on. I lie on my back to rest a bit – which is when a wave breaks over my face and, shocked, I resume an erect position trying to wring the water out of my eyes with one hand, using the other arm in an attempt to keep afloat, while at the same time coughing up what seems like gallons of salt water.

That is when the next wave hits me and shock gives way to terror as I realise I'm in a bit of trouble. Like Stevie Smith in her famous poem, I am too far out, but unlike her, I'm not waving, but drowning. There is nobody anywhere near to help me, assuming they realised I was in difficulties in the first place and secondly, were able to help me. If I came across someone drowning, I wouldn't be able to help them – only keep them company as we went down together.

Under I go. With my eyes screwed up tight, I'm holding whatever breath I've got left in my lungs and I've assumed a horizontal position, kicking my legs up and down like pistons while at the same time, my arms are shovelling great armfuls of sea water behind me as I head towards the shore. Suddenly I have a feeling as if I were being lifted by some mighty external force, like a baby being scooped out of bathwater and I have a curious sensation as if I were flying, weightless, through the air. What has happened, of course, is I have been picked up by a massive wave and carried yards further towards the shore – and safety.

Up I come, whooping, sucking in air, gasping for breath – it feels like my last, the very last – spluttering, coughing, squeezing water out of my eyes, doggy-paddling furiously enough to keep afloat on the bubbles I must be creating, though I am too blind with sea water to see them. It hardly seems possible after all the time I'd spent going out that I could be, in the seconds since I turned back, so close to shore. I still can't feel the ground beneath my feet, but I feel with one or two helpful waves behind me, I could make it to safety quite easily.

Well, that was fun! I think I'll try that again. Not the drowning bit, but swimming out to the tip of the rock again – only this time, I'm going to keep facing the waves. I'm not going to let them take me by surprise like that again. I'll just stop and doggy-paddle when my arms have had enough, knowing that when I turn for home, I'll not need much strength – I'll be assisted by wave power. Besides, it's a bit too early to be going back yet. Better give Iona time to get back and nurse her foot and her wrath, hoping I'll catch it on the ebb by the time I get back.

And that's what I do, taking it slowly – not because that was my decision, but because against the power of these waves, that's all I can do. I am just about level with the rock now, and to swim out to the tip seems a great deal further than I have the energy for. Besides, the water looks distinctly choppier there, not to mention the shore a long way back for someone of my limited swimming skills. No. For someone who normally takes no exercise at all, I've had quite enough. I've no intention of tempting fate to its limits. I don't want to be getting a heart attack, not out here. It's time to head for shore.

Effortlessly I am borne to safety. I can feel the sand beneath my feet now and, emboldened, duck down and swim under the water. I'm not far from dry land now, and use the breaststroke to swim the final few yards. I grab hold of a rock in order to haul myself out of the water, and am just about to stand up when a wave lifts me up, knocks me off balance and wrenches my grip free of the rock. Next second I am spluttering on my back on the sandy floor. Another wave washes over me, sweeps me towards the rocks and then, before I can stand up, catches me again and hauls me back to where I was before. Blinded and breathless, I feel for a rock to clutch on to. Any one will do.

Ouch! Bloody hell, what was that! I look at my hand, and to my astonishment, see it is pouring with blood. It's probably not as bad as it looks, the water thinning it out, spreading it from the cut in the heel of my palm, to where it drips off my wrist. I wash it in the water. Now I can see it, it's not a big cut, but the blood continues to well up. It looks the kind that will obstinately keep on bleeding.

Before the next wave, I clamber out of the water. These rocks certainly are sore on the feet. That's when I notice the state of them. The blood is flowing liberally from my big right toe and now I stop to think about it, there is a stinging sensation on the sole of my other foot. Sure enough, when I raise it just enough to have a look, there is a spreading red stain emanating from the heel. I look at them both in amazement. The floor of the cove had been uneven and rocky, but it hadn't felt like I was walking on razor blades exactly. Probably I had scraped it on the rocks when I had been swept off my feet.

That's only two of my problems. On my swimming trunks is a big green smear – a slimy, olive-green sort of colour, the colour of cooked spinach or a cowpat or the sort of green that someone may have on their swimming trunks if they have had a near-death experience by drowning and they have been very, very frightened. I can see it on my hip and by twisting my head in one direction and my swimming trunks in the other, I see to my dismay that the slime from those rocks has indeed spread right round to the seat and anyone nearby might well conclude I'd had a very nasty accident indeed – and they weren't thinking of my feet or my hand either, though all three are still leaking copious amounts of blood.

I limp over the rocks to our changing place where Iona has already changed out of her costume. That hardly surprises me. She would scarcely have needed much drying. One good thing about this is *La Belle Dame Sans Merci* will surely have mercy upon me when she sees my wounded condition and will not launch into an attack for having had such a stupid idea as to make her go swimming in this bloody awful place.

And reader she did. But whether had mercy or launched an attack, you can decide for yourself – for you surely know us well enough by now to hazard an educated guess.

30

Ice Cream Heaven

I T'S the walking wounded limping back to the hotel. No chance of my wounds closing, using my feet as I must, to get back along that long and winding road to our room where we can access the travelling first-aid kit which Iona had had the good sense to bring with us. It would never have crossed my mind to pack such a thing. I remember how last week she had raided it herself, taking a headache pill for her aching feet after pounding the streets of Florence and the Boboli Gardens. And she has the cheek to think I am off my head!

Iona opines our injuries were caused by barnacles or shells of some sort, perhaps scallops (neither of us are very up on our marine low-life) clinging to the rocks and whose razor-sharp edges were presented in such a way to cause the optimum damage. It has to be modestly said that Iona's injury is as nothing compared to my lacerations, for the insides of my already disreputable canvas shoes are sticky with blood. I suspect they will not survive the journey home.

When we get back to the hotel, it is to field a message from Karen, our rep, with the good news she has found another couple, the Bennetts, to join us for the Amalfi coast trip and *Thunderbirds Are Go*. What a coincidence! That was the name of one of our number last week, whom I called "Gordon" for want of knowing his real first name.

Priority is to get into the shower and wash the salt off my body, the blood off my feet, and the slime off my trunks. The latter seems a bit stubborn to remove. Even with the application of liberal amounts of shampoo, the stains seem ingrained and the best I can do is reduce them from the appearance of having suffered a virulent attack of diarrhoea to a mild stomach upset.

Meanwhile, my poor feet still look like the aftermath of the St Valentine's Day Massacre. After I've washed the blood off, Florence Addison dutifully sticks plasters over the cuts. This seems to have little effect on stemming the blood, as it is already seeping through them. There's nothing else for it – I'm just going to have to put my feet up and take a medicinal gin until they stop bleeding. A bit earlier than usual, but that can't be helped. Needs must.

The good news is there is still plenty of sun on the balcony and best of all, silence for once, from next door – the Three Degrees are probably at the pool.

"Just you sit down, I'll get your gin for you," says Florence.

"No, no, it's OK, I can manage," says the lame one, heroically getting to his feet.

"You'll just do what you're told and do as little walking as possible until you stop bleeding."

Was this the tone in which Florence Nightingale addressed her patients? It seems to me her bedside manner has little to do with solicitude for the state of my feet and a whole lot more to do with the amount of gin she knows I'll pour for myself if I am left to my own devices.

Having said that, I am lucky to get any at all, and I make no protest at her altruistic gesture as to argue would be useless. I hobble out to the balcony, put my chair where I can tilt it back against the wall, and put my poor feet up on the vacant chair whilst I busy myself with applying my new bottle of sun cream.

As expected, when the gin comes, it's so weak it can hardly crawl out of the glass to my mouth. If it hadn't the tonic in it, I doubt it would even have had the strength to do that. In fact, I wonder if there's any gin in at all, that it's all tonic, just what Florence prescribed, a pick-me-up for my poor feet. Naturally, I don't make any smart-aleck remarks to this effect or she will know (if she doesn't already) that I am accustomed to making them more gin than tonic.

* * *

It is decreed we are going to town now my feet have recovered, or at least appear to have stopped bleeding. Tom, Dick and Harriet have kindly told us about the mother-of-all *gelaterie* at the far end of the Corso (it would have to be!) where there are more flavours of ice cream than are dreamt of in Horatio's – or anybody else's – philosophy. I'm not particularly interested in ice cream myself, but I know someone who is.

For my feet's sake, all I really want to do is go to the supermarket which lies at the other side of Tasso Square, just about within a stone's-throw of the bus and train stations, for beer and gin supplies. I must replenish the Amstel I had from the mini-bar when we first arrived or pay the rip-off prices the hotel charges. And since the phallic factory chimney where the courtesy bus deposits us lies equidistantly between the *gelateria* and the supermarket, the gods are seeing to it that my feet will be put to the test as much as possible as first I will have to go in one direction then retrace my steps and go in the other.

As usual, the Corso is teeming with people, far more than the medieval designer of this street (without pavements) ever envisaged. Modern-day pedestrians are funnelled into it, taking their chances with the traffic. What a great idea it would be if today's city fathers were to make this a one-way pavement system. One for the westerly pedestrians and one for the eastward. It would make things a lot easier for us who know where we are going and just want to get there without being jostled or having to use emergency brakes as people in front, catching sight of something irresistible in a shop window, without as much a by-your-leave, or even so much as a hand-signal, cut across your path to have a look.

And all this in the wrong direction, on crippled feet, just for the sake of a lousy ice cream! It's not as if it was food and you had to have it, like protein, as *La Belle Dame Sans Merci* is constantly banging on about. We'd be better by far going to the supermarket, as I'm sure there's protein in beer and all those hops would soon put a spring in my step again.

It's true what Tom, Dick and Harriet said about this *gelateria*. It is an Aladdin's Cave of ice cream. How can you possibly make a choice from all this, from this artist's palette of colours designed to tempt the palate? Under a curved Perspex cabinet, they are arranged in two long rows, a feast for the eye, a Technicoloured display of flavours with a range of colours enough to turn a rainbow green with envy. What these delights are, is displayed on a little notice below the offering, in Italian and in English.

It begins with *limone*, or "Iona's choice", and beneath, *limoncello*. Ah, that'll be the one flavoured with the lemon liqueur. Hmm! May give that a try. Further along, there's banana. Iona certainly won't be giving that a try, that's for sure. She has a morbid fear of bananas. She can't stand the sight of them, let alone the smell or the taste. On the rare occasion when one comes into our house, donated by my mother-in-law because it has a spot of brown on the skin, I keep it until it is black-all-over which tells me that the flesh is so brown and sloppy, I can practically suck it up through a straw. It's quite amusing to hold the skin up after I've eaten it and waggle it in front of Iona.

There's *ananas*, not translated, but which I know from my French is pineapple and also not to Iona's taste, and crème caramel, which I've never seen before as an ice cream, but which she would kill for. To me, however, it my equivalent of Iona's bananas. Hmm! I can see Iona having a bit of a dilemma here; she may have that as a change from her habitual lemon. It seems a bit pointless, having come all this way, just to have the same boring old thing again. If I know anything at all about my wife, that's what she'll have: the crème caramel.

But what will I have? Well, there are some unusual flavours: *melone* and its twin, *anguria*, which the helpful label below translates as watermelon or I would never have guessed. I've never had them as ice creams before, but I have had *noce di cocco* – coconut. In fact, it is one of my favourites ever since I had it on the Caribbean cruise where the next day it was served as soup. Actually, that's how I preferred it, and I have always mashed my ice cream to a pulp ever since – when it is served on a plate, of course. Like my bananas, I like my ice cream runny. And while on the subject, I can also reveal I prefer my grapes so runny they are actually liquid, and so rotten they have fermented.

There is also Tropicana which is not translated, but which should be, as I've no idea what kind of ice cream that is, and yogurt, which seems another odd choice, but not half so odd as *fico d'India* and another flavour Iona wouldn't give a fig for, but I expect this is the very one Dick had.

There are yet more flavours and even more exotic ones. So many new tastes. How on earth do I choose? Will it be papaya, or kiwi, or *gelso* (mulberry), or *fragolina di bosco* (wild strawberry), or passion fruit, or even *mela verde* (green apple), and I'm not out of the woods yet as far as making a decision is concerned, for there is even a *frutti di bosco*.

I'm no good at making decisions at the best of times and to choose one out of this overwhelming range is an impossible task in the short time I have to make my choice. What I do know is that whichever one I choose, it will be the wrong one. It will be a disappointment and I will wish I had plumped for my second choice. And it's no good trying to cheat the gods by choosing your second choice first, because they are smarter than us and up to all the tricks.

Methinks I should stick to more-familiar-sounding names, such as *albicocca*, which is apricot. Or *lampone*, another of Iona's strong-contenders, since her second-favourite fruit, after lemons, is raspberry. Or *pesca*, which I take to be peach, but could just possibly be fish, thanks to my ill-remembered schoolboy Latin. Fish ice cream is an interesting concept, and if anyone could make that, then the Italians could. And I'm not forgetting that their ancestors, the Romans, were rather partial to that evil-tasting and foul-smelling sauce made from fermented fish guts called *garum*, which they put in everything. I'm sure if they'd had the technology, they would have made an ice cream out of it.

Not quite so unappealing is *variegato fragoline* – strawberry ice cream with Smarties in it, looking as if it has caught some vile disease, though I admit it might appeal to the kids. And if you think that's not very disgusting, then what about this – no kidding – *formaggio e basilico*. That's right. Cheese-and-basil ice cream. Now do you see why it could have been fish ice cream?

The funny thing is that while all the other tubs are half-full, this one has not been touched at all. Isn't that a remarkable thing! Basil leaves have been artistically strewn over the top to make it look attractive, but – despite that – no-one has been tempted.

Which just goes to show you, it doesn't matter how much you dress things up, you can't disguise the reprehensible, as Iona would agree with reference to Mrs Scanty-Panties.

31

A Little Shopping

WELL, that's it – the complete range. No more choices. Decision time. I am betting Iona will have the crème caramel, but I still haven't a clue which one I will have.

"Which one do you want?" I ask.

"Hmm! Don't know. I don't think I'll have the lemon. Perhaps I'll have the raspberry... No, I think I'll have the yogurt."

"Yogurt! Don't you want the crème caramel?" It wasn't even a contender apparently.

"God, no!"

"But you like crème caramel!" I protest.

"As a pudding, yes, but definitely not as an ice cream!" She makes it sound as disgusting as fish ice cream.

Ah well, so much for my powers of prediction, but I just can't follow her logic. I know she's fond of yogurt, has it practically every day for lunch because it's good for her bones, or so she has been told. What's the difference between crème caramel for pudding and yogurt for dessert that makes the former disgusting and the second apparently the most desirable ice cream in this entire exotic collection?

"So you're definitely going to have the yogurt then?

"Yes. What are you going to have?"

"Dunno. What do you think I should have?" Since I can't make up my own mind, I may as well let her do it for me.

"Why don't you have the passion fruit?

I give her a sharp look. Perhaps it was the way she paused between "passion" and "fruit" that made me wonder if she was passing a snide personal remark about the state of our marriage or perhaps my sexual orientation.

"No, I don't think so. I think I'll have the coconut." Which just goes to show you I don't listen to a word my wife says.

Out of the shop, where no-one can see us, Iona asks if she can have a lick of mine.

"Mmmm! Delicious! Do you want a taste of mine?"

"May as well."

"Well, what do you think?" she asks expectantly after I've taken my sample.

"I hate yogurts."

Her turn to look at me oddly. Perhaps it was the way I made it sound like I hate your guts, for truth to tell, I don't really hate yogurt at all, I just don't bother eating it that often unless it's one of Iona's a week past its sell-by date and she wants it disposed of. Actually, it isn't that bad, although it's a bit of an odd texture for ice cream. The funny thing is, for once I don't regret choosing the coconut at all as I thought I would. Which just goes to show you, I can be wrong 100% of the time. It's a sort of talent I have.

The ice creams are well and truly finished by the time we pass the cathedral and thread our way through the frenetic square with Torquato Tasso standing on his pedestal, looking supremely disdainful, as if above all that – which of course he is. We emerge at the other side of the square and present ourselves at the supermarket. But what's this? A bunch of people is thronging the entrance and blocking the pavements in both directions. What's going on?

A notice on the big glass doors supplies the answer. It is closed for the afternoon siesta and won't open till 4 pm, which is not for another five minutes. We're so used to shops being open all hours back home, we haven't even considered the possibility that it might be closed. Well at least we did it the right way about, going for the ice creams first. Five minutes isn't all that long to wait. I cross the street to the sunny side whilst Iona remains in the shade to wait.

At four o'clock I am still waiting. At four-past-four I am still waiting, and at eight-minutes-past-four I am getting rather impatient. It's tiring standing around like a stork with my lacerated feet, standing first on one leg then the other to take the weight off one to give the other a rest. There's nothing to do apart from watch the people hanging about, waiting. It's astonishing that, out of all the crowd here, I appear to be the only one who is getting a bit *agitato*. When you consider how Italian drivers can't bear to waste a second behind slower, yet still rapidly-moving vehicles, it's incredible to think how calmly they appear to be taking this waiting-for-the-doors-to-open, just idly chatting away as if they had all the time in the world – which perhaps they have. Of course, a fair number of them will be tourists like me, but even so...

Ah, at last. A youth, who looks as if he has not yet woken up properly, is unhurriedly opening the doors, apparently unconcerned and unworried he might be facing a seething crowd of irate shoppers – and we all surge in.

As I expected and hoped, they do sell Amstel, so I've just saved myself a fortune. They also sell gin, which – I'm pleased to see – is cheaper than the price I'd paid in Rome. We add a couple of litre bottles of sparkling water. That's for Iona mainly, so she can carry that, and she can put the gin in her bag of many zips as she'll be drinking some of that too. I'll carry the beer as she won't be having any of that – an equal and fair distribution of our purchases.

As we make our way back to the bus, still with plenty of time to spare, we happen to bump into Bill and Pat who have also heard about the Bennetts and are looking forward to touring again tomorrow. They too had been down at Cap Sorrento, but had turned to the right where we had turned left and had had a very nice swim (so they said) on a very nice beach. Typical of my luck! They are suitably impressed by the state of my feet, not to mention my hand. They are normally used to seeing me plastered in the metaphorical sense of the word.

They're just strolling about, having a look at the shops. We say our goodbyes and go our separate ways, but we may as well take in the shops too on our way back to the bus, for – as I have already mentioned – I have a birthday present to buy.

We have a look at those shops which sell inlaid boxes, and even whole pictures, some as big as six-feet by four-feet and costing a small fortune – no, a reasonably-sized fortune, actually. The coral – necklaces, brooches and the like – I don't like. I don't care for the colour particularly, and it's a bit chunky for my taste – though admittedly, it's pretty clever to carve out all that stuff so intricately. But we're not really shopping; we're just looking for the present at the moment.

Iona has an agenda. She has spotted a sewing shop in that little square off the Via San Cesareo, where it meets the Via Padre R. Giuliani, the one that is so packed with tables you can scarcely move for the diners dining, the waiters waiting, and the shoppers shopping. Across the square, the old men are playing dominoes in the Sedile Dominova. I loiter outside and watch the activity in the square whilst Iona goes into her shop. I'd rather stand outside in the sun. I can't stand that kind of shop.

Presently she emerges, well satisfied with her little browse; she'll come back later and have a proper look when she has a bit more time. They've got so many nice things in there, she says, she's sure she'll find something to buy.

That's nice.

32

An Incredible Conversation

THE courtesy bus is waiting at the stop. That's good, because this walking has taken its toll on my feet and they are seeping blood again. Gratefully, we sink into a seat together (though you wouldn't think so if you went by the illogical numbering system); I to get the weight off my legs, and Iona to get the weight of the gin and water off her back.

And talking of water, here comes the Man with Two Stomachs who had been on our walking tour of Sorrento. He's got a six-pack of litre bottles of water in his left hand and, just for the sake of balance (I don't think), a cardboard container of a dozen beers in his right. He's sweating profusely, as well he might – great rivulets of perspiration running down his temples, while his oxters and the front and back of his shirt are stained horribly dark.

All this I can see through my seat by the window in the bus. But now he is attempting the ascent of the steps. Perhaps if he weren't bearing his burdens, he might be able to make a full-frontal attack, just about. But with them, it is impossible. He has to come on board sideways, like a crab, and similarly, the passage is too narrow for him to put one foot before the other and he must shuffle up the bus sideways, breathing stertorously.

But even then, such is his girth, his paunches or his buttocks are causing those passengers – like Iona – sitting in the outside seats, to recoil from them as he makes his crustacean-like progress up the narrow confines of the passage. No doubt they are afraid that should he brush against them, they might catch some vile contagion such as crabs, most probably, and be forced to walk sideways forever more.

And then I have a blinding epiphany which makes my blood run cold and makes me break out in a sweat myself – though mine is cold, whereas his is hot and horrible. What if the Man with Two Stomachs is called Bennett? What if he and his probably equally enormous wife are the couple joining us on the tour tomorrow? There wouldn't be room for the rest of us. They'd take up four seats, just the two of them. Gordon Bennett! That's just the sort of trick the gods would play.

I hadn't thought about it till now, had been looking forward to the trip after this day of inactivity, but now I am worried and I must go on worrying because, if I do that, then that will perhaps be sufficient for the gods and they will not make it happen. If I don't worry, on the other hand, it will happen. That, I have learned, is the perverse way the gods operate.

But when I articulate these fears to Iona, she says not to be so ridiculous and to stop being so paranoid.

Well, we'll see tomorrow. In the meantime, there is still time to be paranoid about something else – the Three Degrees. But as we round the corner in the corridor from which we have habitually heard the faint strains of their "music", there is no sound of it at all. As Hamlet famously said, *the rest is silence* – for as we get closer and closer until we finally arrive outside our room, the vile din does not assault our senses. Could it possibly be they have left and we have new neighbours – or even better, no neighbours at all? Somehow I doubt it. I don't ever get that lucky. And if I am lucky in that respect, the gods will make me pay for it tomorrow by making it turn out after all, that the Man with Two Stomachs is none other than Mr Bennett.

And yet, as I sit out on the balcony with my pre-prandial gin in the last segment of sunshine, I have cause for hope, for, from the balcony above me, I can plainly hear a Scottish voice which, equally plainly, belongs to someone who has just arrived. I know this because he is on his mobile phone to someone back home, though why he didn't just shout the information to Scotland and save himself some money I don't know, because he apparently doesn't care who hears what he has to say.

"Yeah, we've just arrived... Yeah, it looks fine... Yeah, the weather's great."

Yeah, yeah, yeah! God preserve me from noisy neighbours! On and on he chunters, giving information about the flight and asking how the people are back home – are they surviving this deprivation from his irresistible personality, or have they been cast into the depths of depression? It is not entirely a one-way conversation, for now he is silent, receiving some information.

On and on the newcomer communicates with his invisible interlocutor. The price of this call is obviously not a consideration, nor is consideration for his neighbours evidently.

But he can't keep this up for ever and the call must draw to a close sooner or later – and however irritating it may be, at least his vowels are preferable to the girls' and infinitely superior to their "music".

But if he has just arrived, is it not possible, does it not give hope that the Three Degrees may have left – that this could be a changeover day? In a hotel this big, it's quite likely that every day is a changeover day, and hope springs up in my breast.

Now there is a conversation of another kind going on above me. The phone call has finally been terminated, praise be, but the caller's neighbour, to his right, above the Three Degrees – evidently alerted by the sound of his voice – has come out onto the balcony to see what all the bloody noise is about and now they have struck up a conversation.

I get up to see if I can see them, but although I can hear them plainly, I can't catch sight of either of them. Perhaps I could if I sat on the balcony and leaned backwards, but I'm not that desperate to fling myself into the void. I'll keep that until the Three Degrees have driven me beyond endurance.

He's been here for a week now, the one above the Three Degrees informs Telephone Sam. Amazing! And he has not registered a protest about the neighbours below! For if there is anyone else bound to be more affected by the "music" than me, it must be he. If only I could see him, when there is a break in the conversation, I might have shouted up to him and asked what he thought about them. But to carry on a disembodied conversation in this fashion doesn't seem the most efficacious way to form an alliance against the Unholy Trinity. Besides, and in all probability, if it had offended him, he would have done something about it, for surely the Three

Degrees could not be so lucky to have another neighbour as wimpish as me, could they?

As I listen to, or fail to shut out their conversation, I learn that Telephone Sam wants to know how you get the metal shutters fully up, for he has apparently ducked under them like a limbo dancer. He also wants to know all about the weather, the hotel, the pool, the food, Sorrento town. It's all excellent, says the experienced one, who is the Fount of All Knowledge, but not a word of warning about Signor Corleone or the Three Degrees. Isn't that an incredible thing!

"And if you get fed up hanging about the pool," continues the Fount, "you can always take a trip to Pompeii."

"Pompeii?" repeats Telephone Sam. "What's that, then?"

Had I been engaged in this conversation, I would certainly have been struck dumb, would have had to pick my jaw up from the ground floor, but the Fount doesn't miss a beat.

"It's a Roman town, just down the road. You can get the train to it quite easily."

"Oh, yeah? What's it like, then?"

"Oh, it's just the remains of some houses. There's some mosaics and stuff, and one or two bodies."

"Bodies?" The speaker sounds incredulous.

"Yeah, from when they were covered up by ash when Vesuvius erupted."

"Oh, yeah?" Plainly Telephone Sam is not impressed or doesn't believe the Fount, whilst I listen more intently and with growing disbelief. Surely this is some big wind-up! If I didn't know better, I might have assumed that they had scripted this for my benefit, but I know they have no idea that I am below them, out of sight, listening to every word.

Never mind me; I wish I could see Telephone Sam, the better to gauge if he is winding up the Fount or not. Can it really be true he has never heard of Pompeii before? I conclude, however incredible it may seem, that this indeed must be the case. The voice sounds too natural, unless the acting is terribly good. Perhaps, like Mr Bennett, alias the Man with Two Stomachs, he is an actor on holiday. But I suspect not. If a technophobe like me has the savvy to work out how to operate the metal shutters, anyone who can't could well be of such little brain they might well never have heard of Pompeii.

"Yeah, it fills in half a day," says the Fount, making it seem the sort of thing you would only do *in extremis*.

"Yeah," says Telephone Sam, but so unenthusiastically I'm left in no doubt that if there are any bodies to be looked at, he's going to study the ones by the pool and he's not going to stir from there unless it is to haul his wife out of the shops in the Corso.

33

Some Unenchanted Evening

I CAN scarcely wait to get back inside and report this in-credible conversation to Iona. Besides, my gin is finished.

"It wasn't even a young voice. I would guess he must be in his thirties anyway," I conclude my story, though that hardly seems an excuse when you would have thought just about every primary school child in the land had heard of Pompeii.

And here's another incredible thing. Although the chances of being overheard were small – not to say infinitesi-mally so – I'd made enough of a fool of myself last week by making inappropriate comments, so this time I am taking no chances and had taken the precaution of closing the glass door onto the balcony behind me.

In the time it had taken me to get some ice and pour another gin (my last, warns *La Belle Dame Sans Merci*), as well as one for her, and tell my story (raising my voice to cov-er the sound of the gin splashing into my glass), I had quite forgotten about the glass door. With a resounding thump, I walked bang into it. It's a wonder it didn't shatter with the shock, which just goes to show you the glass is incredibly strong and how incredibly short is my memory. As well as sore feet, I now have an extremely sore head.

"Serves you right!" says *La Belle Dame Sans Merci*. "You should look where you're going. And what's more," she adds pointedly, "it serves you right for having such a big one." But whether she is referring to my head, the gin, or something else, I'm too dazed to think straight.

She doesn't miss a thing. I wonder if she'll miss me when I am in heaven and there's no-one to whom she can offer advice and try to keep on the straight and narrow. Like it or lump it, that's what she'll have to do one of these days. But in the meantime, my head has a lump on it as if about to sprout an incipient horn. An interesting variation to the angel's wings I thought I was growing last week due to an incredibly itchy feeling in the region of my shoulder blades.

Talking of missing things – where is Signor Corleone? Perhaps it's his day off, as there is no sign of him as we make our way over that oh, so long marble floor which means he can see us coming and which gives him plenty of time to plot where he can seat us to cause the utmost displeasure.

Call me paranoid if you like, but I suspect it's personal. He doesn't do this to everyone, just me, because I got off on the wrong footing with him right from the start. On our way down to the dining room, I had decided I was going to make a stand. I am the *emptor*; beware me. I have decided I am going to take the bull by the horns. I have been rehearsing a speech: *No, I refuse to sit at that table. I want a seat with a view of the bay or, if that's not possible, one where I can see some interesting people.* Preferably Mrs Scanty-Panties, so I can study my wife's face as she looks at her.

I should have foreseen it! When you've screwed your courage to the sticking place, got all the words ready to spout, the gods see to it you've been wasting your breath. Having said that, Signor Corleone has something of the Ancient Mariner about him, and – I am perfectly sure – had he been there, the words would have melted in my mouth and like a lamb, I would have gone without a bleat of protest to our table in the naughty corner at the back of the room, where I would have been shown to the seat facing the wall. Very probably, I would meekly have said: *Thank you very much*, and quietly taken my seat without further demur. Life can be hell when you're a wimp.

There's still no sign of the Godfather as we enter the hallowed precincts of his *demesne*. Like prisoners in reverse, we've managed to reach the inner sanctum without hindrance and we can sit anywhere we like. Not much difficulty about that, for – by some strange conjunction of the planets – our arrival seems to have coincided with the gods having nipped down to the corner shop for some ambrosia. The best table in the room has just been vacated and is ours, just as soon as the waiter has cleared away the debris.

It's the very table where Mrs Scanty-Panties had been facing inwards this morning. From here we have an uninterrupted view of the bay; we can look down on that splendid villa with the Moorish columns which will be mine the day I win the lottery. There, as we dine, we will watch the sky darken, Vesuvius disappear by degrees (like hopefully the Three have), and the fairy lights of Naples and the conurbation of towns strung round the bay will light up the darkness like a necklace of diamonds.

Now the seating is sorted, all we need to complete this demi-paradise is some mouth-watering cuisine. What culinary delights has chef prepared for our delectation tonight? Well, for a starter, there's cream of vegetable soup with *crips*. For the *prima*, there's pasta with *souce*, for the *secundo* there's rump of veal with *artichockes* and *dentex* courgettes. I expect that means they are *al dente*, something to get your teeth into or so hard you end up having to get a false set. I won't be having anything from the sweet trolley as I am not a sweet person, you may remember, but I am on my best behaviour, even sharing the wine out equally, careful not to put a foot wrong.

The gods are smiling on me. Back at the apartment, there is still no sign, or – even better – sound, of the Three Degrees. Perhaps they really have left. What better than to sit outside on the balcony while we can, and while we can enjoy the silence? And why not make the most of the starry night and the warm summer air and sit outside and sip a couple of gins? I'm just an old romantic at heart (especially one of those things). And so, just to make things more ambient and comfortable, I lug the upholstered armchairs out onto the balcony.

Iona's not very sure about this. "We're not going to be out here all night, you know. You're not going to drink yourself legless."

"No, of course not!" I say, giving a hollow laugh. As if I would even contemplate doing such a thing!

Before I sit down, with my glass in hand, I stroll over and look down over the balcony. I wonder if my Dutchman is outside, in his garden. Sure enough, he is.

"Lovely evening," I call down.

"Yes."

"Did you enjoy the fireworks last night?"

"Yes. And you?"

"Yes they were very good, weren't they? They woke my wife up though!"

"Yes, very good!"

"Well, good night!" I say after a pause during which I reflect on whether it is worth explaining to him why it was not very good at all. I decide it's too complicated to explain, especially from this distance.

"Yes, good night!"

Not the most scintillating conversation in the world, but at least it's a conversation of some sort. Not like Iona and me, sitting out here at each side of the table, saying nothing – for there is nothing left to say, nothing to talk about, and I haven't even done anything wrong for which I may be chastised. It would have broken the silence at least.

"This is boring," announces the trouble-and-strife after a while. She is resenting the time she could spend stitching instead of sitting out here, the only light from the stars and overspill from the apartment, not nearly enough for her to be able to see to sew or read even. If I don't distract her soon, she'll announce she's going to bed and she'll make me come too so she can get to sleep. My luxuriating in the velvety-warm darkness of this evening will be over. It's a privilege that comes but rarely to those of us who live in a cold climate, like Scotland. Worse, I'll not be able to have another gin.

What am I to do? If I could only think of something witty to say, conjure up even one joke, I might be able to keep her in stitches, but I can't. The mind is blank. And then I notice something I'd not noticed before. Behind me, in the corner, is what looks like an external socket. If I carry out the standard light and plug it in there, she should be able to sew and I can prolong the dreaded moment when we have to go inside.

"What are you doing now?" Iona wants to know as she sees me beetling purposefully inside.

I make no answer as she'll find out soon enough. God, but this thing is heavy! It doesn't look it, but it is. There must be cement or something in the base to stop it toppling over or to prevent punters from nicking it.

"What are you doing with that thing?"

"If I plug it in here, you should be able to get on with some sewing whilst we sit out here, romantically, in this delightful warm summer evening."

"Don't bother."

"It's no bother," I lie as I hump the dead weight over to where I can make the cord reach the plug. It doesn't do the lump on my head any good: it is throbbing with the exertion.

"If you'd told me what you were intending to do, I would have told you not to bother."

Which is exactly why I hadn't told her. Now for the switch-on of the Great Illuminations. Nothing. Click! Click! Click! But no matter how desperately I operate the switch, the light fails to go on. Ah, perhaps there is a switch on the wall inside. But there isn't. Probably a broken bulb. If only I had thought to think of testing it first. But why should I have? Great! Now I'll have to heave the bloody thing all that way back again, for nothing.

After I have done that, my temples are throbbing to bursting point and the lump on my forehead feels as if it will give birth to the horn imminently. Iona, meanwhile, has finished her gin.

"I'm going in and I'm going to bed," she says with a tone of finality. "Don't be long and don't have any more gin while I'm in the bathroom, right? Can I trust you, or do I have to take the bottle in with me?"

"No, no, it's all right," I tell her. "I'll just finish this and I'll come to bed too. I've got a thumping headache."

I press the button which lets down the shutters, cuts out all light and seals us into our own happy little microcosm, if you pardon the oxymoron. But that's just the sort of thing a moron like me would say.

34

Getting Round the Bends

S OME people have a wash and a brush up, but I am not like other people. This morning, I had a brush to get me up before a wash. I pleaded for just five minutes more. This is, should be, an exciting day, as it is our minibus trip along the Amalfi coast, or the *Costiera Amalfitana* as they call it locally, and although I am looking forward to the trip and eager to start it, the buses won't come any earlier for me getting out of bed five minutes earlier. But *La Belle Dame Sans Merci* won't listen to reason. She doesn't want to be embarrassed by me keeping the others waiting and she's taking no chances, so it was up with Humphrey the hedgehog hairbrush this morning. That's the first time she's had to use it on me this week, unlike last when it was practically a daily occurrence, but – in self-defence – I would point out we had some horrendously early starts last week.

It had been a bad night, as it usually is with me. At some stage I knew that all hope was gone when I heard the thump, thump, thump of "music" through the wall which announced the return of the Three Degrees. My head seemed to pick up the refrain and I could imagine the bump on my forehead pulsing in time to the rhythm. They hadn't woken me exactly, as I hadn't been asleep, but it depressed me unutterably to think they were back and then I worried about the Man with Two Stomachs being Mr Bennett. I lay awake for hours.

Well, at least that wasn't a waste of time, for when we assemble in the foyer after breakfast, Tom, Dick and Harriet; Donald and Helen and us – there is no sign of the Man with Two Stomachs, but there is a normal-sized couple hanging about who look as if they may be waiting for a bus.

"You see, I told you: you were being paranoid," Iona whispers.

And I could have told her that it was only thanks to me worrying about it that the Bennetts turned out to have normal-sized stomachs – but what's the use?

Ah, this could be our drivers now. They have identical crisp, blue-and-white striped shirts and black trousers and, as they cross the foyer floor, I reckon the young driver could be the older man's son. It reminds me of the riddle I used to pose my pupils: Two Eskimos are walking across the snow. A big Eskimo and a little Eskimo. The little Eskimo is the big Eskimo's son but the big Eskimo is not the little Eskimo's father. Who is the big Eskimo? It's amazing how many of them didn't get it and, after some bizarre guesses, I had to tell them the answer – though of course I don't need to tell you, dear reader. It's quite obvious when you stop and think about it for a minute.

What I can tell you is that with a start of recognition, I realise who the big (older) driver is. He is the same man who brought us here from the airport. That's all I know about him, but the Bennetts and he greet each other like long-lost friends. Presumably they have used his taxi before – perhaps many, many times. They get into his vehicle (the same swish Mercedes we came in) and we politely hang back as Tom, Dick and Harriet follow them aboard. That leaves we Scots – and Bill and Pat, who will be picked up at their hotel in the town – with the other driver whom I'm going to call, in Simon and Garfunkel's words, Baby Driver. We did quite a lot with Bill and Pat last week, more than we did with the others. Much of the time it wasn't planned, but sometimes it was – like when we went out for a meal together in Rome and I would say we have become friends rather than just accidental travelling companions on holiday.

Anyway, when we pick them up at their hotel, they seem to be quite satisfied with the choice left to them, which is no choice at all, but of course they would be too polite to express their disappointment anyway. Instead they enquire solicitously about how I came by the lump on my forehead. When I tell them with a straight face that I think I'm turning into a unicorn, they don't know what to say. They don't know whether I'm merely making a bad joke or trying to cover up some sort of domestic dispute, for although I am no stranger to the odd spousal scuffle (witness this morning), they don't know us well enough to have discovered that yet.

Iona hurriedly fills in the awkward silence by explaining that I walked into the balcony door. And if they believe that, that I'm just the kind of idiot who would walk into a door – as well they might, for they had plenty of evidence of it last week. I'm also inclined to think they probably assumed I was under the influence at the time.

Having gone down into Sorrento to pick up our friends, now – according to the laws of Italian logic – it is time to retrace our route, pass our hotel again via the notorious Nostra Verde to Sant'Agata. Evidently we are cutting out the point of the peninsula and going over the hill before descending again to the coastal road, the SS 145, variously known as the Road of a Thousand Bends or, on account of a combination of them, the traffic (many of them tour buses) and the narrowness of the road, it's what I would call "A Driver's Nightmare" – but arguably one of the most scenic roads in the entire Mediterranean.

"This is the way I came when I was stranded the other day," I tell my companions and, principally for the benefit of Donald and Helen – who have not heard the tale before – I entertain them with it now. Bill and Pat, who can't help but overhear me, I'm sure won't mind hearing the enthralling tale again. In fact, how glad they must be they are in the same bus and have the journey enlivened by this cautionary tale.

"That's the grocer's shop and that's where I heard the man say *Salve*! And that's where I did finally catch the bus back. And that's where I tried to get on the other bus –"

There's something very heavy pressing on my foot and when I look down, I see to my astonishment it is another foot. When I follow the foot up to see whose leg it is, it turns out to belong to none other than my nearest and dearest, which is not altogether a surprise as she is sitting next and closest to me. What is a surprise however is that her teeth are clenched and she is my Chinese wife, a.k.a. Scow Ling.

"Shut up!" she hisses under her breath. "You are boring people to death." What! Can she really be serious? Oh well, no matter, I had nearly finished my story anyway. We have passed all the interesting landmarks.

At the top of the mountain, before we start to go down to the coast, we stop to admire the view. From this vantage point, on the apex of this triangular peninsula, with the Capo di Sorrento behind us, we can see the Bay of Naples to our left, and the Amalfi coast to our right – or if you prefer, the Gulf of Solerno, which of course, is in the Mediterranean, but which is also known in these parts as the Tyrrhenian Sea. I suppose that's fair enough. I've got a few other names myself, usually when *La Belle Dame Sans Merci* is mad at me for some reason or other. They tend to be of an insulting (and porcine) nature.

Straight ahead, we can see how the triangle broadens out as range upon range of spectacular mountains tower into the sky before plummeting sheer down to the coast where we can see the interesting phenomenon that I call "the disappearing mountains", as the ranges seem to melt into one another – blue and hazily indistinct, tapering to fingers of land reaching out to the lighter, shimmering-blue waters of the sea.

But up here, on this spine of land, we are standing in the middle of a green sea. As far as the eye can see, vineyards and lemon and olive trees clothe both sides of the mountain with foliage, until they, too, as they recede into the distance, take on the hazy blue of indistinctness. It's incredible how green it is, considering that it has not rained in Italy for months and months.

And incredible how many people live up here too, for amidst all this greenery are what must amount to hundreds upon hundreds of houses. Yet they do not detract from the splendour of the scene before us, but even enhance it, for the ochres and browns of the walls and roofs blend in perfectly with the dark green. Even if they are not old, they look ancient, even timeless, befitting the living that has been scratched out of this soil since time immemorial.

But I am puzzled. Surely all these people can't be engaged in agriculture, can they? I don't know how many people it takes to grow a grape or extract oil from an olive or turn a lemon into limoncello, but I do know that it takes only sixteen men of Tain to produce one of my favourite malts, and they produce thousands of gallons of the stuff – whilst I, altruistically self-sacrificing my liver, do my best to keep them in employment. I wouldn't mind betting that growing all these worthy things is hardly the most labour-intensive of industries. The rest can't all be in the tourist trade, surely?

I am just about to open my mouth and ask what the people here do for a living and thus doubtlessly confirm my companions' impression of me as an idiot, but I reckon it is a risk worth taking. Besides, it is a small audience, but Big Driver – who has been pointing out the landscape to us – suddenly stoops and snaps off a piece of greenery growing at his feet.

"Can anybody tell me what this is?" he calls, holding it out for our inspection.

Now is my chance to show I'm not the idiot everybody thinks I am. Plainly Big Driver expects none of us to know, but I do. There is absolutely no mistaking that long, narrow, indented leaf, a bit like an anorexic oak leaf. It is an ingredient in a salad I first met and fell in love with – it was love at first taste – in Sicily. I used to smother it with all kinds of oils just to make it more interesting but, even in its raw and unadulterated state, I love its peppery bite, and to anyone who says that salads are boring, then they have not tried the salad bar at our hotel in Giardini Naxos.

"It's wild rocket!" I shout out, probably louder than I need to in my triumph, and before anyone else can cut in with the answer.

Big Driver is literally struck speechless.

"Yes, that's right," says he, after he has recovered the power of speech. "It grows all over this place." He seems a bit put out. It's obviously the wrong answer. The correct answer, evidently, is to say you haven't a clue which would then let him act the role of guide and he will tell you, making you feel as if you are getting your money's worth.

It's too late now to get in his good books by asking him what all the people up here do for a living, because he's already marching us back to the buses.

35

Models and Mules

NOW we are on the Amalfi drive proper, descending towards the coast, keeping hard to the right to avoid the on-coming traffic. John Steinbeck and his wife, it is said, were reduced to quivering wrecks by their driver as he pointed out points of scenic and historical interest – and that was in 1953 when, I imagine, the traffic was a lot less dense than now. It seems an endless stream in both directions.

No doubt where we are now is one of the sights which Steinbeck's driver would have pointed out. One good thing about having a Big Driver and a Baby Driver is that we can stop in places where the big tour buses can't, as Karen had pointed out. Perhaps it was the not-stopping that was worrying the Steinbecks – that they might be propelled over the edge onto the rocks below, especially if their driver was looking more at the points of interest than the road.

What we have stopped to look at are the three small islands known as Le Galli or Le Sirenuse, because in former times it was believed to be where the Sirens lived, those murderous maidens whose music was so sweet it lured mariners to their deaths on the rocks.

Le Galli

A hydrofoil is skimming past the islands now, probably on its way from Solerno to Naples via Sorrento, perhaps having called in on the way at Amalfi and Positano or perhaps *en route* for the Isle of Capri or Ischia. Even just pronouncing the names of the places sounds positively musical and magical. No wonder it gave rise to the Sirens myth, particularly when you take into consideration the stunning scenery in which they are located. I can just imagine the sailors "hearing voices" telling them to crash out for a while on one of these enchanting places.

The biggest island looks extraordinarily like a leaping dolphin. There's a villa on it and, according to Big Driver, both were once owned by Rudolf Nureyev who bought it from Léonide Massine – who, as everybody knows (apart from me because I'm a boor, according to Iona), was a famous ballet dancer and choreographer, especially the latter. I have no time for dancing at the best of times; ballet I consider to be the worst of them all.

Many bends later, our shoulders rubbing together as we swing round the corners, we leave the main road round the corniche and take the even more narrow and twisting road to our first real destination – Positano. There, the traffic is more or less at a standstill. Big Driver abandons his vehicle and comes back to tell us we are to get out and he will meet us at the end of the street in half-an-hour. Right. I thought this was meant to be negotiable, but he knows the place better than us, so if he thinks all we need are thirty minutes here, so be it. He seems to have some sort of arrangement with a restaurant – or, more precisely, their car park – and that's where we are to meet. The town and the scenery may be heavenly, but finding a place to park so you can admire it, is sheer hell. Another reason to be glad we are not driving ourselves.

We are on the Via Pasitea, the main thoroughfare of the town which leads to the beach, and the church, Big Driver says, is down that way too. It's called the Santa Maria Assunta and contains a black Madonna from Byzantium which had been pinched by pirates. When they got near Positano, a storm blew up. "Posa! Posa!" cried the statue. Terrified out of their wits, the hardened pirates headed for the shore where they deposited the Madonna. The lady was satisfied, the storm abated, and she has stayed put ever since.

It's not the first time I've heard of miraculous talking statues. I am catholic only in my tastes and the church is not high on my list of priorities, but since Big Driver thinks it's worthy of a mention, I may well spare it a look.

For me there are other attractions: a variety of pastel-coloured villas tumbling down the hill upon a cliff-face so

steep you can't help but marvel at how they could build houses there at all, for it is so vertical that, like seats in a Roman
amphitheatre, not one house blocks the view of the villa behind it. It's also, we are told, where you can have sandals
made for you while you wait (is thirty minutes long enough?),
or you can buy beachwear. But beware of the beach, for there
is a problem with the sanitation, apparently.

We have been deposited outside a clothes shop (be cau-
tious of the prices, let alone the fashions) – and I, who would
normally give a church much more attention than a boutique,
and that is saying something – find it an utter delight. For in
the most unusual display of clothes-for-sale I have ever seen,
instead of mere hangers, the clothes have been placed on
wooden models which are hanging from a rail by means of a
hook through their heads. Although the clothes they are
wearing appear to be identical, each model has a distinctive

The Models

face, not to mention hair colour, or style, or even the jewellery they are sporting.

Most are women – there must be a dozen of them at least, all very attractive in a cartoonish sort of way, but what gets me especially, what really tickles my fancy, is hanging from a rail on the inside of the open door, are three men – one red-head wearing a red shirt (his mum should tell him); one wearing a white shirt, silver-haired – not dyed, just having gone prematurely grey and looking very distinguished; and one black-head, if you pardon the expression, who you can tell, really fancies himself, his teeth gleaming as white as a dental advert out of his bronzed face.

Very amusing, but the *pièce de resistance* is the door-mat of black hair which is not only visible, but unmissable above the scoop of his red singlet which he has deliberately chosen, of course, to show off this manly feature to best advantage. And to cap it all off, naturally, he has a gold necklace from which hangs a medallion of that same glittering metal which draws the eye down to that rug on his chest. I presume it's there for his girlfriends to wipe their feet on when they walk all over him, because, one thing's for sure, this guy may be full of his own importance but I can tell, like the characters in those dreadful green-and-white Penguin crime novels I read, he is a one-dimensional, flat sort of character and he must have a girlfriend at any price, an accessory to show off his own magnificence.

He may have pretensions to two dimensions, but if he stood side-on to you, I swear you'd be hard-pressed to see him at all and that's just what his personality would be like – practically non-existent. I bet he's never read a book in his life. That type never does, relying on their handsome face and physique rather than intellect to pull the birds. In fact, I would bet any money, when he's not doing this part-time modelling job, hanging about this place, his real job is a PE teacher. Trust me on this. I have seen plenty of them and he's the body-beautiful type, not the inner-beauty intellectual sort (like me, for instance).

What a splendid start to this captivating place! And to think that the reason we all come here now, in our hundreds and thousands, including celebrities from rock stars like the Rolling Stones to classical pianists such as Willi Kemff, is all due to John Steinbeck! Yes, the very same who was weeping hysterically along this very coast we have travelled, clutching onto his dear wife, or for dear life, or both. At least they would die together. When he did eventually arrive in Positano he thought he was in heaven, but he had no recollection of dying first.

He wrote an article about it for *Harper's Bazaar* and that was this place's undoing or making, depending on your point of view, although it was a bit slow to catch on at first. It was not until the Sixties, ten years later, that the artists and hippies started descending here (literally) – which makes me wonder if it's fair to lay the blame of this mass invasion of tourism on the pen of poor John. Medallion Man here would be proud to claim the credit, since he is such a babe magnet.

Opposite us, a mule train is snaking its way down an invisible path opposite. We had passed them at the top and it's just as well they have their own route as it would snarl up the traffic no end if they used the same route as the vehicles. This is how they must have done it the days of yore and it adds immensely to the romance of the place to see the old, tried-and-tested methods still in force, even it does take donkeys (and a long time) to get to the top. They are coming down empty. I wonder what they could possibly pack out.

Peep! Peep! Peep! It's a delivery van trying to turn round by reversing into an impossibly tight space, and making that irritating noise that HGVs do when they engage reverse gear to make you get out of their way. Well that's how the goods get in here all right and I can see how some, at least, get out, but how this driver is going to get out of the mess he's in, I have no idea.

It's too nerve-wracking to watch, so we head on down, like the mules, towards the centre of the town.

36

Sounds and Sights of Positano

I T'S a charming walk wending our way down this street, festive with the myriad of colourful clothes festooning the walls on either side, but – even better – at the end of a lane off to our left, through a vista of bougainvillea tumbling from the flat roofs of the shops, a splendid sight in its own right: a view of the houses of Positano. Reds, yellows and browns, but primarily shades of pink, the houses are clambering like a Technicoloured pyramid, high into the sky. It's easy to see why Steinbeck – and thousands of others – have been so captivated by this place.

Now we are nearly at the bottom, and can see the sea at last. Over to our right is a pale pink hotel with white shutters, whose façade – interestingly – follows the curve of the cliff. On the top floor are white wrought-iron balconies on which a profusion of hanging petunias, bulging from their baskets, take the breath away with their sheer number, let alone their beauty, and whose pastel shades perfectly compliment the muted pink and white of the hotel.

But immediately below us, and in front of us, we see something Baby Driver had told us to be on the lookout for. I am not the only person who speaks in riddles, for Baby Driver had asked us if we knew how to tell the lazy Posetanisi from the diligent. (As if we would! Maybe it's a trick question and they are all lazy.) No. The answer is to look at the roofs of their houses. The idea is that in summer, you are meant to paint the roof white to reflect the heat, while in the winter, you should paint it black to keep the heat in.

I'm not sure about the person who lives in this house. You can see where the black is showing through the white, so obviously he did paint it black once and perhaps he has been just too busy, diligently pursuing other pursuits to paint it white again. One thing's for sure though; if I were living here, my roof would always be white. It's not that I'm lazy (although Iona would heartily disagree with that) – it's just I

Positano

can't imagine anything more unattractive than a black roof.

Well, actually, I can. It's noise. And I don't have to imagine it. From the piazza below, dominated by the Santa Maria dell'Assunta, is a din fit enough to split the eardrums asunder. It's the sound of a pneumatic drill. No, there must be half-a-dozen of them at least. This always happens to me. Just when you

248

think you've found paradise, along come the gods and spoil it for you. God knows what they think they are achieving down there, apart from creating a hell of a noise and dust, by digging up the square. Perhaps they are doing something about the sewage system.

So this is the church. It's an unremarkable building with an even less impressive freestand-

Campanile of Santa Maria dell'Assunta, Positano

ing campanile of four tiers in grey and white stone standing in front of it. The dome is made mainly of yellow-and-green majolica tiles, the ribs picked out in a blue-and-white diamond pattern and which they seem to regard very highly in these parts, but which I associate with public toilets. There's nothing to detain us further here, not even a statue that spoke. Besides, this concerto for pneumatic drills and cement mixers with assorted dissonant clangs from the big, beefy guy on the glockenspiel scaffolding is getting on my nerves.

Although the beach is grey and pebbly, they have thoughtfully provided a boardwalk across it, and it is not in the least a monochrome landscape, for colour is provided by fishing boats in a motley of colours, out of their element, jostling for space with the multi-coloured parasols and orange sunbeds and – not least – the colours of the beachwear of the scores of people who are thronging the shore, who evidently appear not to have run the gauntlet of the boutiques unscathed.

Most of them are not lying down sunbathing though – they seem to be gathered to greet a ferry which has just arrived from whence I know not, but what I do know is it that it's only when on the beach, with your back to the sea, you can really appreciate Positano. You cannot fail to marvel at how every inch of this conical mountain has houses clinging to it in a riot of colour. If seeing were not believing, you wouldn't.

Over to the left, I can see a trapezoidal lookout tower which tapers at the top, a clear reminder of the dangers posed by pirates and the Saracens, to name but two, who – amongst others – raided this coast in days gone by. And if that alone wasn't enough to tell you, then the noticeboard plonked distastefully on the roof of that pink-and-white hotel with the magnificent floral display certainly does. It's not very subtle, just like the Saracens themselves were not. In bold letters it proudly announces: Covo dei Saraceni.

A flight of steps leads up to it from the beach where there is a covered terrace and where, I imagine, in exchange for your weekly pension, you can have a refreshment or two. Fortunately we haven't the time for that, to sit down and look at the sea, when there is much more of this village to explore.

But therein a danger lies ahead. Shops. Still, I must admit this is a pretty interesting one, as shops go. If I have never seen anything like Positano before, then I have never seen a shop quite like this before either. It sells a variety of things, such as pottery and trinkets and God knows what else besides, but the thing that captures my attention, just as the beachwear models did, is the most-enormous lemon-scented candle I have ever seen in my life. Or any candle for that matter, which, no doubt is the intention of the owner.

Like a low-light beacon, it is beckoning us towards the delights of the interior. I can't tell you what its circumference is in feet or meters, but note that I speak in those terms, not inches. Suffice it to say I couldn't get my arms around it, should I have an insane desire to hug it. What a handy thing that would be for driving away the midges when I have my barbeques! Perhaps they'd be intimidated by the sheer size of it. Nothing else I know seems to work on the little buggers anyway.

And this must be where they got the scent from. In a basket at the other side of the door, are the biggest lemons I have ever seen in my life. Monster lemons, large as melons – I'd like to see the tree that is capable of producing mutants like this. Even one on a branch would be enough to bend it like a bowstring – more would surely bring the whole tree to its knees. You can imagine the tree moaning, like the mothers you see of the terrible twos (by whom I don't mean twins) who have tantrums in the supermar-

Covo dei Saraceni, Positano

251

ket: *What did I do, oh Lord, to give birth to monsters like these?* You certainly don't get many of these to the pound, but a great deal of lemon meringue pies and enough slices to put in my gin to keep me going all year.

And that's not the only surprise Sorrento has up its sleeve, for we have only just ceased marvelling at the lemons when we see the most peculiar dog either of us has ever seen in our lives. If it has legs, we can't see them. It seems to be propelled on silent wheels like a clockwork toy, and in top gear from the speed with which it is coming towards us. It's not a large dog, not even a foot high, but the astonishing thing about it is that the whole animal seems to ripple with movement, to shimmer even, like a jelly which has just been tipped out of its mould.

It's only when it gets closer we see it is a Rastafarian dog. It's true! Its hair has been pleated all over, even its fringe and its tail. It looks just like the Bettawear brush (a revolution in its time) which my mother used to dust and polish the furniture in one effortless movement, at least once a year. Or, if that simile doesn't create any resonances for you, dear reader, imagine Dougal from *The Magic Roundabout*, only a Dougal with plaits. And if you still don't have a clue what I'm talking about, then it tells me you are of tender years, especially if the most famous dog you've heard of (apart from Lassie) is Scooby Doo.

Suffice it to say we are looking at a brush that walks, well glides really, and wherever he's heading for, he's in a hurry. Perhaps he's late for a very important date (he's taking his girlfriend to a Bob Marley concert) or, more likely, he's just got a job as a French polisher (though he doesn't speak any French) and his lady employer is going to stick a broom handle up his bottom and polish the furniture with him.

252

The author, with Positano in the background

Whatever the case, like greased lightning, he's gone before we have time to snap a photo of him, unfortunately.

What an incredible place this is! And here's another, believe it or not – an oasis of peace and tranquillity, a court-yard, an inner garden, the sort of garden Iona adores. Through an arch, which frames the picture perfectly, we can see a wrought-iron staircase beyond, with terracotta pots on the steps and enormous amphorae in the courtyard, all filled to over-flowing with luxuriant flowers or foliage.

Iona is right. It is a beautiful sight and, as a garden, very low-maintenance. All you would need to do is give it a sweep now and again, or ask Rasta to do a few laps – and at the speed he operates, that wouldn't bother him much. He could make a clean sweep of it before he knew it. In fact, he doesn't even know he's not being kept as a pet, but as a dust-er-buster.

Alas, our time in Positano is up. A pity, really, as who knows what other delights this place has in store? I suppose and hope, we have seen the best of it. Never so much as glimpsed a sandal-maker's shop. Not that I would have ever contemplated buying a pair anyway. Being hand-made, they are bound to be well beyond my price. You can't beat 50p a pair. Thank you Lidl.

I hope they will see me through the remainder of this trip. I definitely don't want to pay Positano sandal prices, wherever they may be sold.

37

On Being Bullied and Being Buried

AS we continue our trip, I hope and pray we will not be involved in an accident. I have never prayed so hard in my life. What a hypocrite!

I can see where the Steinbecks were coming from, apart from California. Italian music is warbling from the cassette deck – fortunately Neapolitan songs, nothing too heavy like screeching sopranos which would be enough to make you want to open the door and hurl yourself into the abyss just to get away from them.

Our driver (Baby Driver, that is) seems to be conducting the singers, or perhaps he is merely pointing out the most splendidly scenic – or, more likely, without these gestures he would be dumb, using them to stress the syllables, especially those at the end of the words which create a glide to the next word and which makes the Italian accent sound so mellifluous and attractive. At any rate (and ours could hardly be described as slow), he is using his right arm to gesture across the vehicle to his right, to the coast and the sea, which lies hundreds of feet below us. It's a good job I'm not nervous, though judging by the expressions on the faces of the others, they are not exhibiting the same *sang-froid* as me. I'm sure they'd prefer less commentary and more attention to the road.

At times, going through the villages: Véttica Maggiore, Praiano, and Conca dei Marini, the road is so narrow it becomes single file, barely wide enough for a bus to pass through – but, says Baby Driver, there is no problem. It is part and parcel of the trip to meet other drivers head-on, and no one minds shunting back and forwards until there is no more than the thickness of a coat of paint between them and they can pass each other easily: *No problema.*

From time to time we make a stop, and although the view is always admirable, there are other things to admire also, such as St Peter's Chapel on top of a rocky promontory, whose walls and everything except the very topmost part of the barrel-vaulted ceiling, are completely covered in ivy. It is set in an oasis of green and terraced gardens, the walls of which end in a precipitous plunge to the depths below. It's just incredible, apart from the natural beauty of the scene, how Man, for once at least, has improved on Nature and has tamed this rocky headland and transformed it into what looks like (from here, at least) the Garden of Eden.

There are tunnels, and arches in the rock, too small to warrant the name "tunnel", and just before we pass through one of them, like thread through a needle, we have time to observe something we probably would have missed had we not been stationary to allow oncoming traffic through.

Someone has constructed a miniature village between the verge of the road and the cliff face, and has even channelled a miniature waterfall so that it appears to have a river flowing through it. It's doubtful many have the chance to appreciate it, even notice it's there, but it is often the fate of artists to have their work ignored by an unappreciative public – and by that I don't just mean painters, but artists of all kinds.

I expect he had fun making it anyway, whoever he was, though how he did so without having his bum shaved by the passing traffic, God alone knows, for we all know what builders' bums are like, especially when they are bending over and their jeans slip down. Which makes me wonder, where did he park his bike while he was doing the construction? There's not a parking place for miles.

It's over in a flash, but there was a glimpse far below us of the Vallone di Furore, the Furore gorge, as we soared over it on the flyover. Interestingly, the Italians have a word for it – *orrido* – which means what it sounds like and which tells you what they think of it. I would call *stupendo*.

Many a time and oft, I have discovered, when you are asked by guides to spot, in natural geographical formations, a likeness to, or a profile of some famous personage or animal, like the elephant rock in Guilin to which I just couldn't see any resemblance, the guides point you in the right direction and say patiently: "See that bit of rock there? Well to the right of that and down a bit – well that's the nose." And when you still can't see it, they tend to get a bit exasperated and say: "Of course you have to use your imagination", which translates as: "What's the use trying to get you to see anything, you're just a bloody moron with zero creative vision."

So, when Baby Driver tells us that in a few minutes we are going to stop to admire a rock which looks just like the Madonna and Child, I am rather sceptical to say the least and I think, in this Catholic-focused country, who else would they see in a rock but those two!

But I have to admit, on this occasion, I need no prompt-
ing at all, for it does bear a striking resemblance to Mary and
Jesus, just as you often see them in statues or paintings – in
three-quarters profile – with Mary holding the Child slightly
away from her to form two distinct figures. This is how we
see it now, from a distance, in silhouette, the difference being
that the Child, bizarrely and prophetically, appears to be
wearing what looks more like a crown of thorns than the halo
with which He is traditionally represented.

We all take photos of this remarkable phenomenon (I'm
sure Baby Driver would be mortally offended if we didn't),
but of course this must be one of the most photographed places on the planet and I don't just mean by the hordes of ama-
teurs either, for this coast forms the setting and background
for innumerable films, so much so that in addition to its other
names, the Amalfi Coast is also known as the Costa Diva.
(And also Costa Fortuna to buy a villa here, I don't doubt.)

Here's one such film. I'm standing in front of a board
which shows stills from a film made by Roberto Rossellini in
1948 called *La Macchina Ammazzacattivi*, and which appears
to show an actress standing in front of the view we can see
now. I've not heard of the film or director before. What can it
be about? What's so special about it that they should deem it
worthy to commemorate it in this way? But as far as the silver
screen is concerned, I'm not so much of a film buff but a film
duffer.

Curiously, as if mirroring my questions, writ in water,
like Keats's epitaph, (which he wrote himself) the opalescent
wake of a motorboat, as it executed a sudden turn, has inscribed a question mark on the blue water below. Well, since
you are asking, motorboat, I'd say it looks as if it may be a war
film, but apart from that, that's all I can tell you, but I bet

there is love in it and I bet the hero dies. (Must remember to look it up when I get home.)

As well as providing the background and setting for movies, this coast is also home to stars such as Sophia Loren. That villa, on the promontory, the big white, square one among the trees, with the orange roof tiles. See it? Big Driver's finger is pointing it out and we can indeed see it. That's it. Franco Zeffirelli, whose villa we cannot see, also has a villa near Positano, he tells us.

We've moved on and stopped at a place where the road has opened out to accommodate restaurants and cafés. Apparently every tourist bus, coach and car on the Amalfi coast has also decided to stop here.

"It's coffee time," Big Driver announces.

Oh, is that right? Was that a democratic decision taken by the five in his bus? It can hardly be so, since there are six in ours for a start, and for another, I would have voted "no" to stopping here – if anyone had bothered to ask my opinion in the first place. Without a doubt, this is not Big Driver speaking but Big Dictator.

He tells us we have fifteen minutes. Translated into Italian, that'll be more like twenty-five. We have places to go and things to see. I resent the time wasted and am annoyed by those hopeless caffeine addicts who can't wait to take the first slug of their drug at breakfast. And since their addiction has such a strong grip on them, and they are incapable of waiting until lunchtime for another fix, they have had to invent the institution known as "Coffee Time". Even then, the lunchtime fix isn't enough to see them through to dinner: they need at least one more top-up before then. Thank God I don't have an addiction like that.

You may wonder why I know so much about this. Reader, I married one. But do I make a big song and dance about it like she does about my occasional little gin in the evenings? "Not bloody likely", if I may quote Eliza Doolittle. I say nothing and do nothing to try and wean her off her habit. A sane person wouldn't come between a tigress and her cub, would he? I don't come between my missus and her drug.

Having no need of a pit stop, or an infusion of caffeine, I wander about on my own (if you don't count the hundreds of people milling about here) and, in due course, I stumble upon an advertisement for an attraction which helps explain the reason why this place is mobbed. We are, seemingly, at the parking for the Grotta dello Smeraldo. It's beneath our feet, actually. You are beamed down there by a lift to a rowing boat which will take you into a grotto, re-discovered in 1932, where light, filtering in from a cleft in the rock, trans-

David and Iona with Amalfi in the distance

forms the water into a translucent emerald colour.

And that's not all, the advert proclaims. See stalactites and stalagmites! See Mussolini's profile! See an underwater Nativity scene! Good grief! What did I tell you about anthropomorphism! I probably wouldn't see any of them, but would rate my chances of getting my money back about as good as Mussolini's of winning the war.

Hmm. I wonder why Big Driver did not tell us we are going there next. But then I realise, he is not only driving the bus, but his own agenda too. Perhaps I'm misjudging him, perhaps when the others come back, he'll tell us about the grotto and he'll ask if we want to visit it and depending on the result of the vote, we may go or may not go.

Not a bit of it. Big Driver waits until my companions have finished lapping up their ice creams, like Mr Salteena and his soup, in Daisy Ashford's delightful comic tale *The Young Visiters*. In this heat it is a challenge to eat an ice cream before it turns to liquid, and he wouldn't want any of that messing up his Merc. Once the last person has completed the final lap, he waves us into the buses without so much as uttering a single word. What was that Karen said about us calling the shots?

As I had predicted, it was far longer than fifteen minutes before we got on the road again, but we're almost in Amalfi now – a lot sooner than if we had gone to the grotto and queued for the lift and then the rowing boats. Maybe the Big Dictator is really the Big Benefactor, and I have rushed to judgement.

We stop once more to have an overview of the town. And very attractive it looks too – a cluster of white houses clinging to the mountain as in Positano, but more strung out, less dramatic and much-less colourful. Down below, the harbour, formed by a natural promontory on one side and an artificial jetty on the other, confines a flotilla of craft. From this distance they appear as mere specks of white. The jetty also serves as a very handy parking place for Dinky cars.

Mine eye, however, is lifted to a massive series of arches that dominate the town from their position high above the town. "That," explains Big Driver, "is the cemetery, once a former monastery. Space is so tight," he goes on, "that you can only be buried for ten years. You buy the plot, but – after that time – what's left of you is dug up and put in the wall."

How fascinating! Mortality becomes mortar.

Our guide warms to his theme. "It is a good way of making money for the town."

If he is being cynical, his lilting accent makes it difficult to detect. "You can't avoid it," he says, by which he means not so much death itself but continuing to have to stump up long after you are dead. "There is only one crematorium in the whole of Italy – and that is in Bologna."

What a remarkable thing! That's the sort of thing the guidebooks don't tell you. I bet he's right. By the time you have paid for the body to be taken to Bologna, plus the cremation fees, not to mention getting the ashes back again, I'd bet any money it's a dearer method of disposing of the dear departed than burying him or her here for ten years. Furthermore, just think of the queue there must be waiting to get into the ever-lasting bonfire in Bologna. Imagine if it were your burning desire to be cremated – you could spend years in cold storage before they wheeled you out. Talk about going from one extreme to the other! I wonder if they bother to thaw you out first?

No, by the time your relation has decayed, a decade later (wonder if that's why they made it ten years) you might well be dead yourself, leaving some poor relation to dispose of *you*. If they weren't poor before, they could be by the time they pay for planting you and then digging you up again. It's not only the dead who will be going to the wall.

Either way, whether they decide to bury you or burn you, it's a hell of a way to get revenge on those relatives you suffered all those years when you were alive.

38

The Dictator Decrees

ALTHOUGH Amalfi comes first, we are going to be visiting it last, says Our Leader, or *Il Duce* in Italian, formerly known as Big Driver. Well, he knows best, after all. He lives here. Perhaps he's like me when I was a boy – I always kept the best on my plate till last, though my sister, interestingly, always did the reverse, eating the nice bits first and leaving the nasty cabbage and other green stuff till last – not forgetting the carrots. I always got rid of them first, as we were never allowed to say things like: *I don't like cabbage.* We were told it was good for us or, as my mother used to put it: *Get it down your bleeding neck.*

Anyway, as regards our trip, they don't call it the *Ravello Coast* do they? If it's a case of keeping the best till last, that suits me fine.

It's a series of hairpin bends from Amalfi to Ravello, and you need the hairpins because it's a bit of a hair-raising trip. I imagine it's worse going down than up. We will discover the truth of that later because, as everyone knows, what goes up must come down. Maybe this is an instance of keeping the worst till last – unless roller-coasters are your thing.

We have parked outside the village. To our left and down a flight of steps, is what appears to be a dead swanky restaurant. The view from the terrace is stupendous. This is where Adam would have dined, at a table for one, naturally, before a certain lady arrived on the scene, because it looks like paradise. But as a seasoned traveller like me knows all too well, while you can devour the scene with your eyes, the food comes at a price – and a great price at that.

Big Driver or *Il Duce*, call him what you will, has a speech to make, now we are all decanted.

"There's a restaurant down to your left there, as you can see (but it's a bit pricey). There's another, if you go straight on, till you reach the Duomo, then if you turn to the left, you'll find a very nice (and cheap) *trattoria*. Or, if you go straight on and walk on a bit, then turn left and then right, or is it left and then right...? Anyway, there's another one up there somewhere and that's the one we are going to, so don't bother to try and follow us, OK. We'll meet you here again at 2:30. *Buon appetito.*"

Well, he didn't actually put it quite like that, but that was the message nevertheless. I look at my watch. It is only

The restaurant at Ravello

11:50. Bloody hell, that's nearly *three* hours – probably will be, Italian time – by the time they get back from their lunch or siesta. That's almost *twice* as long as we have been on this trip. *I don't believe it!* as my hero, Victor Meldrew, would no doubt have said.

But we are far from being victors: we are losers and wimps. Can it possibly be that I am the only person who objects to this arrangement – to subsidising Big and Baby Drivers to a three-hour lunch break? Nice work if you can get it! Drive a little bit, stop for coffee, drive a bit more, then stop for a three-hour lunch because you are so exhausted with all that driving and talking and waving your hands about pointing things out. And the last thing you would want to do is spend even more time with the punters who might spoil your lunch by asking stupid questions during it. Which is why you need to nip off smartish before they have time to ask: "Hey, just a minute! Do we all agree to this?"

Perhaps we are all too stunned, too poleaxed to say anything. Well I am, anyway. And while we are still anaesthetised, too shocked to follow them to what is probably the best restaurant in town, they're off. *Il Duce* (I'm sure that's his name now) is followed by Baby Driver, naturally, the son following in the father's footsteps. Did I hear him right? Did he really say *Buon appetite,* or was he actually saying, "Let's go Benito!"

One thing is for sure. We're not going anywhere for the next three hours. They never even told us what there is to do in this place for one hour, let alone three! And because we were told we were on a guided tour, we hadn't bothered with the guidebooks.

Hanging about here means we are losing a lot of time; time that could well have been spent travelling up the coast to Salerno, which, since it lies at the end of the peninsula, I imagined – expected even – would mark the end of our journey. I recognise that with eleven of us, there would have to be a bit of come and go about our itinerary, but where has been the consultation, where the negotiation, like Karen had led us to believe? And another thing. Since, after here, we are heading back the way to Amalfi, this means that like Simon and Garfunkel sang, we will be *Homeward Bound*, not – as the Neapolitan song nearly has it – *Torna a Salerno*, as we are evidently not going there in the first place.

We could so easily have gone to Salerno if we weren't stopping here for so long. Even if we stopped for an hour, I reckon there would still be plenty of time. I had wanted to go to Salerno, not that I knew anything about it, but that's part of the very reason I wanted to go. And if, in some later reading, I should discover that there is something there I would desperately have loved to see, I am going to be in a very bad mood indeed. I am not in a particularly good one at the moment as it is. We should never have come on this trip without establishing exactly where we were going and what we were going to see. No-one would normally hop in a taxi and say: *Take me where you think I would like to go.* Yet that is exactly the insane thing we all have appeared to have done. And no-one seems to have the courage to complain or suggest that an hour is quite sufficient for lunch either.

So, this is how our tour ends, not with a bang, but with wimps like us. Oh, for the Dutchman we were with on Vesuvius!

Fine dining, Ravello-style

Well, we are here now, so we may as well make the most of the next three hours. We don't need to go into the posh restaurant

268

to be able to see the view. You might even say that the neat, chequered tablecloths with the crisp, white napkins and the sparkling glasses and silverware glinting in the sun, is part of the appeal and you wouldn't want a tramp like me spoiling it with my 50p shoes from Lidl's and what Iona calls my "donkey hat". She says it reminds her of what some of those patient animals wear on the beach as they endlessly parade up and down suffering little children on their backs. What a cross to have to bear!

But looking at that scene below, it's impossible to remain grumpy for long. The height we have gained, climbing all this way up to Ravello, has afforded us an aerial view of the coast with the glittering blue waters flecked with white sails. From this height and distance, they appear motionless. The lush, green hills rush down to dip their toes in the sea. The white houses with their orange-tiled roofs, set among the terraces of lemon groves, add a splash of colour to the velvet-green hillside. It's all quite perfect.

Further down the coast lie the twin villages of Minori and its big sister, Maiori, though we can't see the former as it's hidden behind the nearest ridge. How do I know that? We may not have our guidebooks, but at least we have a map as Iona likes to follow the route. It's something to do with being an ex-geography teacher. It would have been worth having a closer look at those villages too, I don't doubt. They might be, and probably are, utterly charming. Now, thanks to *Il Duce*, we will never know.

Still further along is the intriguingly Scottish-sounding Erchie, the diminutive of "Archibald" which fortunately, since the Cruelty to Children (Christian Names) Act which came into force in the latter half of the 1950s, parents have no longer been allowed to bless their sons with that appalling

The Amalfi coast seen from Ravello

name. After that comes Cetara. Et cetera, et cetera, more villages on the way to Solerno that we will never see now thanks to *Il Duce*'s edict.

We linger a bit, drinking in the view. By the time we have had our fill, the others have drifted off.

The clock on the Duomo in the piazza heralds our arrival. It was very welcoming of it, but it didn't have to go on quite so long about it. Actually it was just chiming the hours. Twelve dongs. That means that ten minutes of our allotted time is already up. We'd better hurry – time is slipping past and we've not really done anything yet.

The afternoon stretches ahead. How on earth will we manage to fill it?

39

A Bloody Miracle

THE piazza is a wide, empty space enlivened by terra-cotta pots over-brimming with brightly-coloured flowers which have placed around the perimeter. The façade of the Duomo, on the other hand, is plain and white and devoid of any ornamentation whatsoever, and I like it all the better for that. It seems to me that when it was first built, it may have been a mere church and achieved promotion at some later stage in its life. I wonder if this pleasing and plain simplicity has been replicated in the interior. Well, we have plenty of time to kill, so why not go in and find out? It's free and, if there is any truth in the adage about the best things in life being free, I should be in for a treat.

The bronze door opens with a protesting creak, as if it doesn't want us to go in, as if it's saying: *Well, go in if you want, but don't say I didn't warn you.* Yes, you did and you were right, oh wise, oh excellent door! What would have been a nice, plain church with white walls and dark pews and a tasteful marble altar, is spoiled by not just one pulpit, but two, facing each other across the nave in adversarial style as in the House of Commons. Now, why on earth would you do that? Surely they don't have debates in here, do they – a holy

The Piazza, Ravello

war of words? And here's another amazing thing – to address the congregation, the priest would have to turn through ninety degrees to address them. How bizarre!

It's the pulpit on the left that immediately draws the attention. For a start, it is higher, mounted on barley-sugar columns, like Bernini's hideous *baldacchino* in St Peter's in Rome, only these are a lot less distasteful. But that's not what I find the worst feature – it's the mosaic geometric ornamentation, rectangles of brown and white with swirling loops along the edges which adorn not only the pulpit, but the flight of stairs up to it. It really is appalling, and the stairs are far bigger than necessary. But then, otherwise, how would the artist have had room to indulge his flight of fancy?

Talking of flight, a bird of prey of some sorts (that species naturally, in a church), has flown up to a pedestal in front of the pulpit and has perched there, looking quite at home. I'm accustomed to seeing eagles in a church, their wings half-spread, like cormorants hanging them out to dry, in order to accommodate a large-print Bible on their backs, presumably for those ministers (and priests) too vain to wear glasses. But this bird has its wings neatly folded along its back and it's too small to be an eagle. I think it's a hawk, and it's there with its legendary eyesight to make sure no-one is having a nap or

Pulpit in the Duomo, Ravello

passing the Pandrops about when the preacher's eyes are reading from the Good Book, or closed when he is saying a prayer.

Or maybe it's just to intimidate the priest in the pulpit opposite. But then he would scarcely need to, as the height already gives him an advantage. The mosaics on this pulpit are a lot more restrained and tasteful. In a way, I quite like it – if it were not for the great, black circles with a figure-of-eight pattern swirling around them on either side of the pulpit, like a pair of demonic eyes. Perhaps, from the perspective of the one-on-high across the nave, it's as if he's being hypnotised and needs the protection of the six stone lions circling and supporting his pulpit.

The lower pulpit is unusual in having stairs on either side. Actually it looks more like a bridge than a pulpit, an impression given further credence by an arched aperture in the middle over which the pulpit projects like an oriel window and which gives the priest a fine view of his adversary across the aisle, as long as he looks up to him – which is probably true in a literal sense only.

In the middle of this pulpit is an eagle, only this time in more conventional pose with its wings half-spread. I think you could rest a Good Book of moderate size on them. More interestingly, on either side of the "bridge" are two turquoise winged serpents with dragons' heads breathing fire, whilst on either side of the opening, sinister and dexter, are a pair of peacocks, rampant, sable. The ancients believed their bodies did not decay after death, and so were adopted by the early Christians as a symbol of immortality.

But wait a minute; here's "something curiouser", as Alice put it. It's a noticeboard, and on it is written in Italian with the English translation beneath:

ANNOUNCEMENT

The Relic of the blood of St Pantaleone, doctor and Martyr and principal patron of Ravello is preserved in the niche over the Tabernacle in the Blessed Sacrament Chapel. In order to see the relic more closely, we invite you to walk behind the altar using either of the two side entrances.

Now, if there's one thing I like, it's a good relic, except very often you can't see them as they are walled up, like the really good ones in St Peter's in Rome (where you would expect the best ones to be), or a piece of the True Cross, which is, supposedly, in the iron cross at the top of the obelisk which marks the centre of the piazza. But here they are positively pleading with you to go and see it.

Blood, eh? Well that's a new one on me. It's usually a body part or a fragment of bone. Imagine that, when you are dead, being butchered like a cow and bits of you being sent here, there and everywhere. It's also a new saint on me, but I can't exactly claim to be an expert in hagiology exactly, so that at least, comes as nothing of a surprise.

I have, however, learned something. I have an inkling of why the ghastly, bigger pulpit with the barley-sugar columns is supported by six lions. It's a pun on the saint's name. If you were a lion having to support all that weight on your back you'd pant a bit too – and they are. Their mouths are half-open as if gasping for breath.

Not a moment to waste. I am standing in front of a rectangular marble tablet in a heavy gilt frame which reads:

ON THE OCCASION OF THE LITURGICAL CELEBRATION OF THE 27TH JULY EACH YEAR WHICH COMMEMORATES THE MARTYRDOM OF SAINT PANTALEONE, IT IS POSSIBLE TO WITNESS A WONDERFUL AND INEXPLICABLE EVENT; THE BLOOD OF THE SAINT, COINTENED IN ITS RELIQUARY WHICH IS SEALED AND NEVER HANDLED, IS USUALLY OPAQUE AND DARK. AT THIS TIME OF YEAR A PART OF THE BLOOD BECOMES CLEAR AND TRANSLUCENT WITH A RUBY COLOUR LIKE THAT OF FRESH BLOOD. IN ORDER TO OBSERVE THIS EXTRAORDINARY PHENOMENEON, LINE UP THE SURFACE OF THE LIQUID SO THAT IT IS JUST VISIBLE BELOW THE NEAREST HORIZONTAL BAR OF THE PROTECTIVE METAL GRILLE.

Someone has helpfully amended the spelling error to CON-TAINED with a marker pen. I can hardly contain my impatience to see this miracle. For them to write it in stone like that must mean they are pretty confident of it happening. And here's the thing. This is July 30th – only three days after this miraculous event is supposed to happen, so there's a pretty good chance that if it has, it'll still show signs of it. Or will it? Will the blood be translucent for that day only?

There it is, behind a heavy iron grille with criss-crossing spikes like the door you might expect to see in a medieval dungeon. A glass ampoule is encased in a ghastly baroque gilt container. It is dark where I am standing, but a light is coming from the stained glass window at the front of the church and bathing the relic in an ethereal light. The blood in the glass, with the light streaming through it, is indeed glowing like a ruby, seeming almost to pulse with life. What's more, it does seem to have separated, translucent at the top, dark at the bottom and quite opaque – just as the tablet has written.

What an amazing thing! I just don't know what to make of it. Could it be something to do with the heat, perhaps? Does blood separate like that when it is heated, which might explain why it doesn't happen until late July? On the other hand, whilst it is boiling hot outside, it's not noticeably warm in here at all. Probably it never does get any warmer than it is at the moment.

Nowadays, since you can't be elevated to the sainthood until you've passed all sorts of tests that can go for years and years – I wonder who it was who first thought of syphoning off Pantaleone's blood whilst his heart was still pumping the stuff around his body, albeit with not a great deal of pressure, presumably. He must have anticipated that the good doctor was bound for sainthood. But how much would you take? Just enough as a memento? Or, following in the tradition of saints' bits being scattered around Christendom, would you not syphon off as much as you think you possibly could without killing the poor bloke off in the process and thus promoting him prematurely to the sainthood?

Not being a medic, I can't reliably say how much there is in the ampule. Definitely not as much as an armful, but more than a fingerful – probably about a handful. What happened to the rest? Maybe they didn't bleed him dry. If that is so, the taxman could take a lesson from that.

Well this has provided more questions than answers, but I must say this is the best relic I have seen since I saw the body of Pope John XXIII, gussied up like Santa Claus in a glass coffin in St Peter's, just last week.

From the outside, this looked one of the most unprepossessing of cathedrals I'd ever seen, but it had turned out to be a real gem – and I'm not just referring to the ruby-red blood either, though that was the best thing of all.

40

A Little Walk in Ravello

ALTHOUGH the cathedral was light and airy – unlike a lot of other cathedrals I have visited – the light outside is almost blinding in its intensity, and the heat like a hammer blow. The cicadas are thrumming, making the air seem to vibrate with the heat. There's no sign of our fellow travellers; in fact, the only other person we had glimpsed since we last saw them was a woman in the Duomo (who had crossed herself furiously at the sight of the blood) and a couple of tourists crossing the piazza, heading towards the souvenir shop at the corner. It's eerily quiet. Apart from them, we could be the only people in Ravello, if we didn't know otherwise. It seems the town has already settled down for its siesta.

Iona catches sight of a tourist information office to the right of the Duomo. Perhaps we can pick up a leaflet about this place, which might tell us what else there is to see here and which also might throw some light on the mysteries we have already witnessed. But we'd better hurry in case it closes soon – if it's not already closed. It should of course, remain open for tourists, but this is Italy and one can't depend on it catering to the whims of eccentric tourists who will insist on wandering about the streets in the middle of the day when they should be tucked up in their beds like normal, respectable citizens.

We make it in time, or perhaps in loads of time; we don't know, but we have a little pamphlet now with a map on one side and the attractions on the other. Let's see now, what does it say about the Duomo? Well, note the doors with their bas-relief panels. Yes, very notable, but what about San Pantaleone? Who and when was he, and why was he martyred? Not a word. And why are those two pulpits facing each other across the nave? Ah, here's something about them. The high one, and the more highly decorated, is called the *Ambo of the Gospel* and was the work of Bartolemo da Foggia in 1273, while the lower one is called the *Ambo of the Epistles* and although, in my view it is much better, the artist is not named. It says here that my fire-breathing dragon-serpents are representations of Jonah being eaten by a sea monster and being regurgitated again. With wings and feet, it's not like any whale I've ever seen before.

It's the work of a moment to go back in and check it out. Ah, yes, I see it now. There is Jonah on the left, a healthy pink, not looking in the least worried about being half-swallowed. On the right, he is seen popping out feet first, as white as an uncooked prawn. Only his limbs are showing, but it looks as if he's been so scared all the blood has drained from his body.

It dates from 1130, so it is nearly 150 years older than the high pulpit. But why they decided they needed a second one and whose handiwork it is, the pamphlet doesn't say. It wouldn't have been da Foggia anyway. And I don't have the foggiest idea about the life and times of San Pantaleone either, if you pardon the pun, as the pamphlet doesn't say.

The main attractions of Ravello appear to be the Villa Rufolo and the Villa Cimbrone, which lies someway out of the town to the west. The Villa Rufolo was originally built between 1270 and 1280, so the pamphlet informs us, but gradually fell into decay until it was bought in 1851 by Sir Nervile [sic] Reid who restored the place and, as a botanist, created a magnificent garden. And it is that garden that is the villa's real claim to fame, for Wagner visited it in 1880 and it was there he found inspiration for Klingsor's magic garden in Act Two of *Parsifal*. For the past half-century, concerts have been held here – as the pamphlet puts it, "in a very suggestive setting".

I make a suggestive remark to Iona – that we go and have a look it. Truth to tell, I'm not much of a Wagner fan. The orchestral music I can take – quite like it, actually – but I don't care for opera, particularly those bloody squawking sopranos. Still, I'd like to see what inspired the maestro.

The lane to the right of the steps of the Duomo is what will take us there and a very pleasant walk it is too, bordered by trees and shrubs and climbers clothing the mellow, grey stone of the walls with green. It leads, straight as an arrow, to an arch in an imposing wall ahead, the sort you might expect to see in a castle. And through that arch when we come to it, lies a cool green place – for the lane has narrowed so the tops of the trees form a canopy overhead, whilst at ground level, shrubs and hedges hug the wall, so the impression is of heading down a green tunnel. At the end is a white wall with a door of a whiter shade – the entrance, no doubt, to the villa we seek.

It certainly looks inviting, but we have a problem. We have to pay. Actually, that's not the problem – it's only €4. No, it's just by the time we have wandered round the house, not to mention the gardens which I'd prefer to do, so as not to miss any sunshine, we won't have a great deal of time left (even with the best part of two hours remaining) to explore the rest of the village. And Iona, who hates garden centres with a passion and cares for gardens scarcely less, is not much inclined to go wandering about a garden in this heat, looking at plants.

So that decides it. We'll wander round the village first, for from what we have seen of it so far, it looks very attractive indeed, and if there is any time left, we'll come back here afterwards. Besides, Iona wants a *gelato,* but preferably something more substantial. She's obsessed about food, she really is. As I would have pointed out to her, had I had the courage, a little fasting never did anyone any harm.

I'm glad I didn't waste my breath, for no sooner had the foolhardy thought come into my head when Iona makes the point she doesn't want a repetition of what happened to her in the Boboli Gardens in Florence last week, when she nearly fainted from lack of nourishment.

She needn't have worried, for when we return to the piazza, who should we see installed at a *trattoria,* but Bill and Pat. We stop to speak and decide we may as well join them. They are sitting in the shade, naturally. They may be English, but they are not mad enough to sit in the full midday sun. *They* may not be, but I am a Scot and I *am.* I move my chair just far enough away so I can feel the rays beating me to death but can also hear and partake of the conversation (not to mention the food). It's also close enough so that passers-by (if there were any) would not assume that because of the dark circles in my pits I have been asked to sit at a distance.

Iona and I share a salad. I have a beer, Bavarian 8.5%, to wash it down. Since I will only be allowed one, I may as well make it a strong one. Iona has a grated iced-lemon concoction which she pronounces the most delicious drink she's had since the squeezed lemon at Pompeii last week. There's no accounting for taste.

So we are both happy, and happy to while the time away with Bill and Pat. This is part of what being on holiday is about, after all, isn't it – relaxing in the sun with good company? You can't be on the go all the time, can you?

All the same, I am itching to go up the street straight ahead – which I see is called the *Via Richard Wagner* – to the left of the Duomo, and which climbs upwards in a series of shallow, cobbled steps, bordered on either side by pink oleanders which have been trained and pruned into slender trees. They are leaning against grey walls, which seem to be sloping backwards at the top. I'm tempted to conclude this is a bit of a laid-back place in more ways than one.

"If you go up to the top and turn right, you can walk all the way round," says Bill, which is what they've been doing, apparently, all the time we were in the Duomo.

"You've not been in the Duomo yet, then?" I ask.

He shakes his head. I tell him about the saint's blood, but somehow it doesn't seem to interest him very much. Perhaps I shouldn't be so surprised. I remember how, when the four of us were exploring St Peter's last week, I was the only one who had taken the trouble to go and see Pope John XXIII. It's funny how some people aren't interested in the most interesting things.

And so we go our separate ways, we to follow the Wagner trail, but whether or not Bill and Pat will take my advice and go to the Duomo we will just have to wait and see.

41

Beauty and the Beastly Duomo

IF it was a pleasant walk to the Villa Rufolo, this is even better, and when we stop at the top and look back, we can see – framed in the oleander blossom and foliage (and, you might say, continuing the opera theme) – the little village of Scala, its white houses rising in a series of terraces up the slope of the hillside opposite.

We have a choice now. We can either turn to the right, along the Via Episcopia, as Bill and Pat did, and which will bring us back round the other side of the Duomo to the piazza again, or we can go left along the Via San Giovanni del Toro. My mother used to say when left momentarily incoherent with rage at some outrage or other I had perpetrated: "By the left!" and that's what we do, not because of my mother's marching orders, but because it looks more interesting.

There's a garden (and it's free), neat geometric beds filled with red flowers whose name I don't know but which look pretty and exotic, and palm trees which are not so pretty, but are exotic, and the whole garden not so large that you can't see it all at once, which meets with Iona's approval. I, on the other hand, think the real appeal of a garden is if it is revealed gradually bit by bit, like some sort of horticultural striptease.

Beyond the garden, through the trees, towers an attractive campanile with the windows divided into pairs by slim, Moorish-style pillars. They seem much too grand for the church to which it belongs, which – according to our map – must be San Giovanni del Toro.

Across the way, what the Americans call kitty-cornered for some obscure and arcane reason (at least to me), but what we call diagonally opposite, is the Belvedere Principessa di Piemonte. It was well worth mounting all those steps on the Via Richard Wagner to come here. A building of some prominence must have stood here once, probably some convent or monastery or some such significant edifice, for in the ruined wall on the Via San Giovanni, we can see what must have been huge windows once, but which now provide a superb location for terracotta pots o'er-brimming with scarlet flowers.

That may be beautiful, but to tell you the truth, and as Keats put it at the end of his *Ode to a Grecian Urn,* but much more poetically and philosophically: *Beauty is truth, truth beauty – that is all/Ye know on earth, and all ye need to know.* And if that sounds a bit enigmatic, should you ever go to Ravello (and you should, if you have not already), then you must come to this belvedere and go to the railings and feast your eyes. Take my word for it, and you can trust me on this as I have travelled far and wide, ye will be hard pressed to find anything on earth more beautiful.

There's another of these *Costa Diva* notice boards here. Italian at the top, with a helpful translation in English below. *IL TESORO DELL' AFRICA* becomes BEAT THE DEVIL, though how the devil they get that from *that,* beats me. It seems to have been an Italian, American and British collaboration and was directed by John Huston in 1953 – the same year that the Steinbecks "discovered" Positano.

It goes on to say that the screenplay was by Truman Capote and gives a list of the stars: Humphrey Bogart, Jennifer Jones, Robert Morley, Peter Lorre, and Gina Lollobrigida. I am reading the English version, but when I look to see what Gina Lollobrigida is in Italian, it's exactly the same and the other names are precisely the same also. Isn't that an amazing thing? I've only been in Italy for just over a week and I've already learned the Italian for John Huston et al.

The real star, however, is not mentioned, but stays modestly in the background letting its human co-stars take their moment in the limelight – the soaring mountain ridges with their serrated edges running down to the jagged coastline. It will be there for millennia after the humans have left the stage and their bones turned to dust. It has all the patience in the world.

Here's something I can't translate, though. It's a modern sculpture which consists of a metal rod, bent into a curve at the top, obviously meant to represent a head, with two stumpy wires lower down, meant to represent arms, but rather too high up and out of proportion. The left one is holding what looks like a ladder, and on and between the rungs are tadpoles

Musical sculpture, Ravello

287

representing musical notes. I can't read music, but note this, I bet it's in German and written by Wagner and I bet it's a bit out of *Parsifal*.

By the time we have finished wandering about the lanes of this enchanted place, there's not enough time left to visit the Villa Rufolo. If we hadn't dallied over lunch we could have, thus we missed out on Ravello's Number One spot. No-one else seems to have visited it either, apart from Tom, Dick and Harriet whose verdict is it was well worth going to, though they don't enlarge on what was so good about it.

The real attraction of Ravello, I suspect, is Ravello it-self. Still, when we get back to the hotel, I'll look up the guidebook and see what I've missed. Iona says it's the maso-chist in me.

Il Duce and Baby Driver, give them their due, are not late. Three hours of a lunch break is probably more than even they can handle without becoming bored with each other's company. They want to know if we had enjoyed ourselves. I haven't the bottle to say we could have done with less time here and more somewhere else.

It's a matter of moments to get to Amalfi. It's downhill, after all.

"You have an hour here," dictates *Il Duce*.

No guided tour here either, then. It's free time, which is what the tour companies call it when they want some free time for the guides or can't think what to do with you. Nice work if you can get it. They have just had three free hours and now they're going to have another hour. There must be lots to tell us about here. There's the Duomo for a start – they could at least tell us about that.

288

I know that in its heyday, as Paul said of another place, Amalfi was "no mean city", so they could tell us a bit about the history of the town for a start. It is the setting for Webster's dark and gory play of murder and intrigue,

The Duomo, Amalfi

The Duchess of Malfi, so why don't they tell us something about her, about the historical and eponymous person in the play? Did she leave her mark hereabouts anywhere? But I don't even bother to ask. I doubt if Il Duce is very much clued up on his English literature.

First impressions are not too favourable. The most noticeable thing about Amalfi is how frenetic it is compared to Ravello. It would have been better, I suspect, to have done it the other way about – to have come here during the siesta, though I doubt if this place ever sleeps, just as I doubt if Ravello ever fully wakens.

And if it lacks the tranquillity of Ravello, then it has none of the charm of Positano either. Perhaps if I had not seen that first, Amalfi might have had a certain appeal, but compared to Positano, it is too strung out, too higgledly-piggledy, too commercial, too busy, too brash – just like its Duomo. For, if the cathedrals of Siena and Florence were bad, then this tops the lot. Its hideousness is quite literally breath-taking.

What is it about the Italians that they like black-and-white stripes so much, as if the only building materials they could find were the contents of the Liquorice Allsorts box – especially the square black-and-white one? That's what they seem to have used here to form the pillars and arches. The rest of the façade consists of geometric designs with, at the top, a mosaic of Christ enthroned, with a host of heavenly angels at His feet and beneath them, the disciples on parade. They are colourful and tasteful, but unfortunately it's the Liquorice Allsorts that draws the eye the most. Taken as a whole, it's a black-and-white horror story which, if the wicked witch had enticed Hansel and Gretel here, and even if they were addicted to liquorice, they would have taken one look at it and not been tempted in the slightest.

It's not all bad, though. The arched windows of the portico, with three slim Moorish pillars in each with a latticework of stone at the top, are very fine indeed. It's just a pity that the rest of the Duomo is so heavy, so in your face, that you tend not to notice them. Inside the portico, the floor is composed of black-and-white squares creating a checkerboard effect which, alas, does not marry well with the arches.

The steep flight of steps up to the Duomo is very impressive, I will give it that – not that there is anything special about them, apart from the fact that they are very wide and there's a great number of them. And to the right, the campanile is not displeasing, for it is plain and unadorned, apart from the Romanesque windows on the second and third storeys. Alas, they have spoiled it with its rather grotesque crowning glory. It looks like the sort of castle you might build for the kids on the beach with your bucket and spade – one big circular tower with four smaller ones hemming it in at each corner, so to speak. That may have been acceptable, but they have seen fit to decorate it with the same green-and-yellow majolica tiles as on the *sedile* in Sorrento.

A notice board announces that this is the Duomo di Sant'Andrea and, if we want to see the interior, then we must go through the museum and buy a ticket. No chance! Probably just some boring ecclesiastical vestments and such like, maybe a bishop's chair such as they have in the cathedral in Sorrento. I wouldn't have minded popping my head in, just to see if the interior is as horrendous as the outside. It probably is, like Siena's, but may not be, but I'm damned if I'm going to pay good money to go in and find out.

42

A Little Bit of Scotland

TURNING our backs on the cathedral, we descend the stairs and in front of the Hotel Fontana, come, appropriately enough, to a fountain with, at its centre, a statue of St Andrew, the patron saint of Scotland (and Russia, Romania, Ukraine and Barbados), but whom they insist on calling "Andrea" here. No doubt that's why he has such a pained expression on his face – giving him a lassie's name like that.

I wouldn't blame him for being annoyed at that, but methinks it's got more to do with the rusty metal halo above his head with the cross of St Andrew in the middle and which is transfixed to his head by an iron spike. He must be suffering from the mother and father of all headaches. It's amazing he's still standing. He appears to have an enormous baguette tucked under his right oxter and another, like a quiver, slung over his back, as if he was off to feed the multitude like his leader did, if only someone first would be so kind as to donate a couple of fish. (You might have thought he would have been the one to provide them, him being an ex-fisherman.) On closer inspection, however, it turns out he is merely posing in front of the equal-armed cross they are going to crucify him on, poor devil – saint, I mean.

But that's not where the real interest lies. Directly below him is a buxom nymph, 38 D, if I am any judge. I am not an authority on these matters, so don't take the figure as gospel. What is beyond dispute is there's more than a handful, for both bosoms are overflowing the confines of her hands, her fingers separated to let her nipples protrude. And in what seems to me a greater cruelty than what they have done to poor Andrea, someone has sickeningly stuck a couple of copper pipes through each nipple. Ouch! Thanks to the drought, nothing is flowing from them now, not even blood.

Meanwhile, above her and on either side are a couple of her well-nourished children with nascent breasts, although they are plainly boy babies. To them this is the height of embarrassment. They can't bear to look, have turned their heads away in horror. Their faces are plainly saying: *Pit them awa' mither. Yir embarrassin' us.*

Well, that was an interesting diversion, but I can't divert Iona any longer from the shops, for they are all around. Indeed, there seems little else to do around here. We must have our daily *gelati* or else the world would stop spinning, so we buy a lemon flavour and a cherry flavour. Some things never change. They are a snip at €6, or £5 each – nectar to sustain the gods, never mind us, as we go about the serious business of window-shopping, or God forbid, *real* shopping.

We have stopped in front of a window in which someone has scrawled on a piece of cardboard which looks as if it has been roughly torn from a box: *Biscotti al Limone €2,80.* What attracts Iona is not the flavour, as you might have supposed, but the name of the biscuits themselves – *Playtime.* A perfect memento to take back to her colleagues. For the uninitiated, in Scotland, the morning break in schools is known as "playtime", even by the teachers, and the snack the children might indulge in at that time, not to mention any games they might play during it, is known as their "playtime piece."

Iona buys a couple of boxes, no doubt hoping if she's lucky, she may get one or two herself. And while we are on the subject of "pieces", reader, you may care to know that in Banffshire, where I was born, a cake with icing on it – or cream, or some such calorific product – is known as a "fancy piece". I feel it is my duty to warn the bucolic natives of that county (which you will not find on any modern map, as it has been absorbed into Aberdeenshire), that when they come down to the big cities in the Central Belt, that that delicacy has an entirely different connotation down there and they should be careful about offering people one, or even worse, asking men, in front of their wives, if they would like to have one.

So that's a memento for Iona's colleagues sorted, but I still have to get something for her birthday. I've come across a shop which sells everything from leather handbags to funny-coloured pasta (but nothing so distasteful as the kind we saw in Sorrento) and, in the window, my eye is caught by a tray of Capodimonte earrings. They look cute to me, but would *she* like them? What do I know about women's jewellery?

"Come and look at these."

She's wandered up ahead, but her hearing is very acute, so that's why this would make an appropriate little present. She comes back and has a look. They seem to meet with her approval. We go into the shop and emerge a few minutes later with the sweetest little pair of Capodimonte earrings you have ever seen in your life – little flowers, like green daisies, with the stamens picked out with little yellow dots.

"This will make a very nice memento of today," she says. "Thank you very much."

"What? *Today?* What about your birthday?" I ask, with the emphasis on *birth*.

"Oh, don't worry about that. We'll find something in Sorrento all right."

So it wasn't a birthday present after all! Just a memento of Amalfi. What she really was saying was "thanks for the memory", like the song.

Our time is nearly up. It's time to head back to the bus already. It's amazing how time goes by so quickly when you are enjoying yourself, not just window-shopping but engaging in real shopping. Apart from the money spent, it is time well spent, some might say. But not me. It *was* all downhill from Ravello as far as I am concerned, with the possible exception of the nymph at St Andrew's fountain. The best certainly was not kept till last.

We have to scamper across the road to avoid being mowed down by a speeding motorist who apparently does not have any brakes. Our object is a roundabout which doubles as yet another fountain, the centrepiece of which is some geezer wearing a hood and a lean and hungry look. I am curious to find out who it is. His dress and skeletal face reminds me of Old Father Time, only he must have put his scythe down somewhere and has forgotten where he put it.

We just make it. I leap onto the safety of the pavement cleanly, but Iona catches the toe of her shoe on the kerb and measures her length on it. She's not hurt very much, more surprised, but her finger is bleeding. Fortunately, in her bag of many zips, she has a plaster. With my plastered feet, and now her finger, we are beginning to look as if we'd been in a fight. With each other, some might suppose.

The person at the centre of the fountain turns out to be Flavio Gioia, whose claim to fame, the notice on the pedestal informs us, is he invented the magnetic compass. Well, maybe he did, but he still looks like Old Father Time to me and he reminds me that our time is up.

Our Leader awaits. Mustn't get on the wrong side of him. You don't mess with dictators. It's time to head back.

43

Strange Encounters of the Missed Kind

S O that was the Amalfi Coast. If I ever come back here again, and who knows, I might, though there are so many places to go, places I have never been, I probably won't, but if I do, I'll do it by water.

Now I'm doing it by the book, looking up what I have missed. Hopefully not too much. Right, let's begin with Positano. So far, so good. Don't seem to have missed anything there. It doesn't say anything about Rastafarian dogs, so that's one up for me.

Ravello. The Villa Rufolo. What does it say about that? Here's a bit about *Parsifal*. Well, I knew about that, but is there anything else I may have missed? Oh, no! What's this? Apparently there are cloisters and if there is anything I like, it's cloisters. I suppose you could call me a cloister lover, which would be nice – just as long as you are female, good-looking, and don't let on to your husband. But there's worse. As you also know by now, if there is one type of architecture I'm partial to, it's the Moorish sort. And what do you think the Villa Rufolo has? That's right – a Moorish cloister. A double whammy.

And, if that were not bad enough, the gardens are described as "enchanting", with superb views over the coast. I don't believe it! If only I'd had this guide with me, or even a human guide who could have told me all this instead of having a prolonged lunch in some *trattoria* or other! Thank you very much, Big and Baby Driver. Thank you very much indeed!

Oh, well, I suppose I have been to the epitome of Moorish architecture, the Alhambra in Granada, and visited the Generalife – arguably the finest gardens in the world. Compared with that, no doubt the Villa Rufolo and its gardens is small beer, but – all the same – I'd have gladly sacrificed my large beer at lunchtime, even if it were a mighty 8.5%, for *e'en a blink*, as Tam O' Shanter put it in a different context, of those cloisters and that sea view.

My misery, you might imagine, gentle reader, is complete; my cup is full and runneth over. But sad to say, it's not – not yet. I read on and discover that D.H. Lawrence wrote part of that seminal ⟦sic⟧ novel, *Lady Chatterley's Lover*, in the Hotel Rufolo. Now, if you are talking about literary heroes, D.H. is one of mine. Well, actually, I think most of his books are a bit pretentious, but *Sons and Lovers* is number four in my list of all-time favourite novels.

If only I had known, I would have paid the Hotel Rufolo more attention. I can't even remember what it looked like. I look up the map we'd got from the tourist information office and discover we hadn't even walked past it. It lies on the road to the Villa Cimbrone, which we hadn't bothered with either, but – if I had known – I would most certainly have made my way to the Villa as straight as any bee.

Once owned by Lord Grimthorpe (who sounds as if he belongs in a Dickensian novel), it was visited by the great and the good of the Thirties, a list of which sounds like an extract from *Who's Who*. As well as D.H. Lawrence aforesaid and to name but some, there was Mr and Mrs Virginia Woolf, Mr and Mrs Vita Sackville-West (he was quite famous in his own right as Harold Nicolson), Henry Moore, T.S. Eliot, and Winston Churchill. Greta Garbo and her lover, the conductor Leopold Stowoski, came here many, many times, though they might only have been good friends and reports of them being lovers may be greatly exaggerated.

Now a very swanky hotel and restaurant, which would never allow the likes of me over the threshold, I could nevertheless have tramped about the gardens which are open to the public, including the belvedere known as the Terrazzo dell'Infinito. It is graced, or perhaps not, by classical busts on pedestals, rudely turning their backs on the stupendous view which – in an interview with an American magazine – Gore Vidal once said was the most beautiful view he had seen in all his travels.

I am indebted to him for something else he said, and which I used in my retirement speech – the story about the Macmillans and the de Gaulles who were having a friendly *tête-à-tête* about their impending retirements.

"Tell me, Yvonne," said Harold, "what are you most looking forward to in retirement?"

You can just about imagine stiff, upper-lipped Harold practically choking on his moustache when he seemed to hear Madame de Gaulle candidly reply: "*A penis*".

Charles probably saved Harold's life that day when he explained: "She means 'appiness."

Vidal lived in Ravello, off and on, for thirty years, and was granted honorary citizenship of the town. I wonder what that entitled him to? Maybe free beer and wine.

So much for Ravello. What about Amalfi? What did we miss there, I wonder? Well, perhaps it's not so surprising we didn't fall instantly in love with Amalfi since it suffered a devastating earthquake in 1343 and most of the old town, and the part we would have liked to see, now lies under the water.

Of the eponymous Duchess, not much remains either – fortunately for me, as I would have hated to have missed that. It says she was a real historical figure, as I knew, and her name was Giovanna d'Aragona or Joan of Arragon (1478-1510). So you see, names *can* be translated from the Italian, just in case you thought I was being a bit ingenuous previously. All that's left which might possibly be connected with her is the Torre dello Zirro, where, according to legend, she and her children were strangled at the instigation of her brothers – one of whom was a cardinal, no less. The lesson is: holy men are not wholly to be trusted.

In case you don't know the story, the reason for this outrage was that after her husband died (to whom the poor girl had been married at the age of 12 in 1490), and while she was acting as regent for her infant son, she fell in love with, secretly married and had children to her steward, Antonio Beccadelli of Bologna. They thought she had married beneath her: they didn't want their blue blood turning into a ghastly shade of purple.

The remains of the Torre are still standing on a ridge between Amalfi and the next village of Atrani, which we must have passed on our way to Ravello but they weren't pointed out to us. But it doesn't matter, as that's probably not where it happened anyway, but actually in a now-ruined Norman castle, further up the ridge.

The Duomo's façade is described as "lovely", arguably the "loveliest cathedral in all of Southern Italy", which just goes to show you that you definitely should not believe everything you read in the guidebooks. It doesn't surprise me in the slightest to discover it is a 19th century "improvement" on the 13th century original, just as the Duomos of Siena and Florence were similarly treated to elaborate ornamentation, but what I would describe as desecration. The campanile, however, from 1276, is mainly original. I wouldn't mind betting my entire pension (it may not be much, but it means a lot to me), that the bit that isn't, is the bit at the top with its ghastly majolica tiles.

The interior, it doesn't surprise me either, was remodelled in the Baroque style and has a baptismal font in porphyry. The Baroque, in my humble opinion, is the worst of architectural styles, and porphyry is the most hideous colour of stone. Well, I'm glad I was spared them at least, but the cloisters, the so-called "Cloister of Paradise", built between 1266 and 1268, is Moorish with pairs of slender pillars and interlaced pointed arches. Damn!

"Hey, listen to this," I read out loud to Iona. "It says here that you can actually see the head of St Andrew in the crypt!"

Now that is very curious indeed, because when we were in St Peter's a mere week ago, we had learned that *it* had St Andrew's head, but Paul VI had given it back to the Eastern Church in 1966. Now that sounds a bit like an own-goal by the Catholic Church to me, as the English commentators might put it, never missing an opportunity to bring up football and the World Cup whenever that particular date is mentioned. There are enough pieces of the True Cross to form a forest if you put them altogether, but how many heads can you claim St Andrew had?

"That's nothing," retorts Iona, who is skimming another guidebook. "It says here they have got his body and his sarcophagus oozes a liquid called *manna* which has miraculous restorative properties and the most holy drink it neat!"

"What!!! Let me see that! I don't believe it!"

Seeing is believing, but remember what I said earlier about not trusting guidebooks. Blimey! Imagine drinking that stuff neat! Like malt whisky, I'm sure it should be diluted with a touch of water to bring out the flavours. It's just too strong otherwise. Not too much, mind you. Any distillery I have visited (and I've been to a few) invariably has a jug of water with pipettes in them so you can add a drop or two of H_2O. The idea is not to drown the precious elixir. (Besides, they wouldn't want you thinning it out to the extent that a bottle lasted twice as long.)

My cup of misery really is full now. Why, that's better even than Santa Panta's blood! It sickens me utterly to think I have missed out on paying homage to the bones of my patron saint. A grave error of mine not to have paid to go into the Duomo, and a serious omission to my collection of graves of famous people. Having said that, I'm not so sure about the omission of the Saint's emission. To be honest, the thought of it makes me feel rather sick.

Don't scoff. Don't dismiss this emission as mere superstition. Apparently St Andrew's bones *were* brought back from Constantinople by the Crusaders in 1206 as a trophy of war, so it could be his bits after all, assuming they nicked the right ones in the first place. Who knows? Considering what else they've said about this place, you've got to take it all with a pinch of salt, especially in the matter of habeas corpus.

Nor, apparently, can you trust what it says on the pedestals of statues, because it says that not only did Favio Gioia *not* invent the compass, but they invented *him* as well. He may not be a real person at all. Can you credit it!

It all stems from a mistranslation from Lucretius where "in" Flavio became "by" Flavio, which became "Flavio Gioia" (a little place down the road) in the way that Chinese Whispers distorts the original. In the fullness of time, this turned into the name of the bloke whom the good citizens of Amalfi claim "invented" the compass about 1300 years after the Chinese actually did.

Which begs the question, why didn't they just put a statue of Pinocchio there if they needed a statue for the centrepiece of a roundabout? But then, of course, he wasn't a local lad. He came from somewhere near Florence, as everyone knows.

44

A Shocking Shopping Experience

NOW we're rested, Iona has had a great idea. Why don't we spend the time before dinner by going to Sorrento and having a look for her birthday present?

"I have often walked down this street before," I sing to her as we are decanted by that chimney in search of a factory. The reason for the song this time is we are going back to the shop where we were yesterday, or rather Iona was, whilst I loitered about outside. This time, however, I do go in and lurk about amongst sewing kits and threads of every hue. It's not the kind of shop any self-respecting man would be seen dead in and, indeed, I am the only member of the species there. I try to look impervious to the curious stares of the women shoppers and console myself with the thought that at least nobody knows me here.

In the end, Iona selects some bibs which have a cheq-uered edge in either blue or pink with a panel at the bottom where she can embroider the name of the new-born.

"Who's having a baby?" I ask.

"No-one at the moment. But people are always having them."

Well, that's true. It never ceases to amaze me how slow some people are before they catch on to what causes babies. And since we don't even know who the parents of this unborn child are, let alone what sex it will be, she buys both pink and blue bibs.

Iona seems to be having some difficulty herself, for she is going through her bag of many zips looking for her Visa card. She's getting more and more flustered as she tries one zip then another. In the end, I give the assistant my card, which of course is just the moment when Iona finds hers. It doesn't matter though, as it's a joint account and my money is her money. And her money is her money too, as she has her own account. And if that doesn't tell me something about who is the boss in this relationship, then I don't know what does.

Now we can get down to the main task of looking for the birthday present. We trail about the town, going from shop to shop, looking at the inlaid jewellery boxes and the coral jewellery and the prices, but it's hopeless really as it's impossible to compare like with like, so in the end we decide if Iona sees something she likes in the next shop, we'll just go for it. But, as it happens, there is nothing in the window that we do like particularly. Iona, however, is sure there must be something inside she could find to buy. We won't know unless we try.

It's not a large shop and has a surprisingly dim interior, conveying the sense that it has not been altered in generations. Occupying just about the entire floor space, is a glass-topped cabinet full of wares. At a desk at the back, under a bright light, an old man wearing a jeweller's eyepiece is hunched over something. He appears to be using something like a dentist's drill. It sounds like one anyway, and it's enough to set your teeth on edge. Intrigued, I go over to investigate. He's carving a piece of pink coral into a rose. So that's how they do it! I hadn't cared much for the coral jewellery up till now but seeing this flower emerge from the raw material, seeming to bloom like the real thing, I am impressed. I suppose, to damn it with faint praise, you could call it OK Coral.

Fortunately slipping his eyepiece out first – I would not care for my face to be observed that closely – the old-timer stops his handiwork and shows us the contents of the big glass cabinet, or Coral Island as it must be called, or – if it is not – it should be. Yet it is not the coral that draws our attention so much, though that is by far the most dominant product on display, but something else which we have not seen before in all our peregrinations around the town on the Great Birthday Present Hunt.

It's a pendant made out of mother-of-pearl, with the silhouette of a lady, and – judging from the hairstyle – I would guess dating from ancient Roman times, or perhaps, to skip a few centuries, the Regency period. Fashions go and fashions come back. In my view, anyone who follows them is a fool. Just look at me. I am the least dedicated follower of fashion you are ever likely to meet in your life, and it's never held me back. Or has it? What do you think, Signor Corleone?

As regards the jewellery, the profile of the lady is in white, on a light-blue background, rather like a piece of Wedgwood pottery. Iona asks to see it and when she holds it up to the light, it has a translucent quality.

"I made it myself," says the old man. "Everything you see here, I made myself."

"Did you really!" I say, impressed for the second time in two minutes, not doubting it for a minute. He must have spent a lot of time, hours and hours, days and days, carving all these *objects d'art*. Thus he has spent his life and has not wasted it. Here is the proof to show after he passes away that he once passed this way.

Iona also likes the pendant, which is just as well as she'll be the one wearing it. It makes it more special too, to actually buy it from the man who made it. No only will it double as a souvenir of this week in Sorrento, but because of its Roman appearance, of last week also. Yes, I have a bit of a talent for picking birthday presents when I bother to put my mind to it.

It needs a chain too, which I presume the craftsman did not make, but he craftily has a supply of various styles in gold and silver. Iona selects a fine gold chain (expense is no object). The artist selects a box to put them in and, even better for me, begins to wrap it up. All that's left for me is the painful duty of having to stump up with the money. But when I open up my pouch – shock, horror! My Visa card is not there! I can tell right away because there's a little cellophane panel where it should be and it's empty. All the same, I search through it and my pockets just in case. It's to no avail, as I knew in my bones. But in a blinding flash, I realise where it must be – in the sewing shop.

I try to remember if I got it back from the assistant but my mind has gone blank with panic. The old shopkeeper, watching this rigmarole, must be wondering if this is April the 1st, or we are playing some sort of practical joke – letting him wrap up the parcel before we tell him we can't pay and he'll have to go to the bother of unwrapping it again, and – like Iona on her birthday – he won't get any surprises when he opens it.

But he needn't have worried. Iona produces her card, so – leaving her to pay for her own present, as well as leaving her for the present – I gallop back to the sewing shop. It's not the first time I've lost my Visa card, but this is the first time I have lost it when I've actually been *with* her. Actually, it is her fault, because if she had not lost her card in that bag with more zips that Johnny Rotten's trousers, I wouldn't have had to produce mine and, like a baby kangaroo, it would still have been nestling safely in its pouch.

If it's not at the shop, I'm going to be in big trouble. We only take enough money to get us started, relying on our Visa card to pay for things as we go along. If it's lost, we will have to cancel the card and remain moneyless for the remainder of the trip. Panting, I present myself to the lady at the till.

I am just opening my mouth to ask the all-important, potentially life-saving question when the assistant reaches beneath the desk and produces what looks my Visa card. The words "Have you got?" die in my throat as I behold the plastic rectangle. I don't suppose they get many men in here, right enough, so I should think the reason she remembers me has more to do with being a rare visitor and nothing at all to do with my appearance – my green Speedo swimming trunks, my Panama hat, my red face, even redder after trotting round here in the heat as fast as I could.

"You rushed off before we could give it back to you," she says, smiling, holding it out to me. "I knew you would be back for it as soon as you realised it was missing."

Just so, as Rudyard Kipling might have said, but methinks if you were one of the ladies who had devoted your whole life to working in this shop and then tried your hand at writing your memorial epic, you'd call it *A Just Sew Story* wouldn't you?

I expect it would be a very funny book that kept the reader in stiches.

45

Encounters of the Embarrassing Kind

S O, that's the Big Birthday Present Hunt over. Now we can go and relax, go back to the hotel – only whenever I think of that, it fills me with a certain dread as I can't help thinking of the Three Degrees and wondering if they will be in, for I know without doubt that if they are, I will hear them before I see them.

And that, in fact, is just what happens. As we round the bend in the corridor, faint strains of their infernal music reaches my ears. I feel a sense of strain already. Damn! Damn! And double damn! No chance of a nice, quiet relaxing *apéritif* before we go down to dinner. The pool is closed, and in any case, the other drinks police, the real ones who patrol the pool, would have been on duty on the lookout for people consuming their own alcohol.

I could go up to the roof but it's a hassle to go all that way with just one drink, to say nothing of looking a bit stupid wandering about the place with a glass in my hand like an alcoholic who can't last without a drink before making it to the bar. And by the time I got to the roof, it would be finished anyway, so I'd have to go back for another one. Like Sisyphus rolling his boulder up the mountain, I'd never be finished trekking to and fro. No, that won't do.

I could go to the bar but why should I be forced out of my room and have to pay those prices? No, there's nothing else for it, I'll just have to endure the "music". And it's not just that that grates on my nerves – it's the incessant chatter, the shrieks of sudden laughter and above all the southern-English elongated vowels.

"Why do they bother with the bloody music?" I moan to Iona. "I'm sure they're not even listening to it." To them it is just background noise; to me it's an infernal din which I just can't shut out.

"Well, if it bothers you that much, why don't you go and tell them to turn it off instead of moaning to me about it all the time?"

"Why don't you?"

"It's you it's annoying so much. You go."

How can she expect me to do that after not even one glass of gin? There's not a lot of Dutch courage in that.

It seems they are going out on the town tonight and are making their preparations, putting on the war paint and decking themselves in their finery which no doubt means dresses as tight or as miniscule as they can get away with. Well, that's good news of a kind. It should mean they will be away all evening and I will at least be able to have my *digestifs* in peace. Anyway, we'll be going for our meal soon, so there's not much point in getting them to turn it off when I'm not going to be here, is there? No, I've talked myself out of lodging a complaint. I'll just stick it out.

But in the meantime, I have to endure hearing about the niceties of sartorial problems such as: *D'yowh think I should wear this? It doesn't make my bum look fat, does it? A yowh shouwah?* I don't know which of them is speaking. None of them is even remotely fat, but if it is the ugly one, she had better hope there's a lot more ugly girls wherever they are going or that her better-looking friends, especially the really pretty one, can attract some talent.

Not much point in having another *apéritif.* It's no pleasure with this din in the background. May as well give my ears a rest and head down to the restaurant.

So far, so good. No sign of Signor Corleone as we make our way across that sea of polished marble outside the dining room. There are no tables free in the first rank by the window, but there are some in the second rank, over to the left-hand side. Although we haven't discussed it, instinctively we both head towards the third rank, in the middle, for although the view of the bay and Vesuvius is restricted, it still affords a better outlook than from either of the sides.

But just as we are about to park our bums in our chosen seat, seemingly out of nowhere, up pops Signor Corleone to frustrate our plans, beckoning us over to the table *he* has chosen for us, already pulling out the chair that presumably he intends Iona, rather than me, to sit in, and smiling so pleasantly as if he's deriving a great deal of pleasure from helping us like this.

Why didn't we, or rather I say (as I am the man and it's my job, though Iona's the real boss): "No, we'll just sit here if you don't mind" or "Look, it may be *your* restaurant, but *we* are the ones paying the bill, not to mention *your* wages. That should count for something, shouldn't it!"

But it looked like an offer we couldn't refuse and we didn't, and so here we are. We'd prefer to avoid creating a scene than look at the scenery, obviously. I hate being a wimp.

On our way out, it so happens that our course brings us so close to a table that to not acknowledge the diners would be rude. It is my Dutchman and his family.

"Hello."

"Hello."

"Did you have a nice day?"

"Yes, thank you. Did you?"

"Yes. We went down the Amalfi coast."

"Yes, it's beautiful isn't it?"

"Yes it is." Pause. Awkward silence. "Well, enjoy your meal."

"Yes. Thank you. Have a good evening."

"Thank you. And you too. Goodbye."

"Goodbye."

"Goodbye."

Polite nods all round, befitting this nodding acquaintanceship.

And so we make our escape, Iona wanting to know when we are out of their hearing, who they were, since I, rudely, hadn't introduced her to him, nor had he, his family to me. I can envisage the corresponding conversation at the Dutch table.

"Who was that funny man, Daddy?"

"Well, do you remember when we were in Herculaneum, I spoke to a man in the baths? He was wearing swimming trunks, remember? Well, that was him. He shouts something to me from his balcony every night. I don't know what he's saying, so I just say something back and come inside to get away from him."

These short and strained conversations are just too embarrassing for words. In future I'll keep out of his way and step back into the balcony the next time I see him in his garden.

I can hardly believe it, but as we make our way towards the lift, waiting for it – there is no mistaking that profile, that bald pate, that nose that must have launched a thousand sneezes – Mrs Scanty-Panties' accessory. It's funny he should be the one I spot first. *Herman's Hermits'* lesser-known Sixties hit *She's A Must to Avoid* is perfect for this occasion. Iona is determined to avoid her at all costs.

What's to be done? The lift still has not come and we are getting closer every second. Too late to take a body swerve, or stop in her tracks, Iona has now spotted the dreaded enemy. *She* can't see *her* for the very good reason that when you are waiting for a lift, you normally stand facing it, which is why she is presenting her diaphanous back (and buttocks) to Iona which is bound to incite her to further feelings of loathing when she notices her. Meanwhile, I bet the object of her hate is supremely and blissfully unaware of her enemy's existence.

As far as I can see, the lady is wearing the same outfit as when we first saw her and very possibly the same as she was wearing last night. I can't be sure as I only saw her from the front, sitting down. Anyway it was black. Could it be the poor thing only has one outfit and it is so worn and threadbare you can see right through it?

As luck would have it, the lift arrives at precisely the same moment as us. I have experience in these matters and trust me, I know perfectly well luck has absolutely nothing whatsoever to do with it. It's the gods, who knowing Iona's antipathy to Mrs Scanty-Panties, "for their sport" as Aeschylus put it, have contrived all this. When did you ever approach a lift and it did an "Open Sesame" without you even having to lift a finger to summon it?

Mrs Scanty-Panties and accessory step into the lift, go right to the back and turn round, as you do. There's more than enough room for the four of us. The door is gaping wide, yet we do not enter. Iona, ignoring this open invitation, moves across to the other lift, leaving me standing facing them. They must be wondering why on earth I don't come in and why my other half has already pressed the button to summon the other lift.

Mercifully, the doors glide together, bringing to an end this horrendously embarrassing experience. What Mrs Scanty-Panties makes of this pantomime I can't imagine. I'm more accustomed to seeing her from behind or her behind if you want to put it that way, but I've only ever seen one expression on her face, which is to say no expression at all, as if she were entered into the coolest-cucumber-of-the-year competition. Probably it never crosses her mind that anybody could dislike her, especially men, whilst women might admire or envy her, but never hate her.

Perhaps I am beginning to get a glimmer of why Iona hates her so much. But it's still a totally unreasonable attitude. And to think she thinks mine to the Three Degrees is unreasonable!

Huh!

46

Confusion on the Way to Capri

W HEN I got up this morning there was something indefinable, something so infinitesimal that it's difficult to put one's finger on it, but there's a certain haziness in the air which renders Vesuvius rather shadowy, less clearly defined, and Naples rather nebulous as if seen through cheesecloth.

As for us, we're quite clear about what we're doing today. We're heading for Capri. We could have gone on an organised tour for €51 each to Capri (by which they mean the town of) and Anacapri, Capri's second and only other town. That seems rather pricey and, since it goes to neither the world-famous Blue Grotto or to the much lesser-known Villa Jovis, we've decided to do it on our own.

The Villa Jovis may be the lesser attraction but it's the major attraction for us because it was from there that that arch-lecher, the Emperor Tiberius, in self-imposed exile, ran the Empire for a decade, from AD 27 to AD 37 until his death – murdered it is said, by that arch perv, Caligula, who de-

Marina Piccola, Sorrento

scended into further perversions and depravity that would have made even Tiberius's hair stand on end if he had any left. The Villa is in ruins now but that doesn't matter – we just want to see what's left of it and its setting, and we'll let our imaginations do the rest.

We already know where the ferry leaves from – the Marina Piccola, which, although it means "small", according to the rules of Italian logic, is actually the biggest of Sorrento's three harbours and where all the ferries and hydrofoils ply their trade. Hydrofoil or ferry? I can't make my mind up. The hydrofoil is faster but dearer, the ferry cheaper, but slower. I'm not much use at making decisions. That's why I have a boss to tell me what to do. No point in keeping a dog and barking yourself. She says I'm barking enough as it is.

"Oh, we'll take the ferry," says the Boss, not without a certain irritation at my indecision.

"Ferry 'nough," responds the Underling, oh, so wittily (or so he thinks), secretly pleased at the response and not just on economic grounds. It's a lovely, warm, sunny day and we're not in any hurry. Why not enjoy a nice cruise over the Bay of Naples to the romantic Isle of Capri?

Ahead of us, two Dutchmen are in the queue to buy tickets for the ferry, but that is fair enough as they were there before us. I know they are in the ferry queue because there's a separate kiosk for the hydrofoil, though nothing to say where you actually queue for the vessels. Which, no doubt, is how the gods have a laugh at the tourists, who only discover this fact after lining up in the wrong queue for half-an-hour.

The Dutchmen are extremely thin with tattoos on their arms and shoulders, which I can see thanks to the singlets they are wearing. They may have them elsewhere too, but mercifully their shorts are covering them up. Both have their heads shaved down to the wood and earrings in their ears. They are accompanied by two boys aged about eleven, who are twins if I'm not much mistaken and as fat as the men are thin, showing off their pubescent breasts as all they are wearing is a pair of shorts. It's easy to see the reason for their pudginess, for even at their tender years, not to mention this time in the morning, they are slugging from bottles of Heineken. You might have thought their carers could have shown a more caring attitude by saying something like: *Why don't you try the local beer since you're on holiday?*

They want a return ticket to Capri, which shows you that their parenting skills are not the only ones in which they are lacking. You would normally assume a return ticket would be the best buy, but this is Italy and they do things differently here. Iona has done her homework, which is why I know the island is principally a day-trippers' destination – the price of accommodation being as steep as its limestone cliffs. Being so small, it's possible to see everything the island has to offer in a couple of trips at the most.

The thing is this mass invasion also results in a mass exodus at the most popular times, so you end up wasting a great deal of time waiting in the queue for the return ferry in order to be sure of catching it. If you don't make it, it means waiting an hour for the next one. On the other hand, if you buy a single ticket, you have the flexibility of coming back by the hydrofoil which is a lot more frequent.

It seems a no-brainer to buy single tickets in order to maximise our time on the island, so I buy two at €14 each. We are told to queue on the pier, where there is a big Number 1. Ah, yes, I see it now! Our departure time, we are told, is 10:20. For once in my life, I seem to have judged it perfectly – making it not by the skin of my teeth, but not too long to have to wait either.

Part of the scheduling was necessarily dictated by the courtesy bus from the hotel into town and, from there, we had walked rather than taken the bus to the harbour, a decision we might well reverse on the return journey as it would be a pretty steep climb back up. In the meantime, it's very pleasant standing here on the pier in the warm (not hot) sunshine, looking across the harbour and over the pleasure crafts to where Sorrento town is strung across the top of the cliff like a string of pearls.

Well, it *would* be quite an idyllic scene if only that bloody hydrofoil – which has now arrived – would switch off its engines and stop polluting the air with its noxious fumes, not to mention the irritating noise of its engine. I'm also starting to feel a teeny-weeny bit worried. The fact of the matter is there are precious few people hanging about here in the queue for the ferry. Especially worrying, considering how imminent its departure is meant to be.

Furthermore, the Dutchmen and the beer-swigging boys who were with us have now disappeared. I hadn't been paying particular attention to them, and had not noticed they could no longer tolerate my sartorial outfit of bright-yellow shorts and matching lemon shirt. Whatever you think of my prose style, trust me, dear reader, I am an icon of fashion. It's just the world has not followed it yet.

Neither had Iona, who – surprisingly enough – had not been attracted to them very much (by which I mean the Dutchmen), and had paid them scant attention. But, I reassure myself, this is Italy and if the bus timetables are a work of fiction, there is every possibility the ferries do not run to time either.

My understanding of the way Italy works is confirmed when, at last, the ferry putters into the middle of the harbour. It appears to be practically empty. Not so strange really, I reflect, as at this time in the morning, the only passengers would be the ones coming back early from an overnight stop. It's unbelievably good news for us since we will have practically the whole ferry to ourselves and we may sit where we like, which means I will sit in the sun and Iona will sit in the shade – probably at different sides of the vessel and with the prospect of a pleasant little cruise across the Bay of Naples ahead of us. It all seems too perfect. Which of course, it is.

The ferry manoeuvres in mid-harbour and executes an 180° turn before docking. It doesn't take long, and it takes an even shorter time for the passengers to embark, but we are not one of them. The sailor with biceps like Bluto who is taking the tickets, shakes his head and won't let us aboard.

On the way to Capri

"Napoli," he says gruffly. He is a man of few words.

"No. Capri." (Bloody idiot!) I show him on the ticket where it clearly says *Capri*. Can't he read? Why is he picking on me? He let those other people on board, why not me?

"Napoli." He looks very determined. If I didn't speak Italian well enough to know that *Napoli* is Italian for *Naples*, I might have thought from his tone that he was saying *Piss off!* Actually, I think that *is* what he's saying, if the tone and body language is anything to go by.

"Does this ferry go to Naples?" Iona cuts in.

"Si. Napoli."

Like the haze which had been evident earlier this morning but which has now burnt off, the Addison brain sees things a bit more clearly now. So this is the ferry to Naples! Good job Iona was with me or otherwise God knows how long it would be before Bluto knocked some sense into me.

We can see a much larger gathering further up the pier where I can also see a big number 2. I'm sure that's where we should be and if that Dutch family is there, then I know it will be a sign that that is where we should be.

We hasten there and sure enough, there they are, but how they found out that is where they should be – or why we were given the wrong information in the first place – I have absolutely no idea. It confirms my belief that the gods move in mysterious ways, their puerile pranks to perform, and not at all averse to using ferry operators for their nefarious purposes either.

47

Problems on the Way to the Villa Jovis

THERE are seats for everyone but they have put a stupid canopy over them, so unless you get a seat by the rails you have no chance of being exposed to the sun. It's only a half-hour voyage, so I prefer to stand at the stern with a few others and catch some rays. And it's just as well that one of the handful of fellow passengers with me can catch more than rays, otherwise my Panama would have suffered a premature burial at sea. He caught it with his feet, so to speak – stamped upon it, just in the nick of time before it was swept overboard. It may be sunny but it's decidedly the draughtiest place on the boat, as the ferry is fairly ripping along.

Hat not needed on voyage then. I park it beneath my oxter and it's nice to feel the wind whipping my hair. To begin with, we run parallel with the coast – there's the ruins of Pollius' villa, the boardwalk, and the place where we lacerated our feet. And there's the bar the nice lady came down from to tell us not to even *think* about swimming. Then as we change course, it's satisfying to watch the ever-widening gap of water as we leave Sorrento behind and see Capri appear ever more distinctly as we draw closer.

Capri has a narrow, wasp-like waist, as if someone had squeezed one of those sausage-shaped balloons and displaced the air to either side, creating huge cliffs on either side. Very close now, we still can't see any sign of the Villa Jovis at the top of the cliffs – but it was from them that that charming emperor, Tiberius, had his perceived enemies thrown to their deaths. He had a great many of them, as he was paranoid about being assassinated.

We are landing at the Marina Grande, which I bet actually does stand a chance of being the bigger of Capri's two ports for it is buzzing with life and boats. It's a cluster of dazzlingly white houses strung out along the shore, whilst Capri town itself sits atop the craggy, limestone cliffs. As we dock, we can see a funicular railway cautiously making its way down to the port. You can walk up if you are a masochist, but we'll just take the funicular and save time and our energy for the Villa Jovis. It looks as if it will be quite a distance, even from the top of the cliff, to say nothing of all those steps we would need to climb to get up there in the first place.

Marina Grande, Capri

would need to climb to get up there in the first place.

No sooner have we landed than we are accosted by a short, fat man who looks as if he has been blown up by a bicycle pump. At first glance, he appears to have a leech fastened to his upper lip, but on closer inspection, it turns out merely to be a particularly thick and dark moustache – all the more incongruous since his thatch is as grey as mine.

"Taxi?"

"No thanks."

"I take you all round the island," he persists, showing me a map and stabbing at it with a stubby forefinger. "Capri, Anacapri, Grotta Azzurra, La Certosa, Villa San Michele –"

"What about the Villa Jovis?" I cut in.

"No, not possible. No roads."

"No thank you. It's the Villa Jovis we want to go to."

"For you special price. Only €100." He appears not to have heard me.

What! He must be joking! Why, the Amalfi trip had only cost €45 and I had thought that over-priced considering the amount of time we had spent subsidising the drivers' lunch. It does indeed sound like a special price to me, and for me, since I apparently look like the sort of idiot who might agree to it.

"No, thank you," and I push on past him. It's the only way to deal with persistent touts.

The queue for the funicular must the slowest-moving queue in Italy, but there is an information kiosk with hundreds of leaflets which we can read as we wait. In the fullness of time, we are deposited in the Piazza Umberto I, otherwise known as "La Piazzetta". What space not occupied by the cafés is heaving with humanity – a kaleidoscope of colour presided over by the church of Santo Stefano whose white, buttressed walls regard the scene dispassionately through porthole windows, just as they have done since the 17th century. Up above, on the roof, are a series of quaint dormer windows which I've never seen in a church before and which, I must say, lend it a certain charm.

The Piazzetta is just too thronging with people, too hectic, too manic. We want to flee from it as soon as possible and regain the peace and sanity of more tranquil surroundings. But how? There are no signs to be seen to anywhere, never mind the Villa Jovis. Nor are there any directions in the leaflets we had picked up. Fortunately, that interminable queue for the funicular was not all wasted time as I'd overheard the man in front explaining to someone that to get to the Villa Jovis, all you have to do is turn left out of La Piazzetta and follow the signs and that is exactly what we do. And there it is – a sign, the writing on the wall, so to speak. It's an attractive affair made of ceramic tiles with a yellow, green, and blue border and in the middle, *Villa Jovis,* with an arrow pointing the way.

The taxi tout had said there were no roads, but his words were more economical with the truth than his prices, for this road we are on now, the Via Le Botteghe, is a paved road – though rather narrow – and coming downhill towards us at little more than a walking pace is a hybrid between a golf buggy and a pope-mobile.

Presumably this is Capri's answer to transport for the aged and infirm, for as it glides past on silent, pneumatic wheels, I notice the occupants have hair whiter than mine and wrinkles deeper than mine. It looks as if it would be more at home on a fairway than a road, but this is a road that's perfectly capable of taking a taxi. Why is it the taxi drivers hereabouts take you to where *they* want to go and not where *you* do?

After that silent vehicle has passed, it leaves the road and the Isle of Capri to us, apparently. Well, us and the cicadas who are thrumming so loudly that the very air seems to vibrate. It is hot now and it's hot work too, even if the road is easy and the gradient slight, so that when we come to a parting of the ways – up to the left for the Villa Jovis on the Via Tiberio, past the church of San Michele alla Croce, or straight on along the Via Matermania to the grotto of that name and the natural arch, or Arco Naturale. We decide to stop at a strategically-placed café with a delightful terrace (and even better view), to have some refreshment and ponder the dilemma of which route to take.

I order a *birra grande* while, amazingly, Iona orders an iced tea. You can't get more English than that, when abroad. It's incredible, because along with bananas, Iona can't stand the taste, sight or smell of tea. I look at her as if she had gone quite mad, taken tea-leave of her senses, so to speak, but she insists that is what she wants. I detect the hand of Bill and Pat here. They are addicted to the stuff. They are English, after all.

And so we pass a delightful time just relaxing and admiring the view, and it comes to pass that I need to pass that which I had imbibed. As everyone knows, beer goes straight through you, which is why it is a food of the least-fattening kind.

But where is the toilet? I see no sign of it or a sign to it either. There's nothing else for it: I'll just have to ask at the bar and like the poor down-and-out in Edwin Morgan's poem, announce to him

A rare photo of Iona drinking tea

and anyone near enough to hear, my need.

I am given a key and told that after the terrace, I should turn left, go down the hill, turn left again and I'll see what I seek ahead of me. I thank him and thank God I'm not so desperate that I'm dancing, and set off on my trek.

I arrive at my goal and find, to my dismay, that no matter how hard I pull the chain, it stubbornly refuses to flush. It's one of those old-fashioned types with an iron cistern above the throne. It's as old as the ark – except in Noah's case, he had water (and plenty of it). As for me, the best I can get out of this contraption is a promising gurgle, but which regurgitates any water it was about to disgorge again. I've heard of anal-retentive humans, but a water-retentive toilet is something else. It's probably something to do with the drought, but I have a sneaky feeling that it's the gods having a laugh again.

I give up and lock the door again, thanking God that the purpose of my visit was the same number as the one where we had queued originally to catch the ferry, not the one we had actually left from. I'm sorry for the poor person who has to go in after me and – if it happens to be the barman, and he remembers me as the lazy lout and boor with the red face who couldn't be bothered to flush the toilet – it won't matter, as I won't ever be back there again.

Or so I thought. Not until we had toiled up the hill some distance, did Iona think to ask: "Where are your sun-specs?"

It is too much to hope I had left them on the table where we had been sitting. I can see, even before I get there, that our table has not yet been cleared, that the empty bottles and glasses are just as we had left them. Perhaps they had fallen onto the floor? No. I'll just have to ask for the key to the toilet again.

Ah, what a relief! There they are on the toilet-roll dispenser. May as well try to flush again, since I'm here. Perhaps the cistern has had time to fill up again by now. Alas not. The result is as before.

And then I think – what if I have broken it? Gadgets and me just don't get on. I abandon hope, lock the door, return the key to the barman. Even if I am *in extremis* on the way back, I will not ask for that key again.

I'd far rather go in the bushes.

48

The Villa Jovis

IT'S a very pleasant walk up a gentle slope bordered on both sides with pastel-coloured villas and the ubiquitous bougainvillea be-tumbling the whitewashed walls. Here is what must have been, at one time, the last word in elegance and grandeur – a massive villa in huge grounds. Through the bars of locked iron gates, we can see a path bordered by a colonnade of Corinthian pillars leading up to the entrance. But now it has an abandoned air, a look of neglect; the peeling shutters, faded by the sun, seeming to hang dejectedly on the dirty, white-washed walls, as if time had stopped still and Nature had allowed the process of decay to continue unhindered. Miss Havisham might have lived in such a house as this, or perhaps it belonged to one of the literati such as Norman Douglas or Graham Greene or Compton Mackenzie who all had houses here – and this, their paradise on earth, has been allowed to fall into ruin ever since they moved onwards and upwards to that other paradise in the sky.

It's onwards and upwards for us too, especially the latter now we have left the villas behind and the road becomes more of a path (so the taxi driver was not wholly wrong) and begins to climb, ever more steeply, through the pine trees. We can see our destination ahead, can begin to make out some grey stones and walls but most prominently, a massive black statue silhouetted against the cloudless blue of the sky.

"Look, they've erected a statue to the old lecher," I point out to Iona.

It provides a focus, a reference point, as we puff and sweat our way ever nearer in the baking, relentless sun. We are seduced however, by a park on our right, the Parco Asta-rita which affords shade and spectacular views of the main-land across the water on which speedboats are carving their wakes. To our right is the Torre del Faro, or Lighthouse; a red-brick tower, or what remains of it. It was used to send messages to the mainland, apparently. You might have thought it was something to do with shipping, but that's not what our leaflet tells us and it should know.

At our feet is the Salto di Tiberio. So this is it; this is where the poor victims were thrown to their deaths, so it is said. I have no head for heights and don't even want to take the leap of the imagination of what it must have been like to have been hurled into the abyss 900 feet below. I don't sup-

View of the mainland from the Parco Astarita

pose the victims got any comfort from, or counted their blessings, the fact that Tiberius had his villa on this side of the island rather than the other, where the cliffs are a thousand feet higher. Well, actually, according to Tacitus, he had twelve villas on the island and this was merely the largest. It's a bit hard to believe, frankly, the need for so many villas on such a small island.

Over to our left, towards the Villa Jovis, a black-and-white goat is standing on a rock on the practically perpendicular cliff face. It gives us a haughty sort of look over its shoulder and casually disappears over the crest, as if it were doing something as simple as stepping off a pavement instead of making a manoeuvre where one false step would have sent it spinning down the sheer wall of the cliff into the abyss.

This must be one of the indigenous wild goats which gave Capri its name – from the Latin *capre*. Or perhaps not. Some say it is from the Greek *kapros* which means "boar", while others say that is from the Etruscan *capr* which means "rocky". I don't suppose it really matters. The boars have long since gone, as well as the tigers and elephants which once roamed here after the island broke away from the mainland during the Quaternary period – so we are told. I do know, however, that one of my cars, a Ford, was named after it; a poor man's E-Type Jaguar. I thought it the last word in styling but, if you pronounce the island the same way as the car, then you are in deep trouble with the natives as the stress should be on the first syllable, not the last.

Although there is a flight of steps straight ahead leading up to the ruins, we are directed by both an arrow and the curator of the site, to take a path round to the left. Unfortunately there are no leaflets or booklets, no guided tour, so we are on our own, apart from the book which we had bought in Pompeii and which shows the ruins as they are now, including a full-colour artist's impression so we can see what the villa would have looked in its heyday. There are, however, boards with diagrams of the floor plans, colour-coded to show you where you are.

At the moment, we are in the servants' quarters and remarkably well-preserved they are too. They may not look too much from the outside, but it's possible to go into them through a high-vaulted passage. It must be thirty feet high or more and three times as long, with arch upon arch, so the effect is rather like walking down the side-aisle of a cathedral.

Down here too are the cisterns in the centre of the complex, a great square block of them, massive arched vaults which must have contained thousands of gallons each, and – according to the diagram – there were sixteen of them. But then, of course, there would have been quite a number of people living here when you think of how many slaves it takes to look after an emperor. Then there was the water they used for ornamental purposes such as fountains and leisure objectives, the baths and the swimming pool.

If you can trust Suetonius, the Roman historian (and some say you can't), Tiberius had a novel use for the swimming pool. He invented a game where he used to swim about naked, the big fish in the pond, while small boys, who were the little fishes, had to swim underneath him and nibble his unmentionables. No good saying you didn't feel like a swim today or you weren't feeling very peckish, or otherwise you would be thrown from those high cliffs and turned into food for the fish yourself.

Up a flight of broad stairs, we come to the imperial quarters and face-to-face with that monumental statue we had seen from below. But it's not Tiberius. I suppose you don't go around making monuments to your less illustrious citizens. You leave that to Nature, like the image of Mussolini in the Grotta dello Smeraldo near Conca dei Marini, or the one of the same man in a hillside somewhere in Tuscany. Well, the others saw it, but I didn't – which just goes to show you I don't have much of an imagination.

No, it's not Tiberius but someone else. They have built a church here, the Santa Maria del Soccorso, where the imperial quarters used to be, and the statue is none other than the Virgin holding her Infant in precisely the same pose as the natural sculpting we had seen on the Amalfi trip. Not much visual difference between her and Tiberius, really. Anybody could make a mistake like that.

From here, the summit of Monte Tiberio, we are given the most splendid view over the entire island, unless it is surpassed by that from the summit of Monte Solaro at the other end of the island. It is the higher peak, the summit of which can be reached by cable car so you don't have to bust a gut getting up there. We can see it soaring into the sky, whilst the verdant pinched waist of the island is flecked with the white houses of Capri and Anacapri like sheep put out to graze and who have taken the opportunity to scatter themselves widely in search of the sweetest grass.

Turning to the north, there is an unimpeded view of the Cap di Sorrento (of which this island is the offspring), and to the east, the humps of Li Galli islands, home to the Sirens which we had also seen at closer quarters on our Amalfi trip. And if you have

View across Capri from the summit of Monte Tiberio to Monte Solaro

Ruins of Villa Jovis

the nerve, if you look down, straight down, holding onto the charming, but insubstantial-looking rustic fence, you can behold the bottom of the sea as the water is so crystal clear. Which of course reminds you there is a lot further to fall after you have hit the water.

Here at our feet, however, it takes a bit of imagination to work out what the rest of the ruins represent. From where we are standing in the imperial quarters, we can overlook the whole complex – a maze of crumbling walls of varying heights – but with the help of our handy book, we can see that furthest from us are the baths, consisting of five rooms. The cisterns, as we know, are in the centre, and the servants' quarters to the west. The one thing it is easy to recognise, to the east, are the semi-circular remains of the *exedra,* the place where people met to sit and have a chat. All very civilised. What remains, therefore, must be the public rooms, apart from the loggia, which would have been behind where I'm standing. Like the elephants and tigers, not forgetting the wild boars, they have long since disappeared.

There were 300 rooms here, give or take a few, covering an area of 7,000 square metres – more, probably than less, if you can imagine that. I can't, as I have no head for figures, never mind heights, but I *can* imagine the erotic statues and paintings that Suetonius tells us swamped this place. That's not because I have a dirty mind (if that's what you are thinking) but because I remember seeing the very same thing in Pompeii. I'm not sure if the artwork was meant to inspire Tiberius himself or the threesomes whom he commanded to perform in front of him, but you can bet your bottom dollar that if they didn't put on a good show, get him so hot that he felt an urgent need to cool off in the pool, they'd be going for the Big Swim themselves.

No doubt that's why, in the interests of fair play, they were provided with sexual manuals which were written by Elephantis, the pseudonym of a Greek lady (*lady*, please note) who lived at the end of the 1st Century BC, in order to provide them with some fresh ideas on how to use their big parts for the small part they were expected to play in the emperor's titillation.

Alas, none of her manuals survive. Which, says Iona, is a very good thing indeed. No matter. My Latin definitely would not be up to it, nor my ancient Greek for that matter.

There might, of course, have been illustrations.

49

Goodbye to Capri

WE wander about the ruins a bit, then take the steps by the *exedra* to the exit. At the junction where we stopped for the tea and beer, we turn left this time and head for the Arco Naturale, yet another very pleasant walk past villas and bountiful gardens. Descending some steps, we come to the Arco. It is certainly very impressive, curving high above us as we catch our first sight of it as we stand amongst pine trees with apparent suicidal tendencies, as they cling with what looks like a desperate toehold to the thin soil. Far down below, framed in the arch, the hillside opposite is clothed with a carpet of more sensible trees who see that gentler sloping hillside as a much safer des res. But what catches the eye most of all, is the small patch of brilliant turquoise water.

Walking down some steps, we are afforded another perspective of the arch, which – in some ways – is more intriguing than the arch itself, for one of the columns has been eroded right through in three places, creating three tiers of windows, which surely must signal the demise of the arch eventually, as it succumbs to *its* arch-enemy, the weather, combined with its arch-ally, time. Indeed, we can see that

Arco Naturale, Capri

some remedial action has already had to be taken with the support of some metal brackets. Ugly and functional, and like a patient on a life-support machine, putting off the inevitable moment.

At its great age, the arch does deserve a bit of support and I'd like to think I'd get as much in the years of my decline, though, unlike the arch, you may not strive officiously to keep me alive. But then the arch is not just old, but an endangered species. Incredible to think that it is all that remains of a grotto that was once carved out by the sea and that it, and the island, was lifted up in the Palaeolithic era – at the mercy now, no longer of the waves, but the wind and rain instead.

I wouldn't say it was going to rain exactly, but the sky has clouded over as we retrace our steps to Capri and make a beeline for the funicular and the ferry. We're hoping to catch the 4 pm. Amazing to think that by then we will have spent five hours on this idyllic island! And talking of beelines, here's the biggest bee I have ever seen in my life, even bigger than the one at the hotel, sounding like a droning bomber as it comes in to rest on a passion flower. Italians are reputed to be big on passion, and it seems it applies to the bees here too.

Seeing an alternative route round the back of the villas, we decide to take it. If the way up was the garden route, then this, the way down, is the fruit route. Plum tomatoes of various shades of ripeness are bending the vines whilst those other vines, my favourite sort, are merely bringing forth their buds *to set budding more* as Keats would put it, because it is not yet their time to reach maturity.

There are some attractive houses too, like this one with Delft tiles on either side of the gates. There's no getting away from the Dutch, it seems, and it appears as if this is where this Dutch family comes to get away from their fellow citizens. (Some hope!) Or maybe they just like the tiles. A splash of colour is provided by terracotta pots fixed to the whitewashed wall. The next villa has huge pots filled with scarlet geraniums forming a guard of honour up the steps to the front door. The first may or may not be owned by Dutch people, but one thing is for sure: all the villas on this street must be owned by people with pots of money, for if the splendour of the buildings wasn't enough alone to tell you, the security cameras advertise the fact there is something worth stealing inside.

But this house is different. It's a deep-plum colour which seems rather loud and vulgar when compared to all the pastel shades and brilliant whites. Not only that, but it looks square and severe, as if a couple of cardboard boxes had been placed at right angles to each other. There is a plaque on the wall, in Italian, but I can read it quite easily. It tells us that in this house, the famous Russian writer, Maksin Gorkij, lived and worked from March 1909 to February 1911 and where – in 1910 – he was joined by "Vladimir Lenin, the founder of the Soviet state". Here, we are told, they were visited by many eminent representatives of "world culture".

Now that's very interesting indeed. Interesting that I, who have next to no Italian, can understand this without difficulty; interesting that the Italian for "Vladimir Lenin" is just that, but that "Maxim" is different but still recognisable; interesting that they were visited by all these "cultural visitors" which must be the Italian for "revolutionaries". You can just imagine Lenin and Co. fomenting revolution in this ugly house on this beautiful island – perhaps where they got their design idea for those soulless housing blocks throughout the length and breadth of what was to become the Soviet Union and its satellites.

Back through the teeming La Piazzetta again. I would have liked to have visited the church since it looks so interesting from the outside, in particular to see what the roof looks like from the inside, but primarily because the floor is supposedly laid with marble from the Villa Jovis. Who knows – if not in his sandals exactly, I could tread the same floor as Tiberius once did, which is not to say I would follow in his footsteps. But there's a problem. Although we have plenty of time before the ferry, we have two queues to face – firstly the funicular, and if the size of that is anything to go by, the one for the ferry will be even worse, having deposited God knows how many passengers from that already.

And so it proves. It takes an age just to get down to the Marina Grande as two loads descend before us and, as I join the queue for the ferry, I can already see it approaching as big as that bee I saw earlier. By the time I have moved forward five feet, it is as big as a humming bird, and another five feet later, it is a raven and that is what I am, raving mad at the man at the head of the queue.

I am near the head of it, but not *that* near, so close yet so far, and speed is of the essence if we are to catch this ferry. But this moron at the head of the queue seems utterly relaxed, quite unaware of the need for any urgency and, by the lengthy conversation he's having with the ticket vendor, he appears to be negotiating to buy not just tickets, but the whole bloody boat.

344

"Come on, come on, COME ON!" If hostile looks were daggers, this man would be a very dead porcupine indeed, but they are not even pins and powerless to prick him on to greater efforts to get out of the way so we can all get on and go.

At last it is over, and he comes away with a string of tickets as long as my patience is short. We shuffle forward, but when I am five feet from the front of the queue, I can see I am defeated. The ferry, which arrived only a matter of minutes ago, is already making preparations for departure and it dawns on me, *mea culpa*, that had I bought return tickets like the Dutchmen, I would already have been on board. Typical! The gods win again.

If we wait for the next ferry, apart from the slight problem of how we will spend the time, we will not get back to the hotel until 8 pm at the earliest and that, says Iona flatly, is far too long to wait for food. I'm damned if I'm going to let the gods have another joke at my expense by spending money on a meal here at inflated prices when I have already paid for a perfectly good one back at the hotel – even I am not allowed to sit at the table of my choice.

That's why I am now in the queue for the hydrofoil. There's one leaving in twenty minutes and another one fifteen minutes after that, if we don't catch this. Somehow I don't think we will. Apart from the hordes of people ahead of us, it leaves from pier ten – which is just about as far away from the ferry terminal as it's possible to be. Threading our way through the throng is like a salmon swimming upstream.

But perhaps my luck is beginning to change. Whilst I am in the queue, buying the tickets, Iona's eagle eyes spot a euro lying on the ground. It offsets the additional expense of the hydrofoil – not by much, it has to be said, but perhaps it's some sort of compensation from the gods for mucking us about so much.

And indeed my luck does seem to have changed because, against all the odds, we do manage to get on board. It seems to be packed to the gunnels. We don't even bother looking for a seat on the lower deck and head upstairs where I spy, at the pointy end, a couple of seats. We make a beeline for them, pushing our way through the crowd as politely as we can before someone grabs them. It crosses my mind to wonder why other people haven't already. Seems strange so many would prefer to remain standing for the voyage, short though it may be.

If making our way to them wasn't very easy, then it was nothing compared to occupying the actual seats themselves, for we have to clamber our way over the feet and legs of the passengers on the seats facing them. They are hardly making it easy for us by drawing their legs in to make room. In fact, you could say, they are deliberately obstructing us by keeping them stretched out. Not only that, but there is a bag occupying the seat to the right of the male passenger which someone's bum might have warmed.

Charming, I must say.

50

A Close Encounter of the Horrid Kind

I F there is a saying "love at first sight", and there is, there must be a corresponding dictum, a counterbalance, a *ying* to the *yang*, and this is it. One half of the pair of obstructive passengers across from us is a gorgeous girl – she can't be more than twenty-five, raven haired and sultry, brown-eyed and tanned, with a voluptuous figure which her clothes accentuate and in such a revealing manner that it seems rude to stare, but ruder still not to look, since she has gone to such trouble to put her wares on display for our delectation. Naturally, that is the one I fall in love with, instantly, though if I were so stupid to admit as much to *La Belle Dame Sans Merci*, she would just say it was the Tiberius effect and it was just pure lust. As usual, she would be right.

Her partner, to her right, is the yang, the one I take an instant dislike to. It's not because of the way he obstinately persists in keeping his feet and legs in our personal space, obliging us to squeeze our feet, uncomfortably, into the smallest of spaces; it's not because I'm jealous, that someone of his age (he must be twice hers at least), can attract someone as delectable as she; it's not even that he's fat and ugly, and he certainly is. Think Shrek without the charm and the green, and that's him.

And even if he had not shaved his head down to the wood so only vestigial grey stubble around the edges remains, he would still never be an oil-painting – not with that beak and those blubbery lips (how horrendous to kiss!) which, at present, are curled into a sneer which tells me there's either a horrible smell in his vicinity, or he doesn't much like the look of us. I don't have much sense of smell, it's true, but I'm rather inclined to think it's the latter. I can't tell from his eyes just how much he hates us as they are concealed behind dark glasses, but I'm guessing it's quite a lot.

But there's more than his face I don't like about him, though God knows that's enough. He has a thick, gold necklace round a neck as thick as Chaucer's miller and an ostentatious gold watch with a broad gold strap which he uses, not to tell the time, but to proclaim how rich he is – not to mention his lack of taste. On his right wrist he is wearing a glittering gold bracelet, though I would call it a bangle, because – wait till you hear this – he is wearing a pink shirt, white socks, red shoes and, incredibly, red nail varnish to match!

I can't help but notice the latter as his left arm is draped over the young lady's shoulders, allowing his fingertips to rest on the swell of her left breast, whilst his right is resting, less interestingly, on the shoulder bag occupying the seat beside him. And that's another reason why I hate him already – that he allows it to take up the space that someone's bum might occupy – if they could bear the thought of sitting next to someone as repulsive as him, that is.

I suspect, if he's not a member of the Mafia, he is a film director, given how so many of them live hereabouts – and he's presumably casting his eye (the couch being too heavy for him to carry) over this wannabe starlet. Surely it has to be the only reason why anybody like her would go anywhere near *him*, though God knows, she must want to be in the movies very badly indeed. Personally speaking, I'd rather die first, for if there could be anything worse than him in his red-and-pink outfit, it's him in his birthday suit. I try not to imagine it, but it gives me the willies and I can't repress a shudder at the thought.

Suddenly it speaks. Gruffly. "It's broke."

Eh? Was he speaking to me? Can he read my mind? But his gaze seems to be directed at a point somewhere over my head. Because of the limited space, I am already sitting practically side-on, so it's easy to look over my shoulder to see who is being addressed. It appears to be a tall, thin man in a battered hat. He is standing at the top of the stairs amongst scores of others who have not been able to find a seat, which makes Red Fingernails' behaviour all the more reprehensible. The man with the hat is pointing to the seat occupied by the bag, indicating he would like to sit on it.

"It's broke," reiterates Red Fingernails, even more gruffly than before.

This is going to be interesting. Either the tall, thin man is deaf or too stupid to read the signs he's not wanted, or incredibly brave, because he's coming over, squeezing his way through the throng.

Now he is standing at the end of the row of seats, looking over, or overlooking the forest of legs and feet which stand between him and his goal. Red Fingernails lifts the bag up a fraction and for a fraction of a second, and plonks it back on the seat. From my perspective, it was just long enough and high enough for me to see a big crack running the full width of the seat.

"It's broke." Red Fingernails reiterates for a third time, snarling now, his ugly lips curling in a sneer of such open hostility that I can see a row of yellow teeth. The last time I saw anything like them was on a horse.

"It doesn't matter," says the newcomer, without hostility, with infinite patience and with perseverance. I have to hand it to the man. If it had been me, I would have turned and fled (if there had been enough room), possibly even thanked him for saving me the discomfort of sitting in such a seat, perhaps even said I was relieved really not to sit down as I had been on my feet for the best part of five hours and I was quite getting to like the feeling. But then I'm a wimp who can't even tell a trio of teenage girls to turn down their "music".

With as much show of reluctance that even a blind man couldn't fail to notice, Red Fingernails makes a big production of moving his bag, but not his legs, so the newcomer can sit down. Somehow, he manages to make it across the obstacles, more difficult now that Iona and I are here, though we try to ease his passage as much as possible. Incredibly, as soon as he sits down, he strikes up a conversation – not with me, who is opposite him, but with Red Fingernails, to his right.

"Do you speak English?"

"Sometimes," snarls Red Fingernails.

"I don't speaks so well. Speaks Spanish."

"Good. Just shut up then."

In spite of all I have seen, this downright rudeness and nastiness is staggering. Iona and I look at each other in disbelief. Too much of a wimp naturally, to intervene – perhaps to cover up my own embarrassment, but more, I think, as a sort of need to express my horror at this latest outrage – I open my pouch and finding a receipt, write: *What a boor!* I pass it over to Iona who looks at it and passes it back without registering any emotion.

It is my little act of courage. What would I have done if Red Fingernails had snatched it out of my hand and read it? Someone as boorish as him, who had just said what he had, might easily have done such a thing, suspecting the note was about him. It was my calculation that he would not and there-in lies my bravery, or my folly, but also my protest. Because I am not so much of a culture-vulture as Iona, because I can't stand opera and ballet, she tends to regard me as a bit of a boor. This is me stating: *If you want to know what a real boor is like – look at him!*

And what of the newcomer? Is he really, really brave, or really, really foolish? Incredibly, he has ignored this crush-ing put-down as if he has not heard it. He certainly acts as if he hasn't, and immediately launches into introducing himself by explaining that he comes from Argentina. Predictably, his would-be interlocutor receives this information with supreme and undisguised indifference. At least it is an improvement on his previous remark.

Looking at the Argentinian more closely, I can see his ancient and battered hat has a safety-pin attached to the brim from which a thread leads to an anchoring button on his shirt. Now there's an idea! I remember how I had had to park my Panama under my oxter on the way over. If only I had thought of this ingenious device, I could have worn it with impunity, secure in the knowledge that it could not fly any further than the length of the thread. Obviously a man of invention, even of genius, to have thought, in advance, that the crossing would be windy and he had devised this functional – but not exactly fashionable – device, to preserve the longevity of his lid.

Yes, I think this explains everything. The Argentinian is not stupid. Quite the reverse: he is an angel rushing in where fools fear to tread. I *have* got that the right way round, by the way. He's not brave: he's merely too friendly by nature to spot the hostility which washes off him like the water off the proverbial duck's back. It's never occurred to him that other people can be hostile, rude and arrogant. That's why, when he meets it face to face, he can't recognise it. That is why he is an angel. Never in his philosophy, did he dream such hostility was possible.

I'm embarrassed and ashamed to be part of this scenario. It's as if I were a spectator at the Colosseum watching Christians being devoured by lions, though as I happen to know, that is not the most apposite of images. Very often, the starved lions knew not what to do with this new source of protein. Confused and frightened by the noise of the crowd baying for blood, not knowing what was expected of them, they just lay down and did nothing, the big pussycats.

Having exhausted his conversation, or perhaps a scintilla of suspicion having permeated his cranium that Red Fingernails is not remotely interested, to my great relief, like the Christians in the Colosseum, the Argentinian falls silent and does nothing to bring attention to himself. Whilst he had been speaking, I was on tenterhooks that Red Fingernails would say something so blunt and shocking that even he could not fail to notice it and I'd be so offended on his behalf I'd say something to defend him before I could stop myself.

I could visualise my blood splattered all over his oh, so carefully-coloured fingernails, after he had bopped me on the nose.

51

A Chapter of Coincidences

O UR fellow passengers are lost in the mêlée. I hope I never see that pink pig ever again.

Something's wrong – there are lots of buses waiting to receive the disembarking passengers. Isn't that a remarkable thing! Iona knows where to go and which bus to get. When travelling in Italy by bus, it's always safest to have your wife with you. And it's well worth the euro to avoid that climb up to the town centre.

Oh no! I don't believe it! I have the window seat and I can see Red Fingernails and Raven Hair approaching. They are clearly looking for their bus. My heart turns over. Please, God, please don't let it be this one. Even if we don't have to sit anywhere near each other, it would offend me to be in the same one as him, breathing the same air.

But it's all right; they've walked past, heading for a different bus, evidently – just the gods getting their money's worth for that euro they let us find. Now that's a cheering thought – one of us is travelling for free! But here's another thought. Why, if he's a movie director, is he looking for a bus – why isn't he whisking Raven Hair away in his Bentley or at least taking a taxi? And why didn't he take the would-be starlet to Capri in his private yacht, since he's so rich – and if he's not, then how the hell did he get off with her? He doesn't deserve her, doing it on the cheap like that. Cheapskate. That's another thing I hate him for.

Well I hope that is the last I have seen of him, though I wouldn't mind bumping into *her* again, literally. I don't suppose it would be much of a treat for her, but I'm still a lot better-looking than *him*, even if I say so myself. It would be hard not to be.

Since we're in town, we head towards the supermarket to get some supplies to take home. That's the blessing of being in the EU as opposed to countries outside it – you are free to carry as much cheap booze home with you as your wife will let you. I have a method to keep the weight of transportation down and which I gladly pass on here for your benefit, dear reader. I decant my purchases into a plastic bottle that once contained a fizzy drink because it is stronger than an ordinary bottle – proof against those beefy baggage handlers who fling your bag about as if it were as light as a thirty-piece china dinner service, though it started off as a six-piece.

To that end, as well as the booze, I buy some more *tonica* (which I need for the gin anyway) while Iona buys a bottle of sparkling water. Thus laden with our purchases, we make our way back to the phallic factory chimney, that outstanding monument which tells us we are nearing the place where we catch the complimentary bus to the hotel.

I can't believe it! If you put it in a novel, your readers wouldn't, but I swear this is true. Life sometimes *is* stranger than fiction. After that close encounter of the most horrid kind (by which I mean the one with Red Fingernails after we had disembarked), whom should we meet coming towards us, as we approach the bus stop, but the Argentinian, accompanied by a lady whom I take to be his wife.

My instinctive reaction is to stop him, commiserate with him, indulge in a hearty character assassination of Red Fingernails and thus exonerate myself from any tacit – and hence complicit – involvement in his humiliation. But I don't. For a start, he appears to be in a hurry. Secondly, he appears to have his entire luggage with him and thirdly, and not least, he doesn't seem to have the vaguest recognition of ever having seen me before. Not so long ago, he had spent twenty minutes only a couple of feet across from me, our feet actually touching, and already he has forgotten me. Had I been in the company of someone who had seen *me* ritually humiliated, I think I would have remembered them – and the shame.

I say hello as he approaches, to which he mumbles something and hurries on regardless. My guess is he's got a train to catch – very soon. But why had he not taken a taxi? You wouldn't normally choose to haul your luggage all the way to the station, would you? Well, most people wouldn't, but our friend is not like most other people. He must have left his Missus behind to do the packing whilst he cavorted around Capri. That, at least, is typical male behaviour in some circles (but not the ones in which I normally revolve, naturally). And here's another thing: his dear wife must have been having kittens wondering if he was going to make it back in time. It's just as well she couldn't see how close he was to missing the hydrofoil. We were amongst the very last to board and in all likelihood he came after us, otherwise he would have found more agreeable companions to sit beside – and I don't mean Iona and me.

There's something else. There are no hotels at this end of town and, since he was coming from the direction of ours, it can only mean one thing – he must have been staying there too. But how could he possibly have had time to go there and get back to town again, especially hauling all that luggage? It's just not possible. I hate mysteries like that.

Our bus is waiting, but there is still some time before it is due to leave. This is where, the day I went on the Great Bus Tour, I'd been observed by the man on the balcony and where I'd heard the sound of smashing china. I linger outside in the sunshine, despite it being rather hazy, so unlike the searing heat to which we have been accustomed for almost a fortnight now. Iona takes our purchases and the weight off her feet to find a seat on the bus.

The man is not there today and I've only been loitering a few minutes when I hear the most awful stramash. It's coming from the block of flats across the street, indeed the same flat as before, and it's the same woman screeching at the top of her voice – only this time the object of her wrath seems to be some children who are screaming back at her. Then, like before, comes the sound of breaking china, followed by a fresh volley of invective from the woman. And just like the last time, there is no sign of any of the players in this domestic drama.

Oh, to be able to speak Italian – but I reflect, I doubt if I could speak it well enough to make out what was being shouted through the rage from that range. Besides, I doubt if my classes would have taught the sort of language they are using. I wonder how often this woman has to go to the crockery department of the supermarket. You would have thought that she might have cottoned on to plastic plates by now when she is dishing out the invective. Or perhaps she doesn't think they sound so satisfying when she throws them at her family.

* * *

I have decided I'll go to the pool – after I've washed the grime off my feet. If I hurry, I might have time for a quick swim before it closes. Iona decides she'll just stay and do some sewing whilst listening to the *Sound of Silence*, as Simon and Garfunkel might have put it, since there is nothing blasting its way into our private space from next door.

I take the long way round, through the gardens, for no other reason than I fancy a change. It's a mistake. It would be. I'm no good at making decisions, as I told you before. Down to the right, amongst the trees, I can see my Dutch family – well, the female contingent of it anyway. In accordance with my decision of last night, I pretend not to see them. Better that than continue our nodding acquaintance with a few polite words ending in an embarrassed silence. I know they will speak almost perfect English: all the Dutch do.

There are plenty of loungers as most people have gone in for their *apéritifs*, but I have brought a nice cold beer down with me and my Panama, to hide it from the gaze of the pool police who are on patrol, straightening the sunbeds so they are in perfect alignment. I pop the can under it now whilst I do a quick couple of lengths. I get out and go walkabout to dry off – although it has to be said, there's not a great deal of heat in the sun, as it has disappeared behind a skein of cloud.

Would you credit it? Here, coming towards me, is Mrs Scanty-Panties with a friend. She is wearing a top, unlike her friend. I expect she thought it wasn't worth spending the money for the little she's got to cover up. Those beer-swigging

Dutch boys had more than she has, and they would scarcely have filled a trainer bra.

As for Mrs Scanty-Panties, I'm not seeing a great deal more that I haven't already seen – she's merely taken off her outer, diaphanous layer, like a veil. And, I think, that's what I'll do when I go back to the apartment – draw a veil over my meeting with her. No point in stirring up a hornet's nest.

It's amusing to think that whilst I have seen Mrs Scanty-Panties several times, she hasn't the foggiest idea that I exist, nor that my wife hates her with a passion or like poison. Of course, since I have normally been exposed to a full rectal, or whatever the opposite of a full frontal is, she's not likely to recognise me; not unless she has eyes above those other cheeks of hers. And even if she did, she wouldn't have recognised me anyway. I am the invisible man. No one notices me.

It's a strange feeling, walking about, recognising people who don't know me, like a ghost wandering about among the living.

52

Some Fanciful Notions

I T'S not the most absorbing of scenes, pool-watching, since there are very few people about now to attract my interest. So when I finish my beer, I decide I may as well go up to the room. Besides, the strength from this sun, having to penetrate all this cloud, is not doing much for my tan. The cloud cover has not been a passing phase, but has been thickening ever since I came down here. It looks as if the weather may be beginning to change, and I'd better change out of my wet clothes before I get the dreaded nappy rash.

It's not sunny on the balcony but it is still warm, warmer than at the pool, no doubt due to the residual heat trapped in the concrete and warm enough to enjoy a nice, cold beer again as an *apéritif* to the gin *apéritifs*. It's when I go outside to enjoy the sneaking of the second gin I am joined by an unwelcome visitor. It's not my gin it's after, but my blood. It's a mosquito, which has landed on my nose of all places. Does it *want* to die, knowing I can't possibly miss it, or has it got a slapstick sense of humour and has calculated it will be able to become airborne before the blow lands and I'll punch myself on the nose? Probably it's been sent by Red Fingernails since he couldn't punch me himself without the risk of me charging him with assault. It's certainly a curious coincidence, since we've not been bothered by these pests before. I tell it to buzz off and it agrees to go quietly, leaving me with the feeing it's a bad omen of some sort.

Before we go in to dinner, we go out on to the terrace where the people who are not averse to paying the bar prices are at least rewarded with a magnificent view in return. We don't normally do this, but something draws me out there this evening, just to see. Yes, there is something intangible in the atmosphere again, just like this morning, and the air seems very still. And Vesuvius, which you can hardly miss, seems bulkier, more menacing somehow; darker, more brooding, less distinct. There is a bit of a breeze and it does seem chillier than other evenings, but perhaps I'm just imagining it, and – thinking no more about it – we head off to the dining room. There is no mistaking the gently-wafting fronds of the potted palm in the foyer, however.

It's another buffet night, so there will be no battle of wills with Signor Corleone and we can sit where we will. And for our delectation, we have an added ingredient. We have some live music, a two-piece band, a guitar and a mando-lin. They have loose, baggy shirts with puffy sleeves and black trousers with a brightly-coloured cummerbund in case their tight trousers fall down. Evidently it's going to be a Neapoli-tan song evening, all twanging tonsils and vibrating strings.

The artistes are on a roving commission, wandering about wherever they like as Signor Corleone is not there to tell them where to go. Quite relaxing really, in an understated sort of way; more of a background ambience, not like that night we had with the tenors last week where they blasted us against the walls with the volume of their voices. Boy, could those boys project! I'd never heard such power in a voice before and at such close range in such a confined space, it really was awesome.

There was a soprano too, and she really was awful. Well, she was to me at least, though I'm sure she was really terribly good. I'm just a boor who can't stand opera, though Puccini has one or two good tunes I must admit. It's the female singers I can't stand; those insufferable sopranos hitting those high notes. They set my teeth on edge. Having said that, it turned out to be a really good night, not so much due to the tenors, but to one of our company who literally reduced me to tears of laughter as she mimicked them.

Like the Musak in the supermarket of which you are unconscious most of the time (but of which you must nevertheless be subliminally aware, when near to closing time, they play faster tunes to encourage you to shop faster), the Neapolitan music is background noise which is easy to ignore. But when they come round to stand in front of our table and sing to us, I find it excruciatingly embarrassing – enough to make me choke on my pasta. I want to tell them *Basta!* which I think sounds like a really good word to say to people when you want them to leave you alone. But you can't here. I must grin and bear it, look as if I am enjoying being serenaded and nodding my head in what is probably, for me, unsyncopated rhythm, until – finally, giving us a little bow – they pass on to the next table and give them the treatment instead.

Altogether, it's a very civilised dining experience. Eat what you want, as much or as little as you like, just as fast or as slowly as you like and – when you come back from topping your plate up – your dirty plate has been magicked away by those conjurors who wait at tables and who have just been waiting to pounce on them when your back is turned.

And there's another difference tonight. On the three sides of the dining room which have empty window frames, on the floor beneath them, the staff have propped glass panels, ready to be fitted into place. Over at the other side of the room, the tablecloths are fluttering, for it is from that side the wind is coming but where we are sitting, we are relatively unaffected. The waiters seem to be having a bit of trouble fitting the panels, for although they all appear to be of a uniform size to fit the gap, they must be infinitesimally bigger or smaller and only the right window will fit into the right frame.

It's a crucial error, this delay; this lack of logic in not labelling the panels to match the empty spaces. It seems to happen all at once, like the commencement of hostilities. There is an enormous peal of thunder, followed immediately by an incandescent flash of lightning so hard on its heels they were practically together. At the same time, the breeze becomes a tornado and powers its way into the room, sweeping a torrent of rain before it.

There are screams from the women closest to the window as they are drenched by the deluge; there is the scraping of chairs on the tiles as they are hurriedly pushed back from the tables and the crash of a wine bottle (empty I hope), which has been blown onto the floor and which, resiliently, does not break, but – propelled by the wind – rolls across the floor. The waiters redouble their efforts with the panels, made harder now as they have to battle against the elements.

Within seconds, the dining room is transformed from a peaceful, calm room into a place of panic and confusion. It becomes a room of two halves, as the football pundits pronounce when analysing a game. We, at our side, are still not affected by the storm, but those at the side of the prevailing wind have abandoned ship and have gone to dine in the inner room, in that vast area where Signor Corleone and crew lie in wait, and although it is set with tables, in all the time we have been eating here, we've never seen anyone sitting over there. And it is thither that the musicians have also gone, for the curious thing is that all the while that this has been going on, the band has played on. Looking at those abandoned tables, the floor glistening with rain, the tablecloths flapping in the wind and the over-toppled chairs, it's impossible not to recall *The Titanic* and how it is said that whilst everyone was rushing for the lifeboats, the musicians continued to play.

And now there is another huge flash of lightning, the lights go out and all is dark. Someone screams and, a few seconds later, the lights flicker on again. Outside, I can hear the rain drumming on the patio beside the swimming pool and, by the sound of it, it's awash – as if you were to venture out there, you would be hard-pressed to tell where patio ends and pool begins.

At long last, the drought which has been plaguing all Italy since May has ended, and it looks as if it is getting three months' rain all at once. I'm glad about that and glad that it had the good sense to come now, in the evening, when all sight-seeing activities are over for the day, and at night, so we can see the celestial pyrotechnics at their best. There they go again! And the lights go out again, only this time for longer than before, so that when the lightning strikes again, it lights up the entire darkness. For a moment the inky sky glows with an eerie light as if Thor, that celestial blacksmith, had produced an incandescent brand from his fire and is about to smite it. And by this unearthly light, we are able to see a curtain of water as it cascades from the roof in front of the empty window frames. The last time I saw anything like that was when I stood behind Niagara Falls, where there are holes in the rock from where you can stand and marvel at the unceasing volume of water cascading before your eyes.

When the lights go on again, I rush off for my camera. If there's one thing Iona and I like, it is a good thunderstorm and I might be able to catch some good photos of it – though sadly the lightning appears to be of the sheet, rather than the forked, variety. Meanwhile, Iona also abandons the dining room. We can always go back for more food later. There's no way of telling how long this heavenly show may last. I arrange to meet her in the bar in the foyer, where we can stand behind the huge plate-glass window which leads out onto the terrace, and although we can't afford the drinks there, it will afford us an expanse of sky and the best place to see the lightning.

Before I reach the lifts, the lights go out again. Great! This promises to be a fantastic storm, perhaps the mother of all storms! What if the next time the lights go off, this time they stay off! How exciting! There we would all be stumbling about in the dark, like a giant game of charades, falling over each other. And what if, when the lights go on again, there's a body? A real murder mystery like some hotels organise for their guests from time to time. What a lark!

If the corpse was Red Fingernails, however, it would have been just too easy for me to solve, for I have had a flash of inspiration as illuminating as the lightning. The Argentinian was only *pretending* to check out. Actually he had sneaked back, done the deed, and then sneaked out again. But how did he know there was going to be a storm strong enough to put the lights out? Hmm! Now that presents a little problem to my deductions, if not a fatal flaw. But if he didn't do it, there must be tons of others who want to kill Red Fingernails, and maybe even more than I do.

Just about everyone in the hotel who ever had the misfortune to come across him I should think.

53

Misreading the Signs

I'M not so daft as I look and take the stairs up to the room to get my camera. I'm not taking the chance of a power cut leaving me stranded in the lift for hours. It's only three floors, and nothing to a man of my calibre who has already climbed the dome of St Peter's and the Duomo of Florence on this trip and – just the Easter before – La Mangia, or bell tower, in Siena. It only takes a matter of moments and I'm back for the display.

You have to hand it to God; He can put on a pretty good performance when He wants to. The fireworks performance I had seen the other night was pretty impressive and colourful, not to say noisy – as Iona can testify – but you can't beat the hand of God. For a start, He does everything on such a grander scale: the sound effects are louder, the thunder much, much more deafening; the flashes of lightning ten thousand times brighter, for a split second lighting up the entire bay. And there are the accompanying effects of the sound and the sight of the rain as it comes down in sheets. As if that were not enough, what God does, in addition, is He cunningly keeps you in suspense, so you're never quite sure when the next flash is going to come, or precisely from which direction, so that when it does come, it takes your breath away with the power and the glory of it, as Graham Greene might have put it – or even the Master of Pyrotechnics Himself, in His Prayer.

On the way back to the restaurant, who should we come across but my old friend the Dutchman with his family! We could hardly not, since they are seated at one of the tables in the foyer and we must pass them. It's impossible therefore, to pretend not to see them, whilst to merely nod and pass on seems a bit rude, leaving them bewildered as to what they could possibly have done to offend me since we have enjoyed such scintillating conversations in the past.

"Hello."

"Hello."

"Some storm isn't it?"

"Yes."

"We were through in the dining room when it started and it was like *The Titanic.*" Since they look puzzled, I elaborate about the rain coming in and the evacuation and the waiters trying to fit the glass in the frames. "And all the time, the band played on," I conclude. It's not surprising they couldn't understand my allusion, as wherever the band is at the moment they are certainly nowhere to be seen now.

"Ah yes," they nod in understanding.

"In fact, the waiters' efforts reminded me of the time when I was a boy, in the Great Storm of 1953 – how my mother held a tray to the window trying to keep the sea out whilst my father was upstairs making some shutters."

"Yes?"

They seem a bit more interested now, so I plunge on. "Yes, we lived right by the edge of the sea," I add somewhat unnecessarily. "The window had been broken by the force of the water. In fact, I was kneeling on the window ledge watching the waves hit the house when the water came in. The glass cut my knee and I was swept backwards into the room. That's when my mother came with the tray."

My audience seem really interested now. "And the waves were so high that the water was coming down the chimney!" I pause to let that sink in, before I administer my *coup de grâce.* "And when my father went out to fit the shutters, a wave dragged him back and if there had not been a telephone pole outside our house, which he managed to wrap his arms around, he would have been swept out to sea and drowned!"

That shakes them. I have spoken nice and slowly so that they can understand me all the better and it appears they have understood me completely.

"Yes, I remember that storm," says my Dutchman. "It was very bad in Holland too. Much of Friesland was under water."

"Yes, I know." I tell him. "I saw a film about it in Middelburg."

"You did?" He sounds rather surprised that I should know about this Dutch film at all, let alone having seen it in that place. But what I think he thinks the most astonishing thing of all (though of course you would have to ask *him*) is the way I give it the Dutch pronunciation, which is relatively easy for us Scots. All you have to do is pretend you've swallowed a fly like the old woman in the nursery rhyme and you're trying to spit it out before invoking the help of the spider. The only difference is that in Dutch, you bring it up from deeper down in your throat and that's what I do. I give it the full works. I hope he didn't think I was going to be suddenly sick over his wife, who was nearest.

"Yes." I explain. "We have Dutch friends who used to live in Zierikzee, and we saw the film at the museum when we went to stay with them. It was terrible – all those people who had to be evacuated," I add, just to let him see I'm not making it up.

"Ah, yes!" he nods. I'm reading his mind again. I imagine he's thinking: *Here's a man of distinction, not very good-looking, but refined. Not much of a big spender, as I can tell from his clothes, but just because he's too poor to buy clothes that no-one else has worn before, that doesn't make him a bad person.*

I have reason to hope I've gone up in his estimation; I'm not just that madman who shouts down to him from the balcony each evening. And I hope at least one of his daughters realises I'm not so stupid as she first thought when she saw me at the baths in Herculaneum apparently expecting to have a swim since I had come prepared, dressed in my swimming trunks. And I hope all of them think I'm definitely not a boor, but a cultured traveller who has been to their country and not just to Amsterdam either, where in the Sixties, just about everyone went for the sex and drug culture.

"And where do your friends live now?"

This is good. We're having a real conversation.

"In Appingedam. It's a small place outside Groningen." Another excuse to clear my throat and show-off my knowledge of his country. "Do you know it?"

He gives an easy laugh. "Yes, of course. I teach at the University."

"Ah, yes, I see." He means Groningen of course.

I'd like to ask what he teaches but I can see that could lead to problems. What if it's gynaecology? That would be a conversation-stopper. My knowledge in that area is rather limited.

Wouldn't it be curious if my friends knew my Dutchman, lived in the same street even, but the chances of that are so remote I'm not going to make an exhibition of myself by even asking – yet curiouser things have happened, and I've experienced enough coincidences recently that this could be another one. It doesn't look as if I'm ever going to find out though, as he's not volunteering any further information. In fact, the conversation seems to have turned into a cul-de-sac and neither of us seems to know how to proceed. The only thing to do is back out and continue with our meal. Leave now and leave that good impression behind me also.

"Well, it's been nice talking to you. Enjoy your meal."

"Yes, thank you – and you, too."

"Thank you. Bye."

"Goodbye."

We have to take a new table. Thank God the wine was finished or it might have been cleared away too. In fact, I wouldn't have left until it had been finished.

"Well, I think that went rather well, don't you?" I ask Iona after we have collected our sweets. All in all, I am rather pleased with the way I handled the chance encounter; I've not only broken the ice with the Dutch family, but I'm bound to have impressed Iona with the easy way I can chat to perfect strangers with my friendly, outgoing manner – the epitome of Scottish urbanity and charm. You never know: the next conversation might be an invitation to call in on them the next time we go to visit our friends.

"How do you mean?" says my dearest partner in greatness through a mouthful of messy brown mush, which, she informs me, is called *Death by Chocolate*, and it is to die for.

I'm not having any. I'm too young to die, although my hair is white.

"Well, how I got on so well with that Dutch family just now, of course."

"Bored them to tears, you mean." She pronounces this stinging verdict with a casualness which makes it seem all the more brutal, as if it were so obvious that it were scarcely worth mentioning and the dispatch of the pudding far more deserving of her attention than the assassination of my character.

I am thunderstruck. "Do you really think so?" I ask, incredulous.

She nods. Her mouth is glued with goo for the moment. I have to wait until she deals with it. First things first. Meanwhile, I wait in suspenders, as I always wittily remark when I am holding my breath in anticipation.

"What makes you think he's interested in your life history? I bet he doesn't even know your name." Pause. "Does he?"

"Well, no." Pause. "What do you mean, 'life history', anyway?"

"That story you told; is it, or is it not, your first-ever memory?"

"Pretty much."

"Well then, no doubt the next time you meet you'll tell him the next episode. The one about when you went to pat the policeman's nice doggy and your head disappeared down its throat."

"That was before the storm," I point out, "and I don't actually remember the incident either, thank God. And I think it's going a bit far to suggest I'm going to regale him with the story of my life. Besides, he thought it was pretty interesting. Didn't he?" Anybody who had been within ear-shot of us now, had they been interested enough to listen, would have been able to detect a tone of doubt creeping into my voice. I expect she's heard the story so many times before she's forgotten how enthralling it was the first time she heard it.

I have to wait for the oracle to speak. That was her name before she was married – Orr. But she still makes enigmatic utterances, like now for instance.

"No." She speaks without rancour, so it can't have been one of my more toe-curling, cringe-making times when I have embarrassed her in public. If I hadn't brought the subject up, I doubt if she would even have mentioned it. I wish I hadn't now, hadn't been so smug and self-satisfied. "He was merely being polite, because he's not a boor. Could you not see he, and they, were all dying to get on with their meal before it froze on their plates?"

"Well, no." Pause. "Are you *sure*?"

"Well after you had finished your intriguing tale, he didn't exactly prolong the conversation, did he? And he didn't exactly contribute much either, did he?"

That's perfectly true, now she comes to mention it. And I did a similar thing last week in St Peter's apparently, when I thought I'd enthralled our fellow travellers with the life and times of Prince Charles Edward Stewart but bored them to tears, apparently. And in more recent times, there was the Great Bus Misadventure which seemed not to enthral my audience, according to Iona. It looks like I'm not very good at reading the signs. I'm just going to have to stop speaking to strangers in future. Or maybe not give lengthy perorations to people in general.

It's a bit of a blow to the self-esteem. But I'm not downhearted. All is not lost. At least I haven't totally disgraced myself like I did on some other occasions last week. And, if I've not exactly given my Dutch acquaintances the impression I'm the cultured person I had presumed, I don't think they could accuse me of being a boor either.

I am struck with a sudden thought. "You know what's funny?"

"What?"

"You remember Deane's maiden name?" Reminding myself that my little petal, Iona, used to be an Orr kid has reminded me of something else. My Dutch friend, Deane.

"den Boer. What's funny about that?"

"Well all the time I was telling the Dutch people about Zierikzee and Middelburg, I really thought I was impressing them with my knowledge about Holland and the Great Storm especially. And it was mainly thanks to Deane that I could do that."

"So what's funny about that?"

"Well I should have known that something a Boer told me is not likely to impress a University professor!" It's such an amusing notion, I can't help but chuckle at my own wit.

My German wife, Frau Ning, lays down her fork even although she's not quite finished the process of hardening her arteries with all the cholesterol in *Death by Chocolate*. She can't say they didn't warn her. She appears to be defeated, but because she doesn't say anything, let alone raise a smile at my latest little witticism, I can't be sure the fork was redundant because she can't face another mouthful or it's something that came out of my mouth.

I think it might be the latter, because of her Viagra eyes. But then I'm not very good at reading the signs, apparently.

54

Late Night Horror Story

IT'S much later, and as dark as Hades. The storm has stopped, leaving the atmosphere intolerably hot and sticky. It's so humid that to stand outside is rather akin to rolling in dewy grass. We've left the glass door to the balcony open to get some air, but have closed the shutters so it can be as dark as Iona requires to get to sleep. She's not a very good person to sleep with. You see, she has some very peculiar habits in bed. Putting in earplugs so she doesn't hear my alleged snoring is one of them. (Hypocrite. She should hear herself.) Putting a pillow over her eyes is another, and having the room as dark as a badger's bahookie is yet another.

Despite these precautions, it's proving impossible for her to get to sleep: she is tossing and turning. And because of all her thrashing about, I can't get a wink of sleep either. And now we have another problem. There's a mozzie in here and it's after my blood. I can hear it buzzing about my ears. Probably the same one that was on my nose earlier.

My head is the only part of me sticking out from under the sheet, so if it is to dine on me tonight, it must be on my face. The problem for *it* is, as long as I stay awake, I can brush it away. The problem for *me* is, if I don't want to be dinner, I must stay awake until it gives up – or goes to Iona. But by its persistence around my ears, she does not seem to be on the menu. Female solidarity strikes again. As you probably know, dear reader, as far as the mosquito race is concerned, the female of the species is pestlier than the male. They are the ones that bite.

It's no good. This just won't do. Tomorrow we are going to revisit Pompeii which will involve walking miles, and I don't want to be exhausted before I even start. That mozzie is going to have to die. The problem is that I can't see the little blighter.

"Iona! Iona!" I say, loudly enough to penetrate the earplugs. The customary pillow has been discarded as it's far too hot and sweaty.

"What? What is it?" She sounds more drugged with sleep than irritated. "I am trying to get some sleep," she adds, redundantly.

"There's a bloody mozzie in here."

"Hmm."

"Well, I want to put the light on and kill it."

"Hmm."

"Well? Can I?"

"Mmm. Suppose so." You'd think she'd show a bit more interest. I could be killing for both of us.

I am groping for the switch when the body swathed in the sheet speaks again.

"Give me something to put over my eyes."

I reach over and from the floor (where I hang up my clothes overnight), pick up the first thing that comes to hand and pass it over. A hand takes it and presumably places it over her face. At last I can switch on the light and begin the Great Mozzie Hunt. Right. Where are you, you little swine, prepare to die!

Yes, where are you? Who would have thought that a creature with a head as small as a pin could hold a brain big enough to know that I have murder on my mind? It's gone into hiding. So now it's a game of hide and seek. I get up and prowl about, but it's no good – there's no sign of it. It's lying low. Typical. I know what will happen. As soon as I get back into bed and put the light out again, it will be back, buzzing about my head.

A different strategy is required. I may as well get it over with and let it bite me, and then I can get some sleep. I know when I'm beaten and I'll know when I'm bitten. For all my might and superior brainpower (even Iona would have to agree that I *do* at least have the brains of a gnat), this little insect is the mistress now. I just can't win. If it's not one pestilence sent to plague me, it's another: if it's not next-door's "music", it's this bloody mozzie.

I get back into bed and switch the light off.

"Did you get it?"

"Nuh!"

The hand silently passes me back the eye-cover. I drop it on the floor.

"What was that anyway?" She sounds a bit more perky now. My prowling about has not done much to help her sleep.

"My underpants." I had noticed what it was when I was on my murder hunt.

The bed suddenly convulses and becomes a living thing like water does when food pellets are thrown to trout in a fish farm.

"Yeuch!!!"

"What's the matter! I've only been wearing them this week."

"Week!!! Oh, *yeuch*! How could you, you boor!"

"Well, I didn't know!" I protest, getting heated myself. "It was bloody dark, you know! I couldn't actually *see* anything! I didn't pick them deliberately to bug you. I just gave you the first thing that came to hand." I let that sink in for a minute. "I only wear them in the evening when we go down to dinner, you know. It's not as if my bum has been sweating in them all day."

I don't know if I'm winning my case or not as I can't see her. Even if I could, I probably wouldn't be able to read the signs, but at least I'm not feeling seasick anymore – the bed has stopped bucking like a bronco having an epileptic fit.

Then I have another thought. I know how I can convince her that it wasn't such a terrible ordeal.

"You had my pants right across your face, right, all that time, and you never smelled a thing did you? Not even a rat. You didn't even know what –"

"Don't be so revolting!"

The bed goes into convulsions again and I can tell, even in the pitch dark, that I'm in bed with my Chinese wife, Scow Ling, and she has turned her back on me. I may not know much, but there's one thing I certainly *do* know – there's nothing I could say now to retrieve the situation. Once a boor, always a boor, even a week hitting the cultural high spots of Italy has not altered me. I'm still a boor and ever more shall be so.

If I'd been born a woman, it could have been different. Look at my friend, Deane. She was a den Boer once and just look at her now! She's flying high in the sky, a Vlieger now, ever since she married Jeroen (whose English is better than some of my ex-pupils). If you didn't know before, you're just about to learn that *Vlieger* is Dutch for "kite".

Too late, I realise what I've done wrong. I should never have presented my case so convincingly. Even when I'm winning, I'm losing. Why don't I just give up? When will I ever learn that I'm just one of life's losers and nothing will ever change that?

It's too late now but I wish I hadn't sat in that sauna of a balcony and sneaked all those gins past *La Belle Dame Sans Merci*. I'm sure that's what made me so attractive to the mozzie, and why it left Iona the Innocent alone. It's not my blood it's after, but the alcohol in it. Well, if you were a mozzie and had a choice, which restaurant would you choose? The one where the drinks are included of course; you'd be daft not to take advantage of the all-inclusive package.

In that case, welcome, kindred spirit! Drink the spirit from my veins and may you be so intoxicated, that you break your bloody neck when you take off after putting your horrible thingy in me and then we may both rest in peace.

Good night, sweet lady insect! Good night! Good night! May you rot in hell.

55

Public Toilets and
Plaster Casts

I have a spot on my cheek where I was bitten during the
night, but that's nothing. I didn't feel it, and it's not as if
I'm going to miss the blood: a proboscisful out of a face-
ful's a sma' request and I'll never miss't. I've got a whole body
of the stuff. I should have followed the example of my national bard, Burns, who didn't grudge his mouse a nibble, and just
let my mozzie friend get on with it from the start.

On the other hand, Burns's gesture didn't involve an
invasion of his person. I do feel a bit strange, don't feel quite
right this morning. Perhaps it was not so much a case of giving but getting. What if I've been injected with some nasty
virus? If that's the case, it certainly *is* better to give than receive, as the adage has it. My stomach feels a bit queasy. I
don't feel like my normal hearty breakfast, despite having paid
for it. Maybe it's because I've had a bellyful of breakfasts. I
normally don't have anything more than a slice of toast.

In the dining room, looking as cool as a penguin's backside, Mrs Scanty-Panties is having her usual breakfast of black

coffee and a slice of toast with a scraping of butter. Despite the drop in temperature, perhaps the reason she's looking so cool is because the cold front from Iona's frosty glare has reached her as we choose our table.

It seems to be a convention of the enemy. The Three Degrees are at an adjacent table. Because Iona can't bear the sight of Mrs Scanty-Panties, I have to have the seat where she can't see her, but which means I have to sit facing the Three Degrees. I can understand her point of view, appreciate how she feels since I have to look at *them*. Maybe that's why I am not feeling so good, and am off my food. If I have to look at them, as I must, I may as well focus on the pretty one.

As we leave, we bump into Tom, Dick and Harriet, whom we haven't seen for a couple of days. We stop and exchange a few words. Like us, they have been to Capri, but Tom being a rich man, they could afford to go on an organised tour. Ah, that's very interesting! Now I'll be able to find out what I've have missed thanks to my parsimoniousness. (But remember, I am a poor man from a poor family.)

They had been taken to the Arco Naturale and the Certosa di San Giacomo. Yes, I should have liked to have seen that, especially the cloisters which are supposed to be particularly charming, for (as you will remember) I have a particular fondness for cloisters. What's more, they visited the Giardini di Augusto, founded by the emperor himself, no less. Now it's a terraced public park which features a monument to Lenin and Gorky, who, if we hadn't seen the house where they fomented revolution, I might have wondered what on earth such a thing was doing there.

So that's what we missed. But of all they had seen, what did *they* like best?

"Well, the chairlift up to Mount Solaro was pretty good," says Tom, the spokesman, "but we thought the place was full of posers."

Ah, so he had bumped into Red Fingernails too, had he? But was the chairlift really the thing he had liked best about Capri? If *that* was the highlight, while it might have been high – in fact as high as you can get in Capri – I am glad I didn't pay all that money for *that*. I may have missed much, but they hadn't seen the remains of the Villa Jovis. That will always be, for the Missus and me, the highlight of Capri. But then, not everyone is a Roman junkie like us.

Today Tom et al are off to Ischia – not independently, but on another guided tour, even more expensive. It must be wonderful to have so much cash to splash about. All the same, I'd rather go where *I* want to go, not where the tour takes us. That said, I haven't a very good record on that, as I know to my cost. Yes, I have missed things I would have liked to have seen on Capri, but as my illustrious namesake, Joseph, said (I have been unable to establish a familial link): "There is much to be said on both sides."

I tell Tom we are taking the train to Pompeii to explore the *Scavi* on our own. No sooner have I said so when he produces a couple of rail tickets to the destination aforesaid, explaining they had intended to go there but didn't in the end, so we may as well use them.

He's a very nice man, Tom. This surely must be proof that he harbours no grudge for my spraying fig seeds all over Harriet's dress. No greater love hath this man than he forgives another for scattering his seeds upon his wife.

It would seem Tom doesn't care a fig about that sort of thing.

* * *

We are catching the 10:30 complimentary bus, which will give us plenty of time to catch the 11:07 train to Pompeii. Last week we had merely scratched the surface of it. Our guide, Marco, had been excellent: a luminary even. He was a tall and lanky fellow and, when he produced a hat from his hip pocket, unfolded it and plonked it on his head, it looked for all the world like a lampshade on a standard lamp. He told us a lot of things, and now, armed with that knowledge and our guide-books, we will explore the parts we did not reach. We still won't be able to see everything, but the choice is ours – where to go and what to see. No pesky taxi drivers here.

The bus is very crowded and I have to stand. I gradual-ly become aware of a peculiar sensation on my knee, like an insect crawling over it. When I look down to see what it is, to my utter surprise, I discover it is not a mosquito but a hand – and judging by the fingernails, a female hand. When I follow the hand up, I see it belongs to a woman of about my own age. She seems as if in a daze, totally unaware of what she's doing.

God knows what she imagines she's stroking. What could possibly be as hairy and knobbly as my knee? What could be as soothing and calming to the touch as my knee? What could give her a bigger feeling of shock/horror if she were to suddenly realise what she was actually stroking was my knee! Actually, I *have* just thought of something...

Iona's mother never gave her much in the way of sex education, but she did tell her once: "Never put your hand on a man's knee. It gets them excited." Actually, it is not exciting me in the slightest, nor is it causing me the least offence. After last night and my new-found sympathetic attitude to the in-

388

sect world, I decide I may as well let her continue if it is giving her pleasure. Who am I to refuse a woman in need, a knead of my knee?

We've plenty of time to spare when we reach the station, and given the state of my queasy stomach and considering how we'll be wandering the streets of Pompeii for the next few hours, I think it might be expedient to pay a visit to the toilets before that. But where are they? You'd think they might be near here somewhere, where you buy your tickets and validate them. That would be logical, but I can't see them. The cunning Italians have hidden them. Perhaps they are upstairs. Sorrento station lies on two levels. On the other hand, I suppose it might make more sense to have them near the trains, even although it does go against the grain of Italian logic somewhat. And sure enough, after a traipse along the platform, initially in the wrong direction, I eventually find them. A sign would have been helpful. Thank God I am not a man in desperate need of relieving myself.

There are three stations of relief. One "English" and two "French", or – you might say – one less repulsive than the other two. I'll not go into details: dirty and smelly, you'd have to be desperate before you'd enter any of them. I couldn't swear to it – I didn't stay long enough to look properly (that's how bad they were), but I *think* the Johnny Foreigner types had paper. The so-called "English" toilet, scarcely more sanitary than its neighbours, whilst it does offer a seat, does not, however, have torn-off squares of *Il Giorno* to read whilst you are enthroned to keep you entertained. Nor does it have a lock on the door.

That is the one I would have picked, but fortunately I had no desperate need to go at that precise moment, which is why I noticed that vital deficiency. Had I desperately, absolutely, needed to go, it would only have been later, when it was too late, that I would have noticed the lack of paper. That is the way the gods operate; catching you with your trousers down.

No thanks. This sort of place is more likely to give you some horrible bellyache than allow you to relieve the effects. No, I'll just hang on until Pompeii. They're bound to have better ones at the *Scavi*. Not for the first time, I reflect on how curious it is that the ancient Romans had better plumbing than those in the French campsites during our camping days and, so it seems, better than the public lavatories of present-day Italy.

Another thing, which I think rather bizarre, is the ancients' fondness for communal toileting where you performed your business in the full gaze, not only of the people next to you, but also those across from you, where it was *de rigueur* to prolong the whole experience, not by reading *The Tempus*, or even *The Sol*, but by indulging in conversation just as naturally as if you were in a café or some other public place passing the time of day as well as the bodily functions. I couldn't have done that, for if there is one thing which I think must be worse than sitting next to someone doing a poo, it must be doing a poo in front of someone else.

Ignoring such attractions as the Temple of Apollo, the Basilica, the Forum, and the Temple of Jupiter, in a spirit of abandonment (been there, done that), we head down the Via dell'Abbondanza, Pompeii's main thoroughfare on the southern side. At last we come to the House of Geometric Mosaics, so-called because of its black-and-white patterned mosaics on the floor. More than sixty rooms of them. Imagine that! And built towards the end of the 3rd Century BC, so already nearly 400 years old when the final, catastrophic eruption struck in

79 AD. It had previously suffered extensive damage in the earthquake of 62 AD, so not a lot of the original building survived.

And so we come next to the Stabian Baths, the oldest of all the baths in Pompeii, a century old at the time

House of the Geometric Mosaics, Pompeii

of the eruption and actually built over the previous baths dating from the 4th Century BC. Incredible! It's impressive enough now with a large grassy area bordered by a portico of Doric pillars and, in addition to the public baths, there were private baths also. There was also a *natatium*, or swimming pool.

Our book with the transparencies shows what it would have looked like. The grassy area has been paved to form a *palaestra*, or exercise yard, while the *natatium* is a larger, improved version of the plunge pool which normally would have been in the *frigidarium*. The façades of the buildings were richly decorated with frescoed paintings, with friezes of garlands and geometric designs. In fact, you can still see the vestiges of them today. It's all quite splendid. And that's just the outside.

Inside, the baths follow the normal pattern of men's and women's sections (no hanky-panky in those days – that came later) with *frigidarium, tepidarium* and *caldarium* and the changing room, or *apodyterium*. Except the women, I suppose being frigid enough already, apparently didn't need the first. That doesn't surprise me. All the ones I knew in the days of my youth were.

I grew up in the Sixties, the generation which not only discovered sex, but sold it wholesale and also gave it away freely. It was the decade of the "pill" where you could buy, in the toilets of a few select (and seedy) pubs, what was known as a "packet of three" without the cringe-making embarrassment of having to ask the chemist's assistant to serve you. (Remember the scene in *A Kind of Loving* by Stan Barstow, which unerringly put its finger on the pulse of the time.) In one hostelry of my acquaintance, so it was said, if you made such a purchase in the toilets, a bell would ring in the bar and everybody would look at you in a knowing sort of way when you returned.

I should be a bit of a celebrity really, notorious as the only person to come through the sex-infested swinging Sixties not to have swung. I often reflect on this matter as I shave, thinking there must be a reason, but for the life of me, I can't see what it is – apart from the gods having had it in for me even then.

In the Stabian Baths, the changing rooms provided shelves where the bathers could put their clothes. If only my bedroom in the Hotel Monte Somma had such shelves, I wouldn't have had to hang up my clothes on the floor and my underpants wouldn't have been so close to hand and I could have saved myself some grief. Actually, if I'm honest with myself, it wouldn't have made any difference; I still would have dropped them on the floor.

The roof of the *apodyterium* is as fine a piece of artexing as I have ever seen – great swirls, such as we have on several of our ceilings at home, except ours are not nearly so pronounced as this. Nor do we have what they have in here –

display cabinets, at least not like this, and certainly not what they contain.

In this, one of the many poor victims of the eruption has been put on display. That's the pain, and that's the poignancy. The features are so well-preserved you don't need any imagination to wonder what he looked like or how he died. Here he is, bald as a billiard ball, his skin looking as if he were suffering from a bad case of psoriasis, but actually just the plaster from the cast they made in the intriguing method devised by the archaeologist, Giuseppe Fiorelli. Buried under the ash, the body decomposed, creating a cavity and into that cavity, the enterprising Giuseppe poured plaster, which is why no less than 1,100 human bodies, not to mention animals and all other things organic, have risen from the ash.

Seeing this reminds me of one of the most famous corpses of all – I'm sure you must have seen it, the dog on its back, writhing in agony. To me it's one of the saddest icons of this awful tragedy, reminding us it wasn't just people who died that awful day, the 24th August, but every living thing. Thanks to Giuseppe, these plaster casts give a human (and animal) face to the tragedy and remind us that Pompeii is not just some sort of ghost town but where you can see the bodies of the dead.

The poor fellow in the next cabinet is contorted in agony. His left arm looks as if he were suffering from some kind of crippling disease, unless of course he really was in life and it has nothing to do with his death throes. His mouth is half-open and he looks as if he were fighting for breath – frozen for posterity at the moment of death.

Curiously, the victim in the third cabinet looks as if he has merely fallen asleep. He's got a big beak, just like Mrs Scanty-Panties' husband, and he's lying on his side, eyes closed, sleeping like a baby, his head resting on his right wrist. He looks as if he is sleeping the sleep of the just, without a care in the world.

Impossible, surely, in that suffocating heat that he slept on! And the din from that apocalyptic explosion must have been tremendous. Even if he were deaf, some sort of other sensory perception must have alerted him to the fact that he was staring death in the face. Only it seems he didn't. It occurs to me that there are many deaths, and none of us knows what lies before us. My father dropped dead with a heart attack at 59. My mother took three weeks to die with cancer at 85. If it were not for the numbers game, I'd know which one I'd choose – but the choice is not up to me, unfortunately.

Well, he's lucky this bloke, that he died so peacefully. Only he looks very young, so in the end he wasn't lucky at all.

56

Back to the Future and the Past

NOW we are at Stefano's Fullonica, or Stephen the Fuller's, which – as well as being the fuller's – was also the laundry. I'm sure you don't need me to tell you what a fuller does in the manufacturing process of wool, but just to remind you, he fills out the wool by soaking it in liquid. Urine, as I'm sure you'll remember, is that liquid, as it not only fills it out, but bleaches it as well – which is how the Romans got all those snow-white togas. They used to literally take the piss out of people.

Receptacles were provided in various places throughout the city, especially outside the *thermopolia,* what today we would call bars or bistros. This system seems custom-made for the male contributor. And, speaking as a father of two, admittedly a small sample, but as a modern father having changed the nappies of both my children, if my daughter's nappies were anything to go by, the contribution from the female of the species is a lot more potent. The ammonia in

George's nappies was bad enough, but Hélène's used to practically poleaxe me.

If I had been around then, based on that experience (I realise it's a bit like *Back to the Future*), I would have had a business idea, bearing in mind that the contents of the receptacles outside the *cauponae* wouldn't have been very powerful, consisting mainly of water after the donors had imbibed freely. I would have opened a *peeatorium* specifically aimed for ladies out on shopping trips. I would have called it *Pees and Contentment*, and there would have been comfy wooden seats and a lady playing a harp in the background. For this luxury convenience, I would only have charged one *sestertius* (1p in today's money). And whilst they were making a contribution to my other business, they could have a jolly good natter at the same time, as so many ladies like to do.

I'm sure you will have guessed what that other business is. I would have been a fuller of some importance – but not, I hope, full of my own importance, though I would have had good reason to be pleased with myself. My wool would have been whiter-than-white, the whitest in all Pompeii, and would have made me a fortune. (Pity my poor slaves who would have to do the tramping in the tank but, as a benevolent master, I would have provided them with clothes pegs for their noses.)

The next building we come to is the Thermopolium of the Lararium. About ninety *thermopolia* have been found in Pompeii and this is one of the largest and finest. It gets its name from the stuccoed and frescoed shrine behind the serving area dedicated to the worship of the *lares*, or ancestors. Shrines to household gods were commonplace in Roman homes, but because this was also a business, they also worshipped Mercury, the god of commerce, and Dionysus, the god of wine. Funnily enough, I worship the latter myself and I have a couple of shrines dedicated to him in my house: my "cellar" in the garage and the wine rack in the kitchen, to which they are transferred prior to sacrifice.

There's also the spirits cabinet, and I'm not quite sure if that's Dionysus' bailiwick or not, but I religiously pay homage there every single day by sacrificing a single malt. *La Belle Dame Sans Merci* can often be heard to say: *My God, not another one!* By which term of endearment you will be able to deduce just how much *she* worships me and admires my selfless dedication to my religion.

The *lararium* is on the right wall but the main feature is the marble counter in which are set the *dolia,* or terracotta jars in which the hot food was placed. To me, most interesting of all, also set into the counter, is the till, which, when it was excavated, contained the day's takings of 683 *sesterces.* Whether or not that would have been a good day or not, in terms of business, I couldn't say, but what I *can* say is that the household gods didn't do too good a job of their protection duties, did they? Nor did all the rest of the gods either, for that matter. So much for the gods. I've always felt they are more *agin* you than for you.

If it's wonderful to walk down the Via

Frescoed shrine to the lares at the Thermopolium of the Lararium

397

dell'Abbondanza now, it must have been something else then. It must have been like walking down an open-air art gallery. Take the frescoes on the walls of this house for instance – orange seems to be the predominant background colour. And there are several portraits of handsome young men wearing laurel wreaths. And if these frescoes are only some of the sur-vivors, there must have been many more all the way down this street prior to the eruption, their colours much more vi-brant than they are now. Better by far than the unglorious mix-match of clashing styles and colours we see on our high streets nowadays with brash advertisements and neon signs clamouring for our attention.

The next point of interest is the house of D. Octavius Quartio. We know it belonged to him because of a bronze seal that was found embedded in the floor near the *atrium*. That was the central focus of the upper-class house with opening off it, the bedrooms and dining rooms. In the *triclinium*, fres-coes depicting scenes from the *Iliad* can still be seen. In the garden is a smaller dining room, the *biclinium* with two couches. As you no doubt know, the Romans dined lying on their sides.

The frescoes here are not of the highest quality I've ev-er seen, and one I think would have been better-suited to one of the bedrooms. The first is clearly Narcissus, his face reflect-ed in the water. The other shows a bare bloke lying on his back with a young lady wearing a diaphanous sort of robe leaning over him. Or perhaps it's a bloke. It's a bit hard to tell. She's not wearing a bra but, if she does have such a garment in her underwear drawer, her cup size would certainly be an A. And, if she had any sense, she'd buy it in the children's department of Marcus et Sparcus to avoid paying the VAT. Actually, Iona tells me, reading from her guidebook, the scene depicts the tragic tale of *Pyramus and Thisbe*, famously enacted by Peter Quince and his Players in *A Midsummer's Night's Dream*. Ah, right enough: there's a lion loping off at the top of the picture and now I look more closely, Pyramus is dripping with blood.

One of the rooms in the house was dedicated to the cult of Isis, and this Egyptian theme is continued outside into a large

House of D. Octavius Quartio

and magnificent garden, so that Octavius and his family, reclining on their couches in the *biclinium* having their tea, might have imagined themselves not in a house on one of the main thoroughfares of the city, but deep in the countryside surrounded by trees and rippling water.

There is an orchard here today and vines trained up trellises, but the water which would have flowed from a small temple or outdoor shrine called a *sacellum*, in the middle of the main channel is gone, along with the fish that swam in it. It runs the entire length of the garden with plinths for statuary and is bordered on both sides by flowerbeds. It's one of the transparencies in our book and provides an artist's impression of what the garden might have looked like, and it confirms our impression (as if we needed it) just how fantastic this place must once have been.

399

And if that were not amazing enough, there is something else. Believe it or not, the channels were purpose-built to overflow and thus simulate the annual flooding of the Nile! I think that's taking the Egyptian theme a bit far but, once again, it does nothing to lessen the impression I get as if I were in something out of *Homes and Gardens* or at an *Ideal Homes* exhibition.

Across the street is another interesting building, a bit different though – the Schola Armaturarum, home to a military association and armoury, and appropriately decorated with frescoes of military emblems and trophies. And strangely enough, after the symbols of war, in the next house we have the symbols of love – for it is the House of the Venus Marina. It derives from a famous painting which pre-dates Boticelli's famous painting by 1,500 years but which also depicts Venus at sea. She is also in a scallop shell, but seen here reclining

House of the Venus Marina

on its coral-pink interior wearing nothing, not even a smile, as well she might not, because she was supposed to be the protectress of the city. And a fine mess she made of that, not only failing to protect it in 79 AD, but also from the earthquake seventeen years previously. To which you could add, a bomb in 1943.

The painting is not in the same league, artistically, as the Boticelli (the left leg is particularly bad), but what it *has* got in spades, is its location. This house also has a very fine garden and from the back, the eye is drawn towards the Venus on the wall of the loggia down an avenue of low box hedges which has been trimmed in such a way that it looks as if someone had planted a row of lollipops in variegated sizes. The problem is it proves impossible to get an uninterrupted view of the painting

Peristyle of the House of the Venus Marina

because other tourists will insist on walking between it and me. And if that were not enough, they *will* insist on talking loudly and even laughing, if you please – destroying the ambience of the place, making it impossible to imagine what it might have looked like in its heyday.

I hang about waiting for them to go, but it's no good, for here comes another bunch, while the other noisy lot hasn't even vacated the scene yet. It's hopeless. We'll never get this place to ourselves. Not that we had at Octavius' house either, but there were so few people walking around it that in fact we more or less did have it to ourselves.

The Venus painting is actually just the middle and the most arresting part of a triptych, featuring on Venus' right, her right-hand man, so to speak, Mars (love and war again, please note). He looks rather tall and thin, like our guide Marco – not my idea of a scary god of war at all. On her left is a fountain basin with birds. I'm not sure why you would want to paint that exactly when you could have the real thing in the garden, nor does it seem to fit in with the other two, but I rather like it, especially the long-legged heron.

Even better still, a peristyle runs round the entire garden – a sort of cloister with pictures. The Venus triptych was only what occupied the south wall and the vestiges of other frescoes can be seen on the others. It must have been truly magnificent in 79 AD. It's a close-run thing, but I think, if I had to choose between the house of Octavius or this, Venus would have won on account of the peristyle.

But then again, what about this place – the house of Giulia Felice? Unfortunately we are not allowed inside but we can see, through the bars of the gate, a magnificent portico which seems to go on into infinity with fluted square pillars. And it practically does go on forever, for, we are told, this house was so large it occupied the whole block, or *insula*. Like Gaul, the house consisted of three parts: Giulia's mansion; baths for public use (for the prices please see the board at the entrance); and shops, including, I'm pleased to see, a *caupona,* or hostelry. It seems the reason for these changes was the need to raise cash for repairs after the earthquake of AD 62.

It is a magnificent mansion, as you would expect, with a porticoed garden with a fish pond in the centre and ornamental statues everywhere, not to mention the frescoes. The one in the dining room is considered especially fine, as well as another one called *The Nine Muses,* now in the Louvre. The rest are in the National Archaeological Museum in Naples along with the board with the prices for the baths.

Frustrated that I can't see it, I'm sure this must once been the best house in Pompeii. But what I'd dearly like to know is, who was this Giulia Felice? What kind of entrepreneur was she? How did she make her money? Was she a merry widow, or even a serial widow? I bet she was happy all right, owning the largest property in Pompeii. If you looked as nice as your name sounds, Giulia, I'd have taken a chance and applied for the position of next husband.

Don't suppose I'd have got the job, though – not unless I had become that famous fuller and she liked the look of my assets. Could have come in handy after the earthquake.

57

The Theatre and the Telamon

WE'VE come to the amphitheatre. Its walls, seen from the outside, certainly are impressive – all the more so when you consider that the arena was not built into a natural hollow in the landscape, but dug out to a depth of twenty feet and the excavated earth banked up to make the seating for the 20,000 spectators. And they didn't have mechanical diggers either, unless you call the tedious labour of digging this place out day after day, mechanical, for it must have taken many, many days, even if they did have thousands slaving away on the job.

It is one of the oldest amphitheatres in existence, dating from about 80 BC. It was built for gladiatorial combat when the games were in their infancy, long before there were wild beasts which required all the cages and lifts and other contraptions under the arena, and long before they thought of flooding it and staging naval battles.

They did have a battle of a different sort here, however, in 59 AD, between rival fans from Nocera, a neighbouring town. (And we thought that we had invented fighting between rival sets of football fans.) The Romans had the answer to gladiatorial hooligans – they closed the arena for ten years, on Nero's orders (which was a bit rich, I think, coming from him). If they tried that at football grounds nowadays, it would be more likely to provoke riots than teach the fans a lesson. In the event, however, the ban was revoked after the earthquake of 62 AD – Vesuvius' wake-up call for the event seventeen years later, which was to send 2,000 people to sleep forever.

The seating arrangements were unashamedly elitist, considering they were all the same price – free. The best seats, known as the *ima cavea,* were reserved for the dignitaries and upper classes, the *media* was for those of the middling sort, whilst the *summa*, furthest from the action, was for women and slaves. As far as the Romans were concerned, that put them 'in their place' all right. No such thing as sexual equality then. There was also a *velarium* to provide shade for the spectators. Quite right too: it must have been pretty hot work sitting on your bahookie watching those guys slugging it out in the middle of the arena under a baking sun, clad in their sinister helmets and other pieces of armour.

There are two entrances along the axis. Actually, one entrance and one exit, from which the gladiators would leave after strutting their stuff upon the stage, or be taken out, dead or wounded. I don't know which we take as we leave and head for, just a short distance away, the Grand Palaestra, but I certainly feel like the walking wounded, with my feet sore from the amount of walking we have done and with a stitch in my side. The water in the bottle I am carrying is warm and tastes of sweat and sun cream. At least my stomach seems to have settled down. Next time I've got funny guts I might give that remedy a try again.

The Palaestra is closed but we can see it over the top of a gate in one of the entrances, and – if we were a bit taller – over the surrounding wall which has partly tumbled down. They are far less substantial than those of the amphitheatre. It's a vast rectangular exercise yard, bigger than a couple of football pitches placed side-by-side and covered in grass. This is where the young men honed their bodies to reach the peak of fighting fitness. There must have been hundreds of them – thousands of them, even. And that's not all. In the centre was a large swimming pool with a sloping floor for swimming exercises. Apart from its huge size, what makes it impressive is the colonnade which runs round it on three sides. There were ten entrances in all, three in the fourth side which did not have colonnades and which faced the amphitheatre.

Now we head for the city walls in the welcome shade of some majestic pine trees – yes, even for me, a further sign that I haven't quite been feeling myself today. Ahead of us is the Porta Nocera and the Necropolis. On the other side of the gate is the road those hooligans would have come to cause the trouble at the amphitheatre. It's certainly a very impressive approach, with massive tombs flanking it and sad cypresses standing around in little groups like mourners.

But just inside the city walls, in what is euphemistically called the "Garden of the Fugitives", under a Perspex lean-to, is a sadder sight. Here are thirteen victims who died attempting to flee from the eruption. One has raised himself up on his elbow as if to get the last gasp of air; another has his hand over his mouth as if to ward off the falling ash. One is curled up in a foetal position, appearing to be sleeping like a baby, only it's the sleep of the dead. Nearby, pathetically, are a small child and a baby, the latter lying on his back, sleeping the way babies do, his right arm flung out and his left drawn across his breast. He looks peaceful enough, and I hope he had an "easeful" death as Keats said he was half in love with. It looks as if he might, as if he had fallen asleep and had just slipped into the Big Sleep without being aware of having made the transition. In fact, apart from the first two I mentioned, they all look as if they could be slumbering, caught in various positions, like sleepers tossing and turning during the night.

Our route back takes us past the "small" theatre, seating about 1,500, where musical performances and poetry readings (for the more sophisticated audiences) were held. It had a roof to help with the acoustics. Although it is cheek by jowl with the Grand Theatre, we had not visited it on our first trip. How curious, I think, that these people who built these theatres, these centres of culture, and those baths, and those sumptuous villas, who enjoyed the arts, are the same people who also built the amphitheatre and revelled in the display of butchery there. But, I reflect, some of us today enjoy boxing (though admittedly it's hardly in the same league) whilst others used to enjoy fox hunting, revelling in the spectacle of seeing hounds tearing a fox to shreds, as well as other blood sports. I'm not just talking about the aristocracy blasting hapless game birds out of the sky. I'm thinking of those who like nothing better than a good punch-up after a few pints on a Saturday night out – the results of which you can see in any A&E department the length and breadth of the land.

Why not visit the theatre now? After all, the seats are free and, after all the walking we have done, it will be nice to get the weight off our feet and have a seat. It's remarkably well-preserved. Gratefully, I plonk my bum on a seat three or

408

four tiers back, not in the first rank of posh people, but somewhere near the front of the *media*. I'm too weary to take my proper seat in the *summa*. It's such a relief to sit down; the unforgiving stone seat feels as soft as a cushion. I puff out my cheeks with the sheer relief of it all and suddenly, Iona, who has been focusing her camera to take my photograph, lowers it again, unable to hold the camera steady as her shoulders are heaving with mirth.

"What is it? What have I done?" I demand rather irritably. It's not nice to be laughed at just because you're hot and your red face is even redder than usual, and you've had funny guts all day, and your feet are killing you, and that stitch is in your side is back again – not to mention the itch in your backside which is sweating so much, it's just as well you're wearing swimming trunks.

"Take a look to your left," Iona says.

I'm sitting at the end of the row and now she happens to point it out, I see a bloke standing next to me, actually in the row below me. He's short and fat, sporting a beard and a curly coiffure and a pair of bosoms that Mrs Scanty-Panties' friend would be proud to call her own. He's puffing his cheeks out, as well he might, because he has his arms raised shoulder-high, like a weightlifter's just about to exhale before that final thrust to lift the weights above his head.

"Hmm. Interesting. But what's so funny?" I'm still a bit piqued.

"Well, look at him! He looks just like you!"

I look again, though from where I'm sitting, I suppose it's not the best perspective.

"Does he hell!" I can't count the ways in which he is different from me. There must be something seriously wrong with her eyesight.

"It's called a *telamon*," she says.

"What's that?"

"It's an architectural support, like a column."

Ah yes, I see now. A bit like a caryatid, like the ones on the Erechtheion on the Acropolis in Athens, only this is a bloke, and much shorter – and uglier. He is supporting the parapets that form the end of the tiers of seats.

I still don't think he looks like me though, even if, as far as our marriage is concerned, I do play the supporting role.

58

On Worshipping Isis

O NCE we're rested, we exit the theatre by following a red carpet. Yes, strange to tell, believe it or not, there really is one.

"Very nice of them," I remark to Iona, "but how did they know I was coming?"

Predictably, like Queen Victoria, she is not amused.

It leads us to the *quadriporticus,* which, as its name suggests, was a porticoed area on all four sides, though only one side has had its roof restored now. It was here the theatregoers met before the performances, or met during intermission. Yes, they certainly were cultured, these Romans.

But what's this? It says that after the earthquake of 62 AD the *quadriporticus* became the gladiators' barracks. Excavating after the catastrophe of 79 AD, archaeologists found weapons and parade costumes, while the principal room, the *tablinum,* was decorated with frescoes depicting the *Loves of Mars and Venus* amidst gladiatorial trophies. Well, that seems pretty conclusive then. And once again I'm struck with the juxtaposition of love and war and culture and killing. They did nothing by half, the Romans: going to extremes seems to have been more their style.

Unlike the Grand Palaestra, from which we were banned, and which this place rather resembles, we are free to wander around – and very pleasant it is too, almost like being in cloisters. There is a red carpet running down this side too. There's still no sign of my welcoming committee and, what's more, some people have the bloody nerve to be walking on my carpet too.

The Temple of Isis lies in a corner off the Via Stabiana, tucked in between the two theatres. Like the *lupanar,* or brothel, which Marco had taken us to, it was one of the priorities for rebuilding after the earthquake of 62 AD. Amazingly, it survived the disaster of 79 AD virtually intact. So, in a sense, although it began its life at the end of the 2nd century BC, it was only a teenager at the time it was preserved in ash.

The temple lies on a podium in the centre of another *quadriporticus* and had niches for statues related to the Isis cult, such as her son, Harpocrates (better known by his Egyptian name of Horus), and her other son, Anubis, the jackal-headed god. He was conceived after her husband, Osiris, was murdered and chopped to bits by his brother, Seth. She put him together again, like some sort of grisly jigsaw, so she could have sex with him one more time. No greater love hath a goddess for her husband than she does something which all the king's horses and all the king's men couldn't do for Humpty Dumpty.

We mere mortals lead complicated lives, God knows, and some more than others, but that's nothing compared to the way the gods lived. Being immortal, you might think they would have learned some lessons over the millennia. But no, they are immutably dysfunctional. And here's the thing – they're the ones our poor ancestors looked to for guidance. Poor superstitious fools!

Anyway, they believed what they believed, and such was the state of preservation of these statues and others, not to mention the stuccoed paintings, they were removed to the Archaeological Museum in Naples, including an exquisite one of Isis. As a sort of compensation, they have left a photograph of what she looks like so we can see what we're missing.

She's a comely wench with a braided hairstyle (which I'm not very keen on, to be honest), but I do like her clothes. She's wearing a dress of material so thin it leaves nothing to the imagination. It's gathered in, just below the bust, like those Empire Line dresses you see in Jane Austen adaptations, and to which I am also very partial – the dresses, I mean. Like Nina Simone's "baby" in the song, I don't care for clothes, but if ever there was a time for good clothes, it was the Regency period. What would they think of trackie bottoms on the men and T-shirts on the ladies bearing the legend, "Press here"? I can see poor Jane swooning on the spot.

You can see Isis' navel too, and there's a voluptuous swelling to her belly which compliments the sumptuous curves of her breasts. No wonder they worshipped Isis if she looked like this. I am half in love with her myself, even although she has a heart of stone. I do not know the sculptor's name – perhaps nobody does – but I think he was a genius. Move over Michelangelo! We'll definitely have to go to Naples tomorrow, our last whole day, to see her in the flesh, so to speak. We'd always intended to go to the museum anyway.

Apart from the goddess herself, the other thing which interests me about this place are several other smaller buildings, one of which is called a *purgatorium* which I think has a wonderful ring to it. *Get thee to a purgatorium!* What a great way to dump your girlfriend after she has been nasty to you just once too often! Actually, it is a room for purification. As we had seen in the garden in D. Octavius Quartio, they took their Egyptian religion extremely seriously, even to the extent of actually bringing water from the Nile to use in their purification ceremonies.

I wonder if the other gods were worshipped as devotedly as Isis seems to have been. I suppose the good thing about pantheism is if you get tired of the god you're presently worshipping, if he, or she, doesn't come up to scratch, you could just shop about for another one and see if that performed any better. And there were plenty to choose from, with the Empire burgeoning and all those foreign gods coming onstream – why *not* give one of them a go?

The Samnite Palaestra lies behind the temple of Isis. It's a small (comparatively speaking), rectangular area where only the columns of the porticoes which were on three sides are still standing, and not even all of them, either – some are only stumps. There are also the remains of a pedestal where the award trophies were placed, for they held athletic competitions here.

It was here archaeologists found a Roman reproduction of *Polyclitus' Spearman,* otherwise known as the *Doryphoros.* It also is in the museum at Naples. Like Isis, they've provided a photograph of him in lieu of a reproduction. He has classical good looks, as you might expect, coming originally from Greece in 450 BC. He looks a bit sad though, possibly because the tip of his spear is missing, probably a heinous crime – the equivalent of an infantryman losing his rifle. But it could also be that he knows he's rather under-developed in the part that pleases the ladies. Ironic, as he has the most developed set of love handles I've ever seen on anyone under seventeen stone. That said, he has a splendid torso with a perfect set of pectorals. I think we *must* go to Naples tomorrow and check him out also.

And we must go back to the apartment before my feet are worn down to stumps like the columns in the *palaestra*. They are short enough already. However, as it happens, our route takes us to the Triangular Forum which we had passed through last week when we had visited the theatre, but not had time to explore. Now we have.

Apart from its base, there is nothing remaining now of the 6th century BC Doric temple, the oldest in Pompeii. Furthermore, the porticoes which bordered the forum have lost their roofs and, apart from one small section, their architraves. It was *not* one of the priorities in the rebuilding programme after the 62 AD earthquake.

Now, left to nature, trees have taken it over and that's what I like about it – a pleasant, shady oasis with broken columns and the towering walls of the Grand Theatre in the background. It's hard to say what might have attracted the eye most when it was in its prime: the ninety-five column Doric colonnade; or the Doric temple dedicated firstly to Heracles (later to Minerva); or the sacred well with its seven Doric columns arranged in a circle. Or amidst all this manmade splendour, on the third side which does not have a colonnade now, the unimpeded view of Capri rising out of the sea.

Iona is tired; dog-tired, in fact. She says her back is aching, not to mention her feet, and she wants to go back to Sorrento – she's had enough of Pompeii for today. It sounds like the cue for a song and, if I had known the words, I would have sung it to her, it being the song for this occasion. That I don't happen to know the tune to *Torna a Surriento* wouldn't have mattered, as it wouldn't have come out anything like it anyway.

So wordlessly and tunelessly, not to say wearily, we make our way to the exit, but buoyed up by the thought that we've done quite well really, over the two days we've spent here, in seeing the sights.

But there's still so much left to see. If we want to see what we've missed, we'll just have to come back – not just to Sorrento, but Pompeii.

59

Telling and Not Telling Tales

THE Circumvesuviana is rattling us towards Sorrento. The seats opposite us are occupied by a young Swedish couple. I get talking to them, as you do, and am gratified that my guess as to their nationality turns out to be correct. The ventilation system is operating at full throttle – that is to say the windows are open as far as they will go. As a result, we have to raise our voices to be heard. Nevertheless I am able to make out they are staying at the camping site.

"Oh, that's interesting," I shout back. "I know where that is. I passed it in the bus when I was going back to my hotel, only I was on the wrong bus..." and I tell them the whole story in full detail as I know there is plenty of time do so. How they must be glad they're sitting next to a *ranconteur comme moi* instead of some boring old fart who didn't utter a word during the entire journey.

Like us, the girl is pretty tired (and pretty too) after tramping about Pompeii all day, as I catch her stifling a yawn. I'm glad I managed to enliven at least some of the journey for her, but she must have been more tired than I thought because after I've finished my tale, she puts her head on the young man's shoulder and closes her eyes. Amazing how some people can fall asleep anywhere at the drop of a hat and in the most uncomfortable of places! Perhaps that clack-clack of the rails and the swaying motion has had a soporific effect on her. I expect that's it.

Her pretty blue eyes open again just as we pull into Sorrento and we make our farewells. This is where they'll catch the bus to their luxurious tent in the camping site. We used to do a lot of camping when we were younger, when the children were small, as that was all we could afford, but I am grateful now that they have flown the nest and we can afford to stay in our luxurious hotel.

It's a sign I am getting older because I used to enjoy camping then, or "clamping" as we used to call it and still do, because that's what our son, George, used to call it. He used to pester us to "Go clamping! Go clamping!" and we did. We went all over France, visiting Roman sites and, as far as he was concerned, other boring old stones besides. The worst holiday we ever had was in Brittany, where we visited every church and every calvary in the entire peninsula. After that holiday, the only clamping George would have done, if he could, were the wheels of the car so we would never go camping ever again.

"What were you talking about?" Iona wants to know. It had been too difficult for her to hear, so she'd stopped trying to listen. I tell her I've been regaling the Swedes with my bus tale to Sant'Agata.

"Not again! For God's sake!" She's started walking faster now as if she wanted to leave me behind, annoyed with me for some reason. I don't know why she's so irritated. Just because she's heard it twice before doesn't mean that other people can't enjoy it, for God's sake!

Now here's a funny thing; it seems despite her fatigue, the Swedes are not taking the bus to the camping site straight away after all, because is that not them ahead of us, at the other side of the street? It seems the girl has been revitalised after her nap and it looks like they are off for a bit of shopping.

Just for a change, because we have not been along it before, and since it is probably our last chance and we have been along the Corso more times than I have had *gelati* here, we have taken a different street out of the station and are walking along the Via Degli Aranci. It's not the normal route to the centre of town, the Corso being much more direct. If we follow it all the way round, we should avoid the town centre and come, in due course, to our bus stop.

But Iona has changed her mind. It's true this street is not particularly interesting, and besides, she's just had another thought – it seems a pity we should be so near and not pay another visit to the best ice cream parlour in Italy, which means it's probably the best *gelateria* on the planet. It was a good decision, for, as we turn right onto the Via Fuorimura, we come to a splendid gorge. Incredible, in the middle of the town, there should be such a stunning natural geographical feature and yet we were totally unaware of it. The Piazza Tasso straddles it, in fact, though you would never know.

We're certainly aware of it now, standing on this bridge where, across the gorge, the steeply-wooded banks tumble down hundreds of feet to the bottom of the canyon. There's a ruined mill down there, covered in ivy, and as well as giving a sense of perspective and of just how deep the ravine is, it gives the place a certain romanticism, the sort of place that would have inspired Wordsworth or Coleridge. Or it could be the sort of ruin that early 19th century aristocrats used to put in their gardens, designed by Capability Brown and others, to create just that effect. A folly, in other words.

The parapet of the bridge is not very high and it's a long, long way down there. At the moment it's very busy with traffic, especially those infernal Vespas whose buzzing is like a dentist's drill in the brain. Impossible to reflect in tranquillity, like Wordsworth might have done, but I can't help thinking this would be a perfect location, on a dark and deserted night, for the disposal of a spouse who has been getting on your nerves for the past forty years. I give one last look down and can't repress a shudder at the thought. Although it's broad daylight, I move a good distance away from the parapet, just to be on the safe side.

At the palace of ice cream, the basil-and-cheese flavour has been replaced with spaghetti flavour. Can you credit it! The only thing more unbelievable is that some people have actually tried it – out of novelty, one supposes. I think they must produce one bizarre flavour a day. I'm sure, if you stayed in Sorrento long enough, you'd be lucky enough to be tempted by anchovy pizza flavour or, for the real masochists, red-hot chilli flavour. Actually, I might have tried that. The contrasting textures of hot and cold would have been interesting. Instead, I resort to the white chocolate and hazelnut and if I were you, I'd advise you to do the same. It's to die for. It could be your last treat by a merciful spouse on your unwitting way to the parapet of death. You'll never guess what Iona had. Well, if you've been following this narrative, actually you should.

Whilst we wait at the bus stop, for once there's no entertainment from the flats across the road. Perhaps the smashing woman has not yet had time to buy replacements. But in the curious way the gods have of arranging things, who should I see coming towards the bus stop – as well as he might, for does he not live in the same place as us – but my Irish friend with his lovely wife. (Well, she might be after a few gins.) He is the benefactor who had given me the euro to go on the Great Big Bus Adventure, though of course, he had no idea what he was letting me in for. Wait till he hears my story! He'll never have had such great value for a euro in his life before – if only I can get the story told before we get back to the hotel.

Maybe it doesn't matter if I don't manage to finish it, because perhaps I can persuade him to come back to our room for a few gins as a way of saying real thanks for his generosity. And if he can't hear the denouement of my story properly because of the noise interference from next door, being Irish, he'd be the very man to sort those girls out! Actually, the more I think of it, the better an idea it sounds. Even although it is our last night, and therefore the Three Degrees can't annoy me much longer, it would give me a great deal of satisfaction if he gave them a good wigging and, if they've got the slightest sense of shame, it might dawn on their teeny-weeny, teenage, moronic little minds how they had spoiled my holiday with their diabolic "music" and inane conversation.

"That's my Irishman!" I whisper to Iona before he comes within hearing range.

She's quick on the uptake. She knows who I mean.

"Don't you dare tell him the story!" she hisses with a fierceness which makes me look at her in astonishment.

There is no time for further speech before the Irish *are* within hearing range. If I thought her whisper scary, that is nothing to the look on her face. It would make braver men than me tremble in their boots and I am positively quaking. I am in no doubt that if I disobey this order I'll be for the high jump from that bridge over the gorge if only, first, she could make me walk the walk of death.

By good fortune, I happen to have a euro amongst the change from the ice cream and which I proffer to my benefactor. He waves it away as if it were some trivial thing. I hope I haven't insulted him, but I felt the gesture had to be made. At least no words were necessary. Mercifully, he recognises me as the person to whom he had given the euro, not someone offering him charity out of sympathy, as the only clothes he seems to have are an Irish football top and trackie bottoms.

"How did you get on?" he asks after the preliminary greetings.

I shoot a sidelong glance at Iona. It could even be a longing glance, but she is my Chinese wife, Scow Ling, and I dare not, just *dare* not tell him. Of all the people in all Sorrento, in all of Italy, no one deserves to hear the story more than this man and I'm not allowed to tell it!

"Oh, fine!" I lie and he gives me a smile and a brief nod and steps into the bus. *La Belle Dame Sans Merci* gives me a different sort of nod. You might call it a nod of approval, for she is Scow Ling no longer, not even Frau Ning.

The driver has stubbed out his fag and is climbing aboard too. It's time for us to do likewise.

Well, I don't know if the gods enjoyed that but if there's anybody not laughing, it's me.

60

A Hobby is Born

I am laughing, however, when we get back to the room, because there is no sign – or, even better, sound – of the Three Degrees. We can sit back and enjoy the sun on the balcony in peace and quiet. I resist the urge to peek over the edge and see if my Dutchman is below in his garden. Instead, I go and get the gin revivers because it is still a bit early for the *apéritifs*.

It's incredible! It really is! It's not just that the gods have decided to spoil the show; that wouldn't have surprised me – I'm used to that. No, the amazing thing is we are sitting in bright sunshine but it's absolutely chucking it down. The rain is a curtain of water on the other side of the balcony and hitting the parapet so hard it is ricocheting off and spilling onto the floor. Within minutes, it is flooded. Yet, the curious thing is, if we didn't mind getting our feet wet, as well as the occasional splash, we could sit where we were and sunbathe! But we do mind, as it happens, so there's no alternative but to come inside. I decide I may as well get properly wet and have a shower.

I have already said the bathroom is the best place, or rather the worst place, to hear noise from next door, which is why I am receiving it so well now. Bloody, bloody hell! No doubt they were at the pool and have been forced indoors by the weather and putting on the ghetto blaster is as automatic a reaction as switching on a light in a dark room. I speed up my ablutions, thinking dark thoughts of how I might lure them to the bridge over the gorge: *Hey, you three girls look pretty gorgeous – especially one of you. How would you like to see something else gorgeous?* But I know that my time for picking up young ladies has long since passed – if it ever started. Even the ugly one would say: *Get lost, perv!* – if she bothered to say anything at all. She might just give me the same sort of look she would if she found dog poo on her shoe.

I give my back a vigorous towelling for my impure thoughts, like the way the monks of old flagellated themselves for having the sort of thoughts nature intended red-blooded males to have. The sooner I get out of here, the sooner I'll preserve my sanity.

"They're back!" I say between clenched teeth, dressed in a towel.

"Mmm!" says Iona. She's concentrating on her stitching.

"Is that all you can say! Just listen to that din!"

"And it's far too early to have another drink!" says the Drinks Police, seeing me heading towards the fridge.

"No, it's bloody well not," I say. "We're stuck in here, it's teeming outside, there's that fiendish din from next door and I'm not allowed to put on the television. What else is there to do, pray?"

No answer and no protest either, just a withering look as I open the door of the fridge. I may be dressed only in a towel, but also in a little brief authority, so it seems. I'd better make the most of it while it lasts. I keep my back to Iona as I

424

pour out a stiff one and whistle to keep down the sound of the gin sloshing into the glass and also as I pour in the tonic, so she can't tell how strong it is.

Success! She still has said nothing. I don't know whether it was my power dressing, but I seem to have got off with it without a dressing down. This will help me get through the next half hour, if I spin it out – and by the time it's finished, the pain from next door may be deadened. By then I may manage to hold on until *apéritif* time. Things may be beginning to look up.

It may be an anti-depressant, it may have driven the blues away, but the gin hasn't exactly expelled the boredom. A man of my calibre is capable of multi-tasking. I can do more than just sit and drink. I can sit and drink and think. That's three things already. Besides, I am getting on Iona's nerves. I can tell by the way she is looking at me and sighing, she finds the sight of me sitting and doing three things at once is not quite enough for her. I'd better do another thing before she loses her patience. Anyway, if I do another thing it will make the gin last longer and lessen the gap before official opening time.

But what to do? I've finished my green-and-white Penguin crime novel at last, thank God. I've written all the postcards. What else can a man do, now dressed in his wife's face-cover of last night, as well as the covering trousers, you'll be pleased to hear, not to mention a short-sleeved shirt and luminous green socks which have a frog on them croaking *Ribbit Ribbit Ribbit*?

That's it! Those socks have given me an idea. Last week when we were in Rome, Iona had suggested I write a book about our holiday. It annoys her, who has so many hobbies, that I have none at all, unless you count collecting those green-and-whites and doggedly reading them cover to cover, no matter how dire they may be. I'm sure I could write a better book than most of them. I have decided I *will* begin that book! It will occupy the present moment and if want to finish it, I should begin the sooner the better, before I croak, already being well-stricken in years.

As I get up and wander over to the dressing table and open the posh folder which has the hotel writing paper in it, I am aware of Iona's eyes following me across the room. I draw out a blank sheet of writing paper and after a few moments' thought, am still looking at it blankly.

"What are you doing?"

"Thinking."

"What are you thinking?"

"I'm thinking of writing that book."

"That's good," says she. "I'm glad you're going to have a hobby."

"Hmm. Just as long as it does not become my hobbyhorse and you nag me for doing it all the time and start complaining we're not doing things together. Writing is a solitary hobby, you know," I add knowledgeably, although I've only just begun.

She gives me a sharp look.

"If that's the sort of punny thing you're going to write, perhaps you should find another hobby."

The tone is more solicitous than critical, the sort you might use to advise natives of Trinidad and Tobago that taking up the bobsleigh challenge might not be the cleverest choice of ideas.

I pick up the pen and having thought, the finger begins to move and writes: *Like "Jane Eyre" for whom there was no possibility of talking a walk that day to get some air, there is a*

426

distinct possibility that we will not be taking to the air today.
There now! I've begun and if that's not the finest start to a
book since *Pride and Prejudice*, then I don't know what is!

When you've not read many books other than Penguin
green-and-whites for a while, it's a wonder I haven't come
across some arresting openings like the famous, and I suspect
apocryphal: *"Damn!" said the duchess, "but someone's done
my lover in!"* – which is supposed to contain a heady mixture
of sex, violence, exoticism, eroticism and racy language – a
great hook with which to engage the reader. Hmm! Not much
of that in my opening sentence.

Maybe I can work those things in later but the sex is
going to be a bit of a problem. How can I do that when I'm
happily married to *La Belle Dame Sans Merci* and I don't
have a lover? It's all right for the duchess; she's just a character in a book. But I am a real person, a traveller telling a real
tale. The exoticism should come from the locations; the eroticism, I admit, is a problem unless you count Mrs Scanty-
Panties or the statue of Isis. The racy language isn't – I can
easily put in a few "bloodies" – I say that all the time, so that
would be true too. And there's no problem with the violence
either, because it's true *La Belle Dame Sans Merci* often
stamps on my toes, even for the slightest of solecisms. It could
even end in murder, but the problem there is as I'm the one
most likely to be murdered, how am I going to tell the tale?

That's a start, but one thing I mustn't do is put in too
many puns as they are the lowest form of wit, next to sar-
casm. At the moment, the important thing is to follow up on
that opening sentence.

But how? Writer's block already.

61

A Gay Farewell

THE dining room, for some reason, seems busier than ever before, or perhaps we have just struck a busy time, everyone fed up with the torrential rain and come to the trough earlier for want of something better to do. Signor Corleone is rushed off his feet, far too busy to direct us for the last and final time to our table. And so, by default, the last battle is won by me. It's the last battle that wins the war, as the saying has it, so you might say the victory is mine over-all. Not that there's a great choice of tables. We're probably sitting at the very table he would have chosen for us anyway.

Here he comes now, bustling like a black beetle.

"Buona sera!"

"Buona sera!" we reply. Then I go on, in my best Italian. *"Vino bianco de le casa, per favore."*

He fixes me with a steely eye. *"Bian-co!"* he says with emphasis on the last syllable, as if he were dredging something up from the bottom of his throat.

"Co!" I reply, making a horrible rasping sound from my own, suspiciously like a death rattle.

Signor Corleone appears to be satisfied. He bows his head, silently clicks his heels and disappears.

It's very kind of him to help me with my pronunciation like this, but I'm not so sure he wasn't being more critical than helpful. I don't think he's ever forgiven me for my first grand entrance in my tramp's clothes. I've asked for that very same wine every day now for nearly a week (apart from the time when I made a mistake and got an expensive bottle instead). The way I ordered it sounds exactly the same to me as I have been saying it every evening, yet he chooses tonight – the last night – to correct me. Perhaps he couldn't bear to hear his beautiful, musical language massacred by a tramp like me any longer, or perhaps it's his last defiant shot to show he's not vanquished yet.

Time to look around now that we have made up our minds from the menu. Yes, this place is certainly busy tonight. Much, much, busier than before. Something strange is happening.

Over there I can see my Dutchman and his family. They're having their photograph taken by their waiter, and now he's having his photograph taken with them. It must be their last night too. They all seem very happy and appear to be getting on very well together. I can't imagine me having my photograph being taken with Signor Corleone, and certainly not looking happy in it. But then that would not be anything new. I never look happy in photographs. Maybe it's because I *am* grumpy most of the time and, despite my years in amateur dramatics, not much of an actor.

But wait a moment! I know that face! I'd know that ectomorph anywhere! If there were one unforgettable face and body on this entire trip I'll never forget, it belongs to him. He's so tall and thin he looks as if he'd been stretched like an elastic band, and it's so easy to see the skull beneath the skin it makes me queasy just to look at him.

We'd met... well, that's not exactly the right word for it. We'd come in the same bus from the airport at the start of our tour and we had sat opposite each other in the foyer of our hotel in Naples whilst our guide had asked our names, and for some prurient reason, our ages. I had called him "Ramesses" because he looked just like the mummy of the Great Pharaoh in a book I have at home. We'd only seen him that brief moment because he and his wife, Nefertiti, not to mention a great number of others, had gone off on a cruise the next day. I hadn't thought of him from that day to this, and here he is as large as life, although he looks as if he has been dead for 1,500 years.

Now it is clear why the dining room is so busy. The cruise is finished, and it's not just the people who were on our bus who are here, but probably half the ship's company too. They are here for their last night, prior to going to the airport. It's a sign, if ever I needed it, that the holiday is drawing to a close and – like swallows – we are foregathering for departure.

But before that happens I have some rationalising of my purchases to do – that gin must be turned out of the glass bottles and transferred into the empty tonic bottles, not forgetting to top up the hip flask for the journey, of course. Except the tonic bottle is not quite empty, and I'm going to have to empty it to make way for the gin – and I may as well put some gin in the tonic, as that would be a waste of tonic. And there's some beer I need to finish too. It could be quite a pleasant evening, if I can somehow appease the Drinks Police and persuade her to let me finish off these libations. It might help oil the wheels of the creative process and help remove my writer's block.

Now my Dutch family are having their photographs taken with another waiter. How curious this fondness for waiters! Some people choose strange things as a memento of their holidays. Anyway, I had better say goodbye. We are not leaving until the afternoon, but they may be off betimes – and leaving they must surely be, for the photographs with the waiters is surely evidence of that. There may not be a chance tomorrow. Better now than leave it to chance.

"Hello!"

"Hello!"

"Did you have a good day?"

"Yes, thank you. And you?"

"Yes. We went back to Pompeii."

"Oh, yes. We went to Capri."

"Oh, we were there yesterday. Did you like it?"

"Yes, very much. Did you?"

"Yes. It was very nice."

Oh, dear, this is getting embarrassing again. I wish I'd never started this. After our less-stilted conversation of last night, it's back to square one.

"Well, I've just come to say goodbye. We are leaving tomorrow."

"Yes, us too. We go home tomorrow."

"Yes, I thought so, when I saw you having your photograph taken with the waiters. A souvenir of many happy meals, eh?"

"Well, actually, no," replies my Dutchman. "I was taking a photograph of them for my brother."

"Your brother?"

"Yes, you see my brother is homosexual and I thought he would like a photograph of them. He likes the dark-haired Italian type."

"Italian type?" I sound like an echo, left groping for words. I never expected this. If I had a gay brother I don't think I'd go about photographing potential suitors for him. And what about the waiters? Does he think they are gay too? Had they been told about the gay brother, or did they innocently suppose they were being photographed by punters happy with their service? What would they say if they knew they were going to be ogled by a homosexual Dutchman they'd never met? They might even have wives and children, for heaven's sake!

"Yes," continues my Dutchman. "I have five brothers and five sisters and two of my brothers are gay."

Too much information! I'm still at a loss for words. He hardly knows me after our few brief, awkward conversations and yet here I am hearing his intimate family details. And *I* got a row for telling *him* about my earliest and traumatic memory!

Of course the Dutch were always ahead of the game in that sort of thing. I recall how one of my gay colleagues years ago, when homosexuality was still a crime in the UK, used to go to Amsterdam for his holidays each and every year and came back with magazines so graphic I'm sure they must have been illegal.

"Oh... er... well, it's been nice meeting you. I hope you have a good trip home. Goodbye."

"Yes, you too. Goodbye."

And with nods at all the ladies and smiles all round, we part. No invitation to visit them next time we are in Appingedam. Just a holiday romance, obviously. What will they say about us when we're out of range? Though since they know we can't speak Dutch, they could begin as soon as my back's turned.

"Phew, do you think that is the last we'll see of that strange man, daddy?"

"Well, who can tell, my dear? He doesn't mean any harm, you know."

"Hmm. I'm not so sure. He's always chatting you up. Do you think he might be a homosexual too?"

I think he probably thinks not, even if Iona were some sort of elaborate disguise. Despite our halting conversations, he didn't ask to have his photograph taken with me so he could show his brother. But wait a minute! He *might* think I'm gay, only he knows I'm too old and wrinkly for his brother's taste and that's why he didn't ask.

Hadn't thought of that. I don't know whether to be glad or sad.

62

The Psychic Limoncello Man

THAT was the last night in the queen-size bed. It may have been a wonderful bed and, although I slept quite well by my standards, I'm still tired when I haul myself out of bed at nine. I sit on the edge of the bed and run my fingers through my hair, which, like that of *Timothy Winters*, remains standing straight up like an exclamation mark whilst I gather my strength for the next step. I don't think it was a mosquito which bit me the other night after all, but a tsetse fly, and it wasn't a stomach ache I was suffering from yesterday, but sleeping sickness, and I am still suffering from it now. That is my excuse at least, but it gets short shrift from *La Belle Dame Sans Merci*.

"All you need is some *Brylcreem* and a thin moustache and then you'd look really disgusting."

"Well, thank you very much!" I mutter as I hobble off to the bathroom. I'm not offended. I may not look good at the best of times, may not have my photograph paraded in Holland, but in the mornings, before my shower, I freely admit, I *am* truly frightful.

After my ablutions, with my hair tamed, the sleep washed out of my eyes, I think I look a lot better. Cue for a song.

"There once was an ugly duckling," and then I make that quacking noise which Danny Kaye used to make with his lips in the song.

"What was that?" Iona wants to know, busy at the mirror taming her own hair.

"What was what?"

"That farting noise. Did you let off a barrage?"

"No, I bloody well did not! I was singing!" I reply indignantly.

"Is that what you call it!"

Just another happy start to another day in the Addison household. But not an ordinary day, as we must – after breakfast – take our luggage down to the luggage room and after that, we are homeless. I hate that, not being able to go to your room whenever you please, not being able to have a shower when you want, because even although there is a courtesy room, you can bet your bottom dollar that when you want to use it, so does half the hotel.

Although it is hot and muggy, the windows are still in place from the night of the storm. They may as well take them out now. Don't they know I'm leaving and I'll be taking the rain with me? It'll be back to dry, sunny weather from now on.

As well as the sunshine, in the luggage room, I spot something else I'm going to be missing, but this I'll be glad to. Perched on top of a case is the object of my hate – the ghetto blaster. For a moment I harbour dark thoughts of accidentally bashing into it with my case, hoping it will smash into smithereens. It's bound to belong to the Three Degrees. As I suspected from the start, it's the only ghetto blaster in the whole hotel out of this week's cohort of guests, and it *had* to be in the room next to me – probably the only person in the entire hotel who was offended by it. Of course, there wouldn't be any point in the gods arranging it any other way.

So that's it. Officially homeless for the next five hours – more or less. Plenty of time to make it to Naples and back, but we've decided not to go. Well, Iona was the one to propose the veto. It was not so much the thought of the walk down to the port (we had planned to go by sea rather than train) but the thought of the walk up to the Archaeological Museum and then back again, not to mention the trail round the museum. Too poor and too scared of being ripped off by the taxis, walking is what we had decided to do. It might have been different if we knew where to catch a bus and which one, but we don't, and the thought of returning to the hotel, hot and sweaty and with the possibly of not getting a shower, or having to rake in our cases for a change of clothes if we did, is just too tiresome to contemplate. So when Iona suggests we don't bother, it sounds like music to me and willingly, I agree.

It's a pleasant prospect, since it's such a nice day, to spend most of it by the pool. As for missing seeing that sexy statue of Isis, well, she's just stone – and if I'm lucky, I might see some comely flesh-and-blood ladies instead. Besides, it will be a good chance to get on with writing that book whilst I soak up some sunshine, not to mention some beers. I had either bought too many or I just didn't drink enough, or wasn't allowed to. The latter, I think. One thing's for sure, I don't want to carry them home with me. The problem is they won't be as cold as I'd like, but you can't have everything.

What we *must* do is liberate a bottle of *limoncello* liqueur from the Lucky 13 – that elixir which, if I am lucky, may keep *La Belle Dame Sans Merci* sweet. I know not to be too optimistic, however. I have found such things don't travel well, rarely taste as good when you get back home. Besides, it doesn't pay to be optimistic with the gods tuning in to your every thought.

Although we have lost the little card which directs us to it, we just about manage to find our way there. I should think we've passed it nearly every day since we came here. As well as the *limoncello,* this is an Aladdin's Cave of other liqueurs, wines and spirits – my kind of shop, in fact. I'm sure they are a lot cheaper than at home, but I just haven't the room, unfortunately – nor, do I suspect, the weight allowance, especially since being homeless now, I can't transfer it into the lighter, unbreakable bottles.

"Have you had a happy holiday?" the proprietor asks, conversationally, as he wraps up my purchase.

I'm a bit taken aback. My conversations seem to have been following this sort of pattern lately – leaving me speechless. How on earth did he know I was leaving today? I suppose the answer is a lot of people must come in for a bottle before they leave, and it was just a lucky guess. Or maybe he recognises me from when we were taken here on the tour, the time when I missed out on the free sample, and he can count up to seven and knows it's my departure day. But out of so many faces, how is it possible he remembers mine? Whilst I admit to being a letter short of an Adonis, I am not so plug ugly either it's the sort of face that's been haunting his dreams ever since.

"Yes, thank you."

"And did you like your hotel, the Monte Somma?"

Now I know he's psychic. My jaw feels as if it is hitting the ground. After an age, my tongue comes out of paralysis and I find my voice.

"Is your name Sherlock Holmes, by any chance?"

He chuckles. He should have left it like that. Said nothing, let me go away wondering how he did it – like whenever a conjuror's trick is revealed, you always feel disappointed, cheated even, thinking how it's so simple you wonder how you'd never spotted it. You feel a bit of an idiot, really.

"No, no! It's just that Monte Somma leaves today..." and he then reels off a lot of other hotels, enumerating the days their guests leave. Committed to memory. That's a feat on its own.

So *that's* how Sorrento does it. A revolving door of tourists. And that's how *he* did it too! Simple really! In fact, so simple I'd prefer not to have known, rather have had the mystery.

But then I get to thinking. How did he know I was staying at the Monte Somma, since it's one of many hotels whose exodus is today? And how could he tell I wasn't staying on for another week?

I'm not so sure his name isn't Sherlock after all.

63

A Poolside Encounter

A
T the hotel, it's a case of packing the *limoncello* and unpacking the beer and towels and sun cream and heading off for the pool. One good thing about wearing swimming trunks all the time is you don't have to faff about changing.

I'm glad I've got the book to write, otherwise it would be a bit boring. The trouble is that writing our tale reminds me of the trauma we had in getting here – how the check-in staff at BA was on strike, and how we only made our flight to Naples by forking out £320 for a single flight to Heathrow. As we left, the strike had supposedly been settled, but the dispute had flared up again and now the words of the lady at the BA customer services desk as I made my way down the tunnel to the aircraft are ringing in my ears: *When you get to Naples, I'd advise you to confirm your return flight.* Of course, I hadn't. Hadn't known where to go to do such a thing and, besides, we were swept up with the rest of our fellow travellers. The next day we were off to Florence and, after that, as the tour got into its swing, I forgot all about it.

But now, as the flight-time approaches, though it is still many hours away, the old fears and doubts are beginning to creep back and I am reminded of the joys of modern-day air travel. Could the Grand Tourists of yesteryear, without the advantages of the comforts and conveniences of today's travellers, possibly have had it easier? Is the strike over? Will there be any delays, or will we be stranded for hours in Naples airport? At least we don't have a connecting flight to catch. Unfortunately our flight, even if it were on time, arrives too late for the last shuttle to Edinburgh. Blessed are they who live within travelling distance of the London airports, for they don't have to bother with such things and can save themselves a fortune by taking advantage of bargain fares as well. On the other hand, I don't envy them their property prices – or their traffic, either.

Oops! A close encounter again, just like yesterday. The Dutch family are in the garden. They won't have spotted us though as they are facing the bay and we are behind them, but we hurry past, pretending not to see them, just in case. I've no intention of speaking to them again. Having said my goodbyes, let that be an end to it.

The garden appears to be a favourite haunt of theirs. Being Northern Europeans with a climate almost as bad as Scotland's, they are not used to the heat or the sunshine and seem to prefer the deep shade offered by the trees. Still, you would think that that would be the very reason why they would try and catch some rays, like Donald and Helen here – who, like us, were also caught up in the strike, but who are in even a worse position than us because their tickets down to London were even more expensive than ours, if you can believe that. Except they probably weren't so stupid as me and didn't lose the receipt for the tickets as soon as they'd bought them. If there's any compensation going, this act of folly is not going to help my case.

By the looks of it, Donald and Helen have been here a while already as their white, sensitive, Scottish skins are already turning red as they sunbathe. We walk softly past them so as not to tread on their dreams.

It's pretty busy at the poolside, so not much chance of being spotted by the pool drinks police – though I can hardly avoid being spotted by that other Drinks Police, the one I'm married to. I may as well have the first of my three beers because, the sooner I do so, the less warm it will be. Besides, have I not worked up a thirst walking around the streets of Sorrento?

So, here we are. Iona's in stitches, although I have not said anything amusing and I may appear to be doing nothing, but I am searching for the right word before I begin writing. It's good to have a hobby and not get on each other's nerves. Hmm! Wait till she sees what I've called her in the book and what I say about her. I may need to find a new travelling companion for my next book – if I live to tell the tale.

And here are more of our travelling companions coming along now. Tom, Dick and Harriet. They've been making a last shopping trip, so they tell us, by which they no doubt mean Harriet has been shopping and has taken Tom and Dick along as beasts of burden. In which case, Tom will want a beer. I can see him looking at it, and lift my Panama to where the others lie concealed to offer him one. He politely refuses it, perhaps because he recognises it as illicit. I've known him for the best part of two weeks now. He's a pretty nice bloke but he's pretty straight, and I'm sure he wouldn't take as much as a sip from a drink that hadn't been bought from the poolside bar. It's all right for him; he can afford those prices. I'm sure he'll go to heaven one of these days. But no need to say goodbye to him or his family just yet; just "See you later", for we surely will – on the bus to the airport, if not before.

It is said that if you stand at Piccadilly Circus for long enough, you are bound to see someone you know before too long, and so it is here. Our sunbeds seem to be on the main thoroughfare from the hotel to the pool and here comes my Irish friend. He's alone – and so am I, for Iona has had enough of sun and stitches and has gone I know not where. I wave at him, in a casual sort of way, with my beer arm, which happens to still have a can in it.

"Would you care for a beer?" I ask him.

It's a bit of a no-brainer, offering a beer to a Celt. We don't need to be asked twice. He sits down on Iona's bed. Now the story that he deserves to hear can be told – but I don't launch into it straight away, like the Ancient Mariner. Despite what Iona thinks, I do have some finesse. I ask him where he comes from exactly and he asks me the same. And if I were moaning about the extra expense of coming from Scotland, then I should try living in Ireland. He arrived in Sorrento later than us and has some good news: the strike, it appears, has been settled. But have I got news for him!

"Do you remember that euro you gave me?"

He takes a swig of the beer and nods at me over the rim of the can.

"Well..." and I launch into the story. My fear is *La Belle Dame Sans Merci* will come back before it's finished and I'll have to terminate it hastily, thus missing out some of the details which add life and colour to the tale.

It's all right though. My story and his beer are finished, by an amazing coincidence, at the same time. If I were asked, I couldn't say which he enjoyed the more. He stands up to go.

"Well, thanks for the beer," he says.

"You're welcome. Care for another?"

"No, no thanks. I'd better be going. My wife will be wondering where I am."

That sounds a lame sort of excuse to me. He doesn't look the sort of man who's scared of his wife. He looks much more manly, not a wimp like me. I think it's much more likely he's noticed there's only one beer left and he's too polite to take it, or possibly he reckons it'll be too warm by now to be at its best.

"Well, have a good holiday."

"Yeah, thanks. Have a good flight."

"Right, thanks."

Pity he didn't stay for that beer. I could have regaled him with how we managed to get a flight to Naples by the skin of our teeth. Oh, well; his loss. He'll never know what he's missing – not unless, by some remote chance, he reads my book one day, and recognises himself as the benevolent Irishman. Then he'll come to the part where I describe his wife, at which point he would become transmogrified into a belligerent Irishman and it would be just as well for my sake we hadn't swapped names and addresses.

64

A Problem with the Bar Bill

MAY as well have the last swim. Alas, as I come out, I have a close encounter of the third kind – the third person or people I have met since I came out to the pool. It's the Dutch ladies, on their way for a swim. Amazingly, they are all wearing brown swimsuits. Maybe they think that will make them appear to the casual observer as if they have good tans, and that's why they don't bother with all that tedious business of lying in the sun.

"Hello."

"Hello."

And we pass on without stopping, so no halting, embarrassing conversation this time. I expect they are relieved that I'm not engaging them in a further desultory conversation.

After a while, along comes my manager to give me my orders. She looks as if she's washed, dried and polished, ready for travel.

The Streets of Sorrento (Image Credit: Pixabay)

"It's time you were getting ready. And you'd better go and pay the bar bill," she says. "Everyone else is."

I suppose I had better. I had been putting it off, as I know it will not make pleasant reading. Anyway, I can't do any more writing as I have just run out of the hotel notepaper. It's the end of the sun for me for another year. I hope it has charged up my batteries enough to see me through the dismal winter ahead, just as I hope the batteries I charged for my iPod last night will see me through the following week.

In the courtesy room – which, amazingly, I get into at the first time of asking – someone has left a copy of *The Sun*, so the sun wasn't quite over for me after all. It's not the sort of paper I can use to write my words, but I can read it on the plane, or look at the pictures if I find the text too challenging. Just as long as no one thinks that I bought it. If that's the good thing about the courtesy room (*if* it is), the bad thing about it is that I must be about the last, probably the very last, to use it, and that no doubt explains why I was able to get into it without waiting.

448

It looks like the Chinese laundry from hell. It's impossible not to get into the shower without climbing into it by means of a soft, wet, white stepladder of discarded towels. But that's not the problem. The problem is that the only dry towel left is not even big enough to cover my modesty if someone were to walk in unexpectedly now. It's not that I am boasting – far from it. It begs the question why you would bother making such a stupid little thing like that in the first place. It wouldn't even dry your face.

There's nothing else for it – I'm going to have to use one of those discarded on the floor, or even several of them. Not this one, though. I drop it hurriedly. It's got suspicious brown marks on it. I don't know what they are, but I'm not going to look too closely. It's a warning and a sign that the gods are not entirely cruel. Normally they would have let me dry my face with it before I noticed.

It's not the most pleasant thing in the world to dry yourself with someone else's dirty, wet towel, even though it's dirty only in the sense that it was used before me. I know, because I checked them before I used them. And now, dry, and I hope, cleaner than before, and not harbouring any infectious contagion, I have presented myself at reception to pay my bar bill.

"Room 334. I've come to pay my bar bill, please." I don't know why I said "please" as if I were begging them to pay, when I'd really rather not do so at all.

"Just a moment." The receptionist is an attractive young lady. I don't mind waiting looking at the scenery whilst she does something with the computer.

"Yes, Mr Allison. That'll be €129."

Good grief! That's what they called me when I first arrived. And good grief, that's a lot of wine! Nearly £120! Can that really be right? As far as my name is concerned, I don't want to keep whining on about it, and it's hardly worth sorting it out now anyway. Maybe like the Chinese – with their "l"s and "r"s – it's an Italian thing, they can't tell the difference between their "l"s and their "d"s. As far as the bill is concerned, I knew it would be bad, but I didn't expect it to be *that* bad. I study the printout. Just a minute!

"It says here, €3 for the mini-bar bill. I didn't have anything from the mini-bar."

"Yes, Mr Allison – you had a Coca-Cola from the mini-bar."

"Was that a real Coke or a diet?"

"A regular, Mr Allison."

Now I *know* it's a mistake. I know *I* didn't have a Coke and, if Iona had – which I doubt, as she is well-trained in how to be parsimonious – she would never had a "regular". And while I'm on the subject, that's another thing that annoys me; the way foreigners use American terms and think they are conversing in English.

"No, it's impossible. We wouldn't have had such a thing."

"Well the mini-bar was checked and a bottle of Coke was missing."

"I didn't drink it."

She shrugs hers shoulders. Translated from the Italian and rendered into Mandy Rice-Davies speak, she is saying: *You would say that, wouldn't you, if you didn't want to pay for it?*

It's stalemate. I wonder if I can get off with it by saying some bloke called Allison drank it and that's the very sort of drink a bloke with that name *would* drink, and it's nothing to do with me. But the best thing to do is pay up before she calls the manager and accuses me of refusing to pay my bill. I console myself with the thought that it's only €3 or to put it another way, nearly £3 – for a tiny bottle of Coke! Bad enough, but even worse when I never had it in the first place. Oh, well, it seems that's the price I must pay for using their fridge to cool my beer and gin. Just as well I'm smuggling some of their electricity back in my batteries. Grumpily, I sign the Visa slip.

So this is the way Sorrento and the stay in the Monte Somma ends, I reflect. Not with a bang, but a whimper.

I had thought it all looked so promising at the start.

Sorrento (Image Credit: Pixabay)

About the Author

A native of Banff, Scotland, David M. Addison is a graduate of Aberdeen University. In addition to essays in various publications, he has written nine books, mainly about his travels.

As well as a short spell teaching English as a foreign language in Poland when the Solidarity movement at its height, he spent a year (1978-79) as an exchange teacher in Montana.

He regards his decision to apply for the exchange as one of the best things he ever did, for not only did it give him the chance to travel extensively in the US and Canada but during the course of the year he made a number of enduring friendships. The story of his time in North America is recounted in his *Innocent Abroad* series, also published by Extremis Publishing.

Since taking early retirement (he is not as old as he looks), he has more time but less money to indulge his unquenchable thirst for travel (and his wife would say for Cabernet Sauvignon and malt whisky). He is doing his best to spend the children's inheritance by travelling as far and wide and as often as he can.

Also Available from Extremis Publishing

An Innocent Abroad
The Misadventures of an Exchange Teacher in Montana: Award-Winner's Edition

By David M. Addison

An Award-Winning Book in the 2015 Bookbzz Prize Writer Competition for Biography and Memoir

WINNER

When, in 1978, taking a bold step into the unknown, the author, accompanied by his wife and young family, swapped his boring existence in Grangemouth in central Scotland for life in Missoula, Montana, in the western United States, he could never have foreseen just how much of a life-changing experience it would turn out to be.

As an exchange teacher, he was prepared for a less formal atmosphere in the classroom, while, for their part, his students had been warned that he would be "Mr Strict". It was not long before this clash of cultures reared its ugly head and the author found life far more "exciting" than he had bargained for. Within a matter of days of taking up his post, he found himself harangued in public by an irate parent, while another reported him to the principal for "corrupting" young minds.

Outwith the classroom, he found daily life just as shocking. Lulled by a common language into a false sense of a "lack of foreignness", he was totally unprepared for the series of culture shocks that awaited him from the moment he stepped into his home for the year – the house from *Psycho*.

There were times when he wished he had stayed at home in his boring but safe existence in Scotland, but mainly this is a heart-warming and humorous tale of how this Innocent abroad, reeling from one surprising event to the next, gradually begins to adapt to his new life. And thanks to a whole array of colourful personalities and kind people (hostile parents not withstanding), he finally comes to realise that this exchange was the best thing he had ever done.

This award-winning book, the opening volume of the *Innocent Abroad* series, charts the first months of the author's adventures and misadventures in a land which he finds surprisingly different.

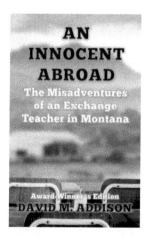

www.extremispublishing.com

Also Available from Extremis Publishing

Still Innocent Abroad

Further Misadventures of an Exchange Teacher in Montana

By David M. Addison

In the sequel to his award-winning *An Innocent Abroad*, Scot David M. Addison continues his account of a year spent as an exchange teacher in Missoula, Montana in the western United States.

When he embarked on the exchange, the author vowed he would embrace every experience (within reason) that came his way and mostly they *were* reasonable, though there were some he would not care to repeat.

In the course of this book, he experiences seasonal activities such as Hallowe'en (American style), Kris Kringle and Thanksgiving. He also sits his driving test in his wreck of a wagon which he not-so-fondly dubs "The Big Blue Mean Machine" and whose malfunctions continue to plague him in this book, just as they did in the last.

Nevertheless the author and his young family put their trust in it to take them, in winter, on the 1,200 mile round trip over the snow-clad Rockies to visit relations in Canada – just for a long weekend. Which just goes to show you that although he may have learned some things, this author from a small island is still very much an innocent abroad in this vast and mountainous land to even contemplate embarking on such an expedition – particularly since he set out so ill equipped.

Meanwhile, at school, he is on his best behaviour as he tries not to repeat the shocks and alarms of the first few days when he found himself up to his neck in trouble with parents out to get his guts for garters. The reader will not be disappointed to discover that he still finds some parents and students challenging. At the same time, he is also on his guard for attacks from the "enemy" within – his practical-joker colleagues who are all too keen to exploit his innocence for their own amusement.

The narrative ends with the traumatic events on Christmas Day. It would have been a memorable day whatever happened, but no-one bargained for the Addisons turning their hosts' Christmas Day into one they would not forget in a hurry.

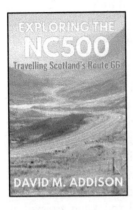

Exploring the NC500

Travelling Scotland's Route 66

By David M. Addison

Travelling anti-clockwise, David M. Addison seeks his kicks on Scotland's equivalent of Route 66. Otherwise known as NC500, the route takes you through five hundred miles of some of Scotland's most spectacular scenery. No wonder it has been voted as one of the world's five most scenic road journeys.

There are many ways of exploring the NC500. You can drive it, cycle it, motorbike it or even walk it, even if you are not one of The Proclaimers! And there are as many activities, places of interest and sights to be seen along the way as there are miles.

This is a personal account of the author's exploration of the NC500 as well as some detours from it, such as to the Black Isle, Strathpeffer and Dingwall. Whatever your reason or reasons for exploring the NC500 may be, you should read this book before you go, or take it with you as a *vade mecum*. It will enhance your appreciation of the NC500 as you learn about the history behind the turbulent past of the many castles; hear folk tales, myths and legends connected with the area; become acquainted with the ancient peoples who once lived in this timeless landscape, and read about the lives of more recent heroes such as the good Hugh Miller who met a tragic end and villains such as the notorious Duke of Sutherland, who died in his bed (and may not be quite as bad as he is painted). There are a good number of other characters too of whom you may have never heard: some colourful, some eccentric, some *very* eccentric.

You may not necessarily wish to follow in the author's footsteps in all that he did, but if you read this book you will certainly see the landscape through more informed eyes as you do whatever you want to do *en route* NC500.

Sit in your car and enjoy the scenery for its own sake (and remember you get a different perspective from a different direction, so you may want to come back and do it again to get an alternative point of view!), or get out and explore it at closer quarters – the choice is yours, but this book will complement your experience, whatever you decide.

Also Available from Extremis Publishing

Travels Through Time in Italy
Eight Cities Past and Present

By David M. Addison

Long before Thomas Cook made mass tourism to Italy possible in the 1860s there was the Grand Tour which, believe it or not, goes back a couple of centuries before that. Seen as a sort of educational finishing school for aristocrats, the Tour took in the Classical and Renaissance sights of Italy, finishing up in Naples and Pompeii.

Now, on a package tour, along comes David M. Addison accompanied by his wife, aka La Belle Dame Sans Merci, who thinks he could do with a bit of polishing up as they take in the cultural hotspots of Naples, Pompeii, Assisi, Florence, Pisa, Siena, Rome and the Vatican.

The sweep of this book takes the reader from Roman times to the Renaissance, from emperors to kings – including the artists and architects, the politicians and popes, the saints and sinners – all of whom exercised a major influence on their times. With an eye for the off-beat and the extraordinary, this is a personal account of what most impressed the author on his latter-day educational Tour.

Also Available from Extremis Publishing

The Grocer's Boy
A Slice of His Life
in 1950s Scotland

By Robert Murray

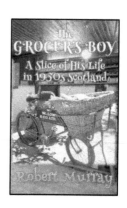

The 1950s in Carnoustie: a beautiful seaside town on the Tayside coast, and a place which was to see rapid social and technological advancement during one of the fastest-moving periods of cultural change in recent British history.

In *The Grocer's Boy*, Robert Murray relates his account of an eventful childhood in post-War Scotland, drawing on fond memories of his loving family, his droll and often mischievous group of friends, and the many inspirational people who influenced him and helped to shape his early life.

Join Robert on his adventures in retail as he advances from his humble beginnings as a delivery boy for the famous William Low grocery firm, all the way to becoming the youngest manager in the company's history at just nineteen years of age. Read tales of his hectic, hard-working time as an apprentice grocer — sometimes humorous, occasionally nerve-wracking, but never less than entertaining.

From Robert's early romances and passion for stage performance to his long-running battle of wits with his temperamental delivery bike, *The Grocer's Boy* is a story of charm and nostalgia; the celebration of a happy youth in a distinctive bygone age.

Also Available from Extremis Publishing

The Fearn Bobby
Reflections from a Life
in Scottish Policing

By Ian McNeish

'It's all about the community', the words of Kenneth Ross, Chief Constable of Ross and Sutherland Constabulary, guided Ian McNeish through thirty years of police service. They were true then, back in 1974, and they are true now.

Ian held a police warrant card for three decades, serving communities across Scotland. In that time, his work saw him moving from the northerly constabulary where he policed the rural Hill of Fearn to the social challenges that presented themselves amongst the urban landscape of Central Scotland.

From his formative years in post-War Scotland through to his application to join the police service, Ian has led a rich and varied professional life that ranged from working in iron foundries to building electronic parts for the Kestrel Jump Jet and legendary Concorde aircraft. But once he had joined the police service, he found himself faced with a whole new range of life-changing experiences – some of them surprising, a few even shocking, but all of them memorable.

Leading the reader through his involvement in front line situations, Ian explains the effects of anti-social behaviour and attending criminal court appearances, in addition to dealing with death and the responsibilities of informing those left behind. He considers topics such as ethics, public interest, police and firearms, drug issues, causes of crime, and a lot more besides.

In a career where his duties ranged from policing national strikes to providing comfort and support through personal tragedies, Ian advanced through the ranks and saw first-hand the vital importance of effective management and good teamwork. Whether as the 'Fearn Bobby', policing a remote countryside outpost, as a seconded officer working for the Chief Executive of a Regional Council, or as a Local Unit Commander in Bo'ness, Ian always knew the importance of putting the community first. Comparing today's policing techniques with his own professional experiences and examining both the good times and the harrowing pitfalls of the job, his account of life in the force is heartfelt, entertaining, and always completely honest.

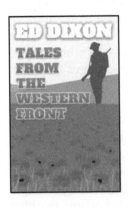

Tales from the Western Front

By Ed Dixon

Tales from the Western Front is a collection of stories about the people and places encountered by the author during more than three decades of visiting the battlefields, graveyards, towns and villages of France and Belgium.

Characters tragic and comic, famous and humble live within these pages, each connected by the common thread of the Great War. Meet Harry Lauder, the great Scottish entertainer and first international superstar; Tommy Armour, golf champion and war hero; "Hoodoo" Kinross, VC, the Pride of Lougheed; the Winslow Boy; Albert Ball, and Jackie the Soldier Baboon among many others.

Each chapter is a story in itself and fully illustrated with photos past and present.

For details of new and forthcoming books
from Extremis Publishing,
please visit our official website at:

www.extremispublishing.com

or follow us on social media at:

www.facebook.com/extremispublishing

www.linkedin.com/company/extremis-publishing-ltd-/

Lightning Source UK Ltd.
Milton Keynes UK
UKHW010758051218
333470UK00005B/468/P